# TRAVEL LETTERS

**TRAVEL LETTERS**
by the Venerable Sangharakshita



Letters first published in *Shabda*,
the monthly Newsletter of the
Western Buddhist Order, 1979-83
This edition, June 1985

Copy preparation and Typesetting by Lion's Roar,
1 Cedar Road, Norwich, Norfolk

Design by Chris Krupa

Printed by F. Crowe and Sons Ltd.,
11 Concorde Road, Norwich, Norfolk

Published by Windhorse Publications,
136 Renfield St., Glasgow G2 3AU

ISBN 0 904766 17 9

# TRAVEL LETTERS

SANGHARAKSHITA

Windhorse

*by the same author:*

Messengers From Tibet and other Poems
A Survey of Buddhism
Anagarika Dharmapala: A Biographical Sketch
The Three Jewels: An Introduction to Buddhism
The Essence of Zen
Crossing the Stream
The Path of the Inner Life
The Thousand-Petalled Lotus: An English Buddhist in India
The Endlessly Fascinating Cry
Buddhism and Blasphemy
Human Enlightenment
The Religion of Art
The Bodhisattva: Evolution and Self-Transcendence
The Ten Pillars of Buddhism
The Threefold Refuge
The Way to Wisdom
Auspicious Signs
Salutation to the Three Jewels
The Eternal Legacy

## CONTENTS

# PREFACE

AN astrologer friend once told me that I would never stay long in one place. Though I do not believe that our lives are governed by the stars, it is certainly true that for much of my life I have been 'on the move' to a far greater extent than I really wanted to be. Given a perfectly free choice, I would probably have preferred to spend the whole of my time in some solitary mountain retreat, quietly pursuing a regular programme of study, meditation and literary work.

But this has not been possible. Both in India and in England I have had to consider — and have been happy to consider — the needs of the growing number of people 'with little dust in their eyes' who are 'perishing for not hearing the Dharma', and this has inevitably entailed a good deal of travelling. Of few years was this more true than 1979. In 1979 I visited India after an absence of twelve years, paid my first visits to Malaysia and Australia, and also paid my second visit to New Zealand. These travels provided me with a rich crop of impressions, and these impressions I wanted to share with my friends, especially with the members of the Western Buddhist Order. From time to time I therefore wrote a sort of circular letter to all Upasakas and Upasikas. These letters were published in *Shabda*, the Order's unedited monthly newsletter.

On my return to England it occurred to me that my experiences in England might be as interesting to Order Members in India and New Zealand as my experiences in India and New Zealand had been to Order Members in England. In any case, in principle I belonged no more to one part of the world than to another. Thus it was that between May 1979 and September 1983 I wrote altogether seven Letters for publication in *Shabda*, three from New Zealand, three from England, and one from Wales. The first four Letters, and the first part of the fifth, were written in 1979 itself, the remainder of the fifth and the first part of the sixth, in 1980, while the seventh was written in 1983. Thus there is a two year gap between the sixth and seventh Letters. This was due mainly to the fact that during this period so much was happening that I had no time to write about it. Indeed, from the very beginning I found that I could not write fast enough to keep up with my own experiences and, since things did not stop happening while I was writing, I fell farther and farther behind. The result was that in later Letters I not only had to go back and continue the story from the point I had reached in my previous Letter but also continue it from the point at which I had stopped writing that Letter itself.

This accounts for the rather curious structure of the Letters. In each one I describe both very recent experiences and experiences that had occurred weeks and even months earlier. Thus in my 'Second Letter from New Zealand', written in Christchurch, I first bring the story of my experiences in New Zealand itself up to date and then, going back to the story of my experiences in Malaysia and picking up the thread where I had dropped it at the end of my '(First) Letter from New Zealand', written in Auckland, I describe my last days in Penang and the four days I spent in Sydney. In subsequent Letters this interleaving of past and present becomes more elaborate and, perhaps, a little contrived. At first, as I have indicated, the particular structure of the Letters was imposed on them due to the fact that literature could not keep up with life, or that life outran literature. Subsequently, I tended to think of this structure as constituting a distinctive literary form — though whether I had been able to use that form successfully was another matter. Whatever the case might be, such a 'scrambling' of the record meant that I did not have to adhere to a single, continuous narrative line and could, therefore, do greater justice to the many-layered, many-faceted nature of my experience as I travelled from one place to another. In particular, it enabled me to do greater justice to the fact that the past is not simply the past but that, in a sense, it also exists in the present, so that one's so-called present experience actually consists of the 'present' plus the 'past'.

# PREFACE

Whether the original readers of these seven Letters noticed their curious structure I am unable to say, but now that they are all being published together in book form that structure will perhaps stand out more clearly. What certainly does stand out more clearly is the extent of the changes that have taken place, both within the Western Buddhist Order and within the wider Movement of which it is a part, since these Letters were written. To take a simple and obvious example, the salutations with which I began the first five Letters was 'Dear Upasakas and Upasikas'. Since 1982, however, the term Upasakas has been replaced by Dharmachari and Upasika by Dharmacharini. This is in order to emphasise the fact that members of the Order are primarily 'practisers of the Dharma' and that their commitment is to the Three Jewels rather than to any particular life style, whether that of the monk or nun or the layman or laywoman. (The reason why I did not begin the last two Letters with a salutation was probably that by that time my Letters had begun to assume the character of essays.) It will also be noticed that Sydney, described in my 'Second Letter from New Zealand' as 'an ideal place for an FWBO centre' now has four Order Members and a meditation community that doubles as a public Centre, while in Glasgow the spacious premises in Sauchiehall Street that, according to my 'Second Letter from England, I' were pointed out to me by Kovida as the location of the new Glasgow centre, have long since been occupied.

The extent of the changes that have taken place since these Letters were written is nowhere more evident than in India, where many times the modest £10,000 that was mentioned as being needed by Lokamitra for our work in Poona ('First Letter from New Zealand') has already been raised and spent and where our social, educational and religious activities have increased proportionately. On the other hand, the FWBO Auckland has had to give up the pleasantly decorated rooms where I had admired the way in which the beautiful New Zealand woods had been used to the best advantage ('Second Letter from England, I'), while my own plans to move into a house in Bungay, Suffolk, with Prasannasiddhi and a few other friends after my return from Wales ('Letter from Wales, I') met with no better success than my earlier project of retiring to a property in the South of France, near Carcassonne. Contrary to what might have been expected I am, therefore, still living at Padmaloka.

## PREFACE

But though I am still living at Padmaloka, there too changes have taken place since these Letters were written. All nine members of the community mentioned in 'Letter from England, I' left within a year or two, though one of them has since returned. Abhaya is now Chairman of the Norwich Buddhist Centre, Kulananda has started up Windhorse Trading, Sona has established FWBO Stockholm, Virabhadra is in charge of the medical work at Dapodi (Poona), and so on. Besides changing in terms of membership, the Padmaloka community has more than doubled in size, and at present consists of twenty-three men from three different countries. The Padmaloka complex in fact now comprises two separate though interrelated communities, the thirteen Dharmachari members of which form a single Order Chapter. There is a Retreat Community, which is responsible for organising all the retreats that are held at Padmaloka, and an Order Office Community, which is responsible for assisting me in carrying out my duties as Head of the Western Buddhist Order and President of each of the autonomous local FWBOs. The work of both these communities has increased enormously over the last two years, and continues to increase. Padmaloka is therefore a very busy place, and I am probably not the least busy person in it. So busy am I, in fact, that I no longer have time to listen to music or to go out for even an occasional drive in the countryside, as described in 'Third Letter from England, I' — though I must admit that I do still sometimes spend a few minutes doing absolutely nothing.

It was because I was so busy, especially with other kinds of literary work, that I could not write any more of these Letters. I was not even able to write the two further Letters from Wales that I had originally planned to write. In the first of these two Letters I had intended to give an account of life at Tyddyn Rhydderch, the stone cottage in which Prasannasiddhi and I spent three cold and rainy months after attending the sixth annual Mystics and Scientists Conference at Winchester ('Letter from Wales, I'), as well as a description of the surrounding countryside. Such a description would have included at least a passing reference not only to Vajraloka, the Buddhist Meditation Centre of North Wales, but also to Blaenddol, *then* simply a deserted and slightly derelict stone farmhouse but *now* — thanks mainly to Prakasha — the abode of a study and meditation community. In the second Letter I had intended to give an account of my first and second journeys to Il Convento, the former Christian monastery near Grosseto, in Tuscany (Italy), where since 1981 we have been holding our annual men's Pre-Ordination Course. I particularly wanted to say something about Aachen (the northern capital of Charlemagne's empire), which I had visited on my way to Tuscany 1981, something about Carcassonne (one of the most important cities of the Cathars), which I had visited three months later on my way back to England, and something about Avignon (the seat of the Papacy for the greater part of the 14th century), which I had visited on my way to Tuscany '82. It had also been my intention to include in one or other of these Letters a few reflections on the general state of the Movement.

But as I have said, I was too busy to write any more Letters, and these intentions remained unfulfilled. Nor were the two further Letters from Wales the only ones that I was too busy to write. Later on I had the idea of writing Letters from India, where I spent three months during the Winter of 1981-82 and three weeks in December 1983, and also Letters from Italy, where I of course attended both Tuscany '83 and Tuscany '84. In both cases there was so much I wanted to write about. There were so many impressions, so many experiences. But again I was too busy. I had more and more to do and (it seemed) less and less time in which to do it. Moreover, with every year that passed, and every Letter that remained unwritten, literature was proving less and less able to keep up with life, or life was outrunning literature to an ever greater extent. Indeed, so far as these Letters are concerned literature has given up the struggle altogether and is content to acknowledge defeat. Since there will probably be no more Letters, therefore, I have gathered together the seven that I wrote from New Zealand, England, and Wales, and have issued them in their present form in the hope of being able to share with a wider circle of friends than that to which they were originally addressed some of the impressions and experiences of a rapidly receding period of my life.

SANGHARAKSHITA

Padmaloka
Norfolk
29 March 1985

CHAPTER ONE

## LETTER FROM NEW ZEALAND

Dear Upasakas and Upasikas,

IT is 10 a.m. in Auckland, New Zealand. The sky is grey and overcast, but the weather is not at all cold. At Suvarnaketu ('Golden Comet'), the men's community at 46 Sarsfield Street, we have just finished breakfast, and the lads have scattered over the house to get on with various jobs — Purna to 'phone Vijaya about my arrangements for visiting Christchurch next month. Priyananda and I arrived from Sydney the day before yesterday, March 15th, [1979] at about 6.30 (local time), exactly one calendar month after our departure from England. Megha, Purna, Udaya and Priyananda's brother Tony were waiting for us at the barrier, and within minutes we were driving through the warm night air of Auckland in the direction of Sarsfield Street.

Here I was soon installed in the two rooms, a bedroom and an office, which had been got ready for me. On the chest of drawers was a large, hand painted greetings card depicting a rising sun and hordes of joyful Mitras and Friends apparently engaged in welcoming Bhante to New Zealand. It was signed by all those who had decided to greet me in this way rather than 'overwhelm' me at the airport. Also on the chest of drawers were framed photographs of Jamyang Khyentse Rimpoche and Dhardo Rimpoche and lots of flowers — roses, michaelmas daisies and chrysanthemums, and a yellow, poppy-like New Zealand flower that I couldn't identify. My journey was at an end. I had reached New Zealand at last. After an absence of four years I was back in the Land of the Long White Cloud. No doubt a lot is going to happen during the next two months, so before getting into my New Zealand programme I think I had better stop and tell you something about our journey out here and our experiences in India, Malaysia and Australia, since impressions of the earlier stages of the journey are already becoming a little blurred.

Letters that were waiting for me here tell me that it is already Spring in England, and that the daffodils are out at Padmaloka. When we left England there was snow on the ground. Owing to a strike in Bombay, we had to go by Air India instead of Qantas, on which we had booked. We also left two hours late, had to go via New Delhi, instead of direct to Bombay, and owing to another strike had to wait altogether six (or was it eight?) hours in New Delhi (in the plane). This meant that we reached Bombay exactly twelve hours late. However there were compensations. On leaving New Delhi we saw a fiery-gold sunrise pouring itself like molten gold over a vast pavement of greyish-white cloud, and on approaching Bombay there was a marvellous view of the fantastically weathered brown sandstone peaks of the Western Ghats. Neither Priyananda nor I suffered much from the delay. The real sufferer was Lokamitra, who had been waiting for us all night in the very crowded and uncomfortable conditions of the Santa Cruz airport. However, he was overjoyed to see us as we emerged (Priyananda not entirely unscathed) from the Customs, and in fact looked very well.

Followed the all-too-familiar tussle with taxi drivers, coolies, beggars, touts and policemen. Eventually we were honking our way through the suburbs in one of the yellow-and-black Bombay taxis, eagerly exchanging news. I could not help looking about me. Had things changed since my last visit, thirteen years ago? There were lots of dusty palm trees. There were ugly blocks of flats, obviously put up recently, but already a dingy white and crumbling. In between the blocks of flats there were indescribably squalid shanty towns of the most wretched type. And of course there were people. Thousands upon thousands of people. And there was the strong, friendly sun — perhaps the best thing in India. As we drove down through the inner suburbs it seemed as though everything had not only decayed but proliferated. Buildings seemed to bulge out into the streets, bursting at the seams as they did so, and spilling heaps of rubble and garbage. The streets seemed narrower, and even more aswarm with people than before. The Japanese Buddhist temple at Worli was squeezed in by a block of flats, and half hidden by a huge bill-board. It seemed to have shrunk. Whenever the taxi stopped, which it did frequently, either because of traffic lights or because of traffic jams, beseeching faces would appear in the open windows: beggars. As we approached the end of the peninsular enormous blocks of high rise flats, dazzlingly white in the sunshine, towered immaculate above the urban undergrowth against a brilliant blue sky, some of them unfinished. They were all new, and some already showed signs of decay. Soon we were whirling along the graceful curve of Marine Drive. It was more open here. On our right was the Arabian Sea. To our left, the two or three miles of what, twenty or thirty years ago, had been luxury flats, but which had begun to crumble even before my departure for England in 1964, and some of which were now in a very bad way indeed.

After personally investigating thirty hotels (he showed us the names and addresses on a piece of paper, neatly ticked off), Lokamitra had discovered the Strand. Here he had booked two rooms, one large and one small, *en suite*, with attached bathroom. (For some reason or other, there was no running water. Water was brought in plastic buckets by a servant: perhaps the proprietor found it cheaper to employ a servant than to get the plumbing fixed.) There were several pieces of furniture, apart from the beds, and there was a carpet on the floor. By Indian standards it was quite luxurious — and quite expensive, though not immoderately so (the equivalent of about £10 a night for the three of us). Clearly Lokamitra did not want Bhante to get too bad an impression of India. The best thing about our rooms, however, was the fact that they were on the second floor and commanded a fine view of the sea and, in the distance, Elephanta. After an early lunch, ordered from the depths of the hotel, and which took a long time to come (Lokamitra kept complaining to the supervisor), Priyananda and I had a short sleep from which we arose feeling very refreshed. Lokamitra, who seemed full of energy, spent the time studying. After we had had tea, and enjoyed a further exchange of news and views, I had a visitor. This was Ardeshir Mehta, the son of my old friend Dr. Dinshaw Mehta (now in New Delhi), with whom I used to stay in Bombay. Lokamitra had 'phoned him while I was asleep, and he now came bringing a legal friend who had attended some of my lectures many years ago. I had known Ardeshir as a small boy, and he had visited me in London when I was still at the Hampstead Vihara (he is now about forty), and we were very glad to see each other. He studied agriculture for six years in Israel, has lived in kibbutzim, and is very interested in the setting up of what we would call farm-based spiritual communities. We all had a pleasant talk, and before leaving Ardeshir invited us to lunch the following day. Lokamitra, Priyananda and I then had a walk along the front, and then round through some streets where we looked in the windows of two or three antique shops, as Priyananda was in search of a good Buddha image. Then back to the hotel, a glass of hot milk, and bed. Thus ended our first day in India.

Next morning I slept till about 10, having not been able to sleep until quite late. After breakfast and a hot bath (yes, hot), I wrote my first two picture postcards — the first of many. The three of us then went off to lunch with Ardeshir, with me still in my civvies, as I was in no hurry to change from Norfolk country gentleman (?) into professional Indian holy man. Lunch was in the shrine (Zarathustra, Buddha and Jesus Mary 'n' Joseph) of the NC Corporation Pvt. Ltd., one of the 'earning arms' of the Society of Servants of God, Dr. Mehta's organisation, where I had given many lectures in the fifties and early sixties. It was in fact not lunch but what Dr. Mehta calls 'the spiritual meal', a balanced vegetarian meal cheap enough for the ordinary Indian to be able to afford. It is called 'the spiritual meal' because it is supposedly blessed by God, everything in India of course requiring some kind of 'religious' sanction. Despite God's interference, we found the spiritual meal quite palatable. I had, in fact, sampled it a number of times before, at an early stage of its evolution, when though undoubtedly nutritious it was neither very palatable nor very digestible. Ardeshir gave me some of his father's publications (regarded within the Society as coming straight from God), and promised one of his own. He (Ardeshir) is an extremely likeable person, and we all found him very intelligent and sympathetic. Since he had spent so much time in the West there was no difficulty of communication.

Though he accepted many of his father's ideas (on their own merits though), and indeed worked for the NC Corporation, he clearly found it a bit inhibiting to work under the direct control of God's personal representative (indeed, of God himself, in a sense). Who wouldn't! One of the things we discussed was the possibility of the FWBO importing handicrafts from India. Ardeshir was willing to help.

After arranging to meet again in the evening, and meet members of the Society, Lokamitra, Priyananda and I went to the Fort area, where we called in at Chetana's bookshop (where we saw the Indian edition of *Crossing the Stream* on sale) and had a quick look round the Prince of Wales Museum. Here we saw some fine Buddha images and, to our great delight, Li Gotami's copies of four of the Tsaparang frescoes depicting scenes from the life of the Buddha. They were very distinctive in style, and brilliantly coloured, and it is a pity that full size reproductions are not available. From the Museum we went to the Government Handicrafts Emporium, Priyananda being still in quest of an image, but it was closed owing to a strike and there was a red flag planted ominously on the locked gates. At 4 o'clock we were due to have tea at Marine Drive with Dinoo Dubash, an old friend of mine who receives the Newsletter regularly and follows the progress of the FWBO with keen interest. She was not only delighted to see me but pleased that I was in civvies instead of robes, gave us a magnificent tea, and asked lots of questions. Despite her seventy-seven years, and her deafness, she was very bright and lively indeed. Knowing that she was a great reader, I had brought her a copy of *The Thousand-Petalled Lotus* and a couple of Windhorse publications and these she was pleased to receive. Before we knew where we were nearly three hours had passed and we were having to be on our way to our next appointment. Before we left Dinoo gave Lokamitra a very generous donation to cover the expenses of my stay in India.

Our next appointment was at Mayfair, Malabar Hill, the Bombay headquarters of Dr. Mehta's Society. Here we had another spiritual meal, and I met about a dozen members of the Society, most of whom were well known to me. I told them all about the FWBO, particularly about our threefold structure of centre, community, and co-operative, and the emphasis which we place on spiritual community, and found them extremely interested. Altogether it was a warm and friendly meeting. I also pointed out to Lokamitra and Priyananda, hanging on the wall, the thangka which Jamyang Khyentse Rimpoche had had painted for me after I had received from him the initiations of Manjughosha, Avalokiteshvara, Vajrapani and Tara. The thangka depicts these four 'deities' together with the principal teachers of all the spiritual lineages which Jamyang Khyentse transmitted to me on the occasion of this initiation, among them being Padmasambhava, Milarepa, and Longchenpa. In the early sixties I brought this thangka to Bombay for safe keeping with Dr. Mehta (it was the time of the Chinese invasion,) and he eventually came to consider it as the property of the Society. However, I asked Lokamitra to get it photographed so that the names of the teachers of the various lineages, which are written under their portraits, could be deciphered. On my arrival at Mayfair I 'phoned Dr. Mehta, who was eagerly waiting for the call in New Delhi. As the line was very bad we could have only a short chat. He insisted that I should spend at least a month with him on my way back to England, but I was able to promise only a few days.

Sunday morning saw the arrival of Virabhadra. Before Priyananda and I were up, Lokamitra was off to the Victoria Terminus to meet the New Delhi express by which he was expected, and returned with him by 10 o'clock, the train having arrived two hours late. It was a joyful reunion. There were now four members of the Western Buddhist Order together in India. After Virabhadra had told us his news (he was looking extremely well, and clearly enjoying his stay in India), and we had told him ours, and after we had all had something to eat, we packed our bags and took a taxi to Dadar, a suburb of Bombay, where, after a short delay, we managed to get another taxi which took us all the way to Poona. What with the brilliant sunshine, and the breeze coming in at the windows, it was a delightful journey, and we took about three and a half hours to cover the hundred-odd miles — roughly the distance between London and Norwich.

After we had left the city, and crossed the bridge that links Bombay with the hinterland, the scene started to change. Houses and industrial estates thinned out, then disappeared. Flowering trees appeared amidst the jungle on either side of the road, among them the coral tree, with its big, blood-red flowers, almost like lumps of raw meat, and its leafless branches. Soon we started winding our way up into the bare brown hills, with their strangely eroded peaks, passed through the pleasant hill resorts of Lonavla and Khandela, and of course stopped half way for a cup of tea. Outside the restaurant hovered a Rajneesh follower, a Caucasian, in the usual gear, and with a rather vacant look — the first of many that we were to see. As we had left the plains behind us the weather had changed, from hot and humid becoming hot and dry, while the sunshine seemed to grow more brilliant and the sky bluer. Thirty or so miles from Poona we saw in the distance on our left the Karle Buddhist cave temples, the famous 'horseshoe arch' facade of the principal cave being just visible. Soon we were passing through the suburbs of Poona, some of them with smart new industrial estates, then through the outskirts of the city and over the bridge to Parnakuti and, finally, to the Ambedkar Housing Society and the tiny semi-detached bungalow on the edge of the colony which was the FWBO's temporary home and was to be my own base for the next two weeks. As the taxi stopped outside the Pancha Shila Vihara (the place's original name), and Padmavajra came out to meet us, men, women and children emerged from their bungalows to watch our arrival with unabashed interest and curiosity. They were evidently glad to see us, or rather, discarding false modesty, perhaps I should say they were glad to see *me*. By this time I was wearing my 'robes', into which I had changed that morning for the journey, and was now the familiar yellow-clad figure that many of them had seen anything from thirteen to twenty or more years ago.

The two weeks that I spent in Poona, from Sunday 18th February to Monday 5th March [1979] were among the fullest and busiest that I have had for a long time, and it will not be possible for me to give a day by day account of my experiences, as I have done so far. Instead, I shall give a summary of the events of this period and make a few general remarks. In any case Priyananda, Lokamitra, and probably Padmavajra and others too, will be writing their own accounts, so that readers of *Shabda* will be able to see my visit to Poona from several different points of view. But first a few words about the Vihara. This was situated, as I have already said, at the edge of the Ambedkar Housing Society's colony, and had been placed at the FWBO's disposal some three months earlier by one of our Mitras, a retired Government servant. It consisted of two main rooms, both quite small, plus a kind of vestibule, a kitchen, a bathroom, and a toilet. By the standards of our Indian Buddhist friends it was comfortable, even luxurious, and quite spacious. The front room, to which there was access from the vestibule, served as the shrine and meeting room, and at a pinch could accommodate thirty or more people, while the back room, normally occupied by Lokamitra, had been made over to me for the duration of my stay. It contained a bed, table and chair, and, for my greater comfort, a deck-chair, which suddenly collapsed one day when I was sitting in it, to the great distress of our friend the Government servant, who was talking with me at the time. We also had the use of the front rooms of the two adjoining houses, one of them being our dining-room and the other a dormitory. This, then, was my headquarters for two weeks.

In front of the bungalow was an uneven stretch of sandy, sunburnt ground (much of it used as a public toilet) at the far end of which stood a continuous row of hovels such as the tenants of the Ambedkar Housing Society colony must have moved out of not so many years ago. From the hovels one descended into what Lokamitra called 'hell', a kind of sink into which flowed all sorts of human refuse in the form of the poor, the diseased, the criminal, and the dying, perhaps several thousand strong. On the farther side of 'hell', adjacent to it, was the local bazaar area, with its colourful shops and stalls, beyond the bazaar area a busy crossroads, usually congested with taxis and bicycles, and beyond the crossroads the bridge that led from Parnakuti into the city. Behind the bungalow was, of course, the Ambedkar Housing Society colony. From the window of my room I looked out onto the corresponding bungalow in the next row, which was only a few feet away. By Indian standards the room was quiet. During the day, but especially in the morning, the principal source of disturbance was the shrieking of women and the squalling of children. At night there was a kind of 'village watchman' going his rounds and calling out the hours and, towards dawn, knocking thunderously on the doors of those who had to get up and go to work. As he moved from house to house he would be accompanied by a terrific barking and howling of dogs, of whom there were many living in the colony. At first the racket used to waken me up, but after a few days I got used to it and slept on. The lads, certainly, never complained of losing any sleep.

To this room in the Vihara, then, many people came to see me, from the old and illiterate to the young and Western-educated, those who had attended lectures and classes many years ago and those who were seeing me for the first time; men, women, and children. They started coming within minutes of my arrival, and the flow continued until I left, though Lokamitra so arranged things that I could follow my usual practice of reserving my mornings strictly for myself.

Among my first visitors were Mr. and Mrs. Maheshkar, who had arranged so many of my programmes in the old days. They were very little changed, though Mrs. Maheshkar had certainly grown a trifle stout. Both were very pleased to see me. Mrs. Maheshkar was so moved, in fact, that for several minutes she was unable to speak. When at last she did manage to do so, however, she could not forbear remonstrating with me a little for not visiting Poona for such a long time. As best I could, I explained what I had been doing in England, and the effect it would now have on the work in India. As I did so, my Hindi started coming back, and soon I was as fluent as ever. (Both Mr. and Mrs. Maheshkar speak Hindi well, though their mother tongue is Marathi.)

As more and more visitors poured in it was a strange experience for me to recognise the faces, and in some cases remember the names, of scores and scores, even of hundreds and hundreds, of people that I had known quite well in the fifties and early sixties but of whom I had not, in most cases, thought individually since then. It was like suddenly remembering another life. But though I may not have thought of them they had certainly thought of me. Prior to Lokamitra's visit to Poona in 1977, I had imagined that after the lapse of so many years most of my old friends and pupils would have forgotten me, for all practical purposes at least; but after making contact with the Maheshkars and others Lokamitra had reported that this was far from being the case, and my own experience in Poona fully confirmed his impressions. People were delighted to see me. In fact, it was as though they not only remembered me but had been waiting for me to come back. Indeed, the longer I stayed in Poona, and the more I saw of people, the more it became evident to me that the lectures which I had given in the late fifties and early sixties (two hundred of them in Poona alone) had made a far greater impression than I had realised at the time. This was shown by the fact that visitors, and invitations to give lectures, were soon coming from all over Maharashtra and beyond. After a few days it dawned on me that my fourteen year absence from the Indian Buddhist scene, far from diminishing my influence, had actually increased it, and that I had become a bit of a legend in my own lifetime. (Grown men enthusiastically recalled attending my lectures as small boys.) This was due partly to the fact that during the time that I had been away there had been hardly any real Buddhist activity in Maharashtra, and certainly no monk doing the sort of Dharma-teaching that I had done, and partly (I think) to the fact that I was now quite old (always an advantage in India) and had behind me twelve or thirteen years of successful Buddhist work in the West. Be that as it may, thanks to all the hard work Lokamitra had put in during the last six months, and his careful preparations for my visit, I felt that I had come back at exactly the right moment and could carry on from where I had left off last time.

This was particularly evident, perhaps, at the public meetings. There were altogether eight of these, five of them being meetings in Buddhist localities and three of them lectures in the compound of the Ahalyashram, a well known social and educational institution established some years ago (long before Dr. Ambedkar's conversion) by an Indian Buddhist social reformer who had been educated in, of all places, Manchester. There are more than eighty Buddhist (formerly Untouchable) localities in Poona, i.e. neighbourhoods occupied mainly or exclusively by Buddhists, of whom there are altogether 300,000 in Poona. (I questioned this figure when Lokamitra first quoted it, but it is apparently correct.) The reason for the existence of these ghettos, as they in fact are, is of course the Hindu caste system. In the villages the 'Untouchables', who were landless labourers doing all the dirty work of the village and receiving only leavings of food and cast-off clothes in return, were forced to inhabit separate areas well away from the main village, where the Caste Hindus lived. When the Untouchables migrated to the cities the same system was followed: hence the 'localities'. In these meetings, all except one of which were held in the open air, and which usually started a little late, there was the same familiar procedure. Lokamitra and I would arrive to find the loudspeakers blaring forth the inevitable popular film music (Lokamitra is determined to ban this one day) and people still turning up in droves, in some cases milling around at the back of the meeting. When it was judged everybody had arrived (though there were always latecomers) we were led to the pandal, a kind of covered and decorated stage at the back of which the image of the Buddha and the picture of Dr. Ambedkar had been set up on a temporary shrine. After I had offered a handful of flowers to the Buddha, and garlanded the picture of Dr. Ambedkar, I would be requested to administer the Three Refuges and Five Precepts. It was good to hear the hearty responses coming from all those thousands of throats. Then followed the speech of welcome, after which I gave my talk.

Sometimes I was garlanded before my talk, sometimes afterwards. Up to thirty or forty garlands, mainly of french marigolds and tuberose blossoms, would be offered, — some of them very magnificent indeed, — as well as posies of various kinds of flowers. Since most of these flowers, many of which grew in trees and shrubs, had no stalks, the heads had been carefully tied onto thin sticks of wood, which meant that they could not be put into water. Since the speech of welcome was usually quite long (I could hear my career being recapitulated, though without mention of my meteoric career in the Roman Catholic Church), I had time to study the audience before speaking. Before me was a sea of eager faces that stretched back into the darkness. Everybody sat on the ground, of course, men on one side, women on the other. (One of the most noticeable, and most pleasant, features of life in India, is the decency of the relations between the sexes, and the total absence of sexual games-playing.) Children sat either with their mothers or separately in the front. Though the standard of the meetings varied somewhat, especially those held in the localities, which Lokamitra had organised through local Mitras, nearly everyone in the audience seemed pleased, happy, and interested — even excited. It was as though they had been starved of the Dharma for a long time and were really glad to be getting it at last. In the localities I spoke — Mr. Maheshkar interpreting into Marathi — on such subjects as Maitri and Prajna, and Lessons of the Life of the Buddha. A vivid description of Padmapani's Windhorse fresco and its symbolism seemed to go down particularly well.

At the Ahalyashram meetings I spoke on 'The Buddha — Man or God?', 'The Path of the Dharma' and 'The Future of the Sangha'. In all these talks I gave as much information as I could about the progress of Buddhism in the West, especially about the work of the FWBO. This was very well received indeed. People seemed to find it not only of great interest but very encouraging. It was as though the fact that a real Buddhist movement could be started in England showed that one could be started in India too, despite all difficulties. As for me, I was delighted to be speaking to such large and very receptive and responsive audiences again, and generally went on for much longer than I had intended or Lokamitra had planned. My style of speaking was naturally rather different from what it is in England. (Lokamitra remarked after one meeting that I had not used a single 'as it were' in my whole talk.) But I need say no more on the subject. Priyananda (rather to my dismay) tape-recorded all my talks in Poona, so those who are interested in hearing Bhante driving home the Dharma with a sledgehammer rather than with some more delicate instrument will be able to do so. After the meeting had ended with the 'Last Vandana', chanted to a very beautiful melody which Padmavajra has learned and will probably be introducing in England, people would usually come surging forward to greet us in such numbers that Lokamitra — laden down with all the garlands and bouquets — and I would have difficulty in making our way to the car.

In addition to speaking at these eight meetings I gave a talk on *Dhammapada* 6 at a *punyanumodana* meeting held in memory of one of our Mitras, who had died shortly before my arrival, and also conducted two Mitra study groups at the Vihara, in the first dealing mainly with Individuality, in the second with Commitment.

While all these public meetings were successful (even though one or two of them were slow to take off), the standard varied somewhat, as I have already said. There was also a noticeable difference between the meetings held in the localities, and those held at the Ahalyashram. This was because the latter, which were better attended, and ran more smoothly, had been organised under the personal supervision of Lokamitra. Indeed, from this as well as from other things I observed, it was clear that Lokamitra had the situation in Poona well in hand and was making a powerful impact on the local Buddhists, and that his particular combination of personal qualities was exactly right for the situation. What he had been able to accomplish in nine months was in fact amazing. On occasions, particularly in the Mitra study groups, I felt that the Dharma really had been revived at last in India, and that with the starting up of the FWBO in Poona something very clear and very pure had started flowing through the stagnant wastes of Maharashtrian Buddhism. It must also be acknowledged that Lokamitra probably would not have been able to achieve so much without the loyal support of Padmavajra, who despite his personal difficulties has taken classes, given talks, typed minutes, looked after the domestic side of the Vihara, etc. with unfailing reliability. When I arrived from Bombay with Lokamitra, Priyananda and Virabhadra he did not say very much, but for the next few days he went about his duties with a smile of quiet satisfaction. When Padmapani and Yuvaraj arrived five days later he was still more pleased. Thereafter I often heard the four lads, as we called them — Priyananda, Padmavajra, Virabhadra and Yuvaraj, — laughing and talking together in the vestibule/kitchen and having what seemed to be a thoroughly happy time. Soon, under Padmavajra's guidance, the other three were paying visits to the bazaar, after which they blossomed forth, — rather shyly at first, — in all sorts of wonderful shirts and lungis, some white and some coloured, Virabhadra favouring a combination of white shirt with white pyjama trousers or bright red lungi, Yuvaraj a combination of white or pale jade green embroidered shirt with flowered light red lungi. At meetings the four of them always sat in a row to the right of the stage, looking very young and very cherubic, and beaming when they were given *their* garlands and bouquets. (Padmapani usually wandered around taking pictures.) In addition to his usual duties, Padmavajra looked after me, putting up my mosquito net at night, bringing me hot water, washing my clothes, making tea, and doing whatever else he could to make my stay in Poona happy and comfortable. (Priyananda was similarly helpful during the whole journey to New Zealand, particularly when it came to dealing with travel agents.) Before long it was evident that life in India tended to bring out people's characters, in one or two cases revealing aspects that I for one had not observed before. Virabhadra looked healthier and happier than ever, and seemed to get on particularly well with our Indian friends. (During the day he worked in a local hospital, or toured nearby villages with a medical team doing preventive work.) Yuvaraj, however, remained in every way — except for the shirts and lungis — the same Yuvaraj that he had been in England. After a couple of days in Poona he got bored, and went off on his own to see the Ajanta caves, returning in time for the Ordination Retreat.

Though it lasted only for three days, including the days of arrival and departure, this retreat was perhaps the culmination of my stay in Poona — indeed, in India. On the morning of Monday 26th February, thirty-three of us, including all the 'English Upasakas' and five Mitras and Friends who had arrived from Ahmedabad the day before, left for Sinhagad. This was a hill fort situated a thousand feet or more above the surrounding countryside some twenty-five miles out of Poona where I had once spent a few days in the early sixties. In those days it was quite bare and deserted, except for a few old-fashioned bungalows that were occasionally occupied at week-ends, but in recent years the Government of Maharashtra had tried to turn the place into a picnic spot, if not into a tourist attraction, and gardens had been laid out and the area generally tidied up. There was also a television aerial that had not been there before. However, these 'improvements' had not really impaired the beauty of the place, though it was not so solitary or so quiet as it had been, especially in the morning, when parties of schoolchildren were brought on what I supposed were educational visits. On all sides round one could see the flowing contours of the bare yellow-brown mountains with their curiously contorted peaks, range after range to the horizon, as well as three more of the hill forts which, like Sinhagad itself, were associated with the name of the 17th century Maratha hero Shivaji, who from these desert fastnesses had resisted the power of the Mogul empire. Below, a few vague patches of cultivation showed green against the prevailing yellow-brown.

After delays and difficulties with the taxis (only one turned up instead of two) Lokamitra and I and Mitra Wanshiv, together with much of the luggage and cooking apparatus, reached Sinhagad at about 10.30. Everybody else came by 'bus, which took them only to the foot of the hill, after which they had a five-mile climb to the top. Lokamitra and I and Wanshiv were luckier. The taxi deposited us outside one of the massive stone gateways of the fort, from which it was only half a mile, up flights of stone steps and through gardens, to where we were staying. For the retreat Lokamitra had hired two bungalows, one belonging to the PWD and one to the Tilak Society. In the first of these he and I stayed, together with the five 'English Upasakas', the five Mitras and Friends from Ahmedabad, and a young Indian Buddhist monk who had attached himself to us, or at least to Lokamitra, and who seemed convinced that the FWBO had all the answers (he had the makings of a good Mitra, which was more than one could say of most of the other monks I met), and here at this bungalow we had our shrine-cum-meditation room. In the other bungalow, a couple of hundred yards away, stayed the women and the rest of the men, and here we had our dining-room and kitchen. After a quick meal (most of the cooking had been done beforehand), the retreat began.

After the confusion of the start, it was astonishing how quickly the retreat got under way, and soon everybody — or almost everybody — was as much into it as though they had been on retreat a week. Lokamitra led. After administering the Refuges and Five Precepts, and giving the opening talk, I retired to my rooms, where I spent the greater part of the retreat, very pleasantly, doing absolutely nothing, just looking out of the window at the yellow-brown hills, or at an unfamiliar bird fluttering among the rose bushes, enjoying the brilliance of the sunshine and the blueness of the sky, and emerging only for Order meetings, a Question and Answer session and, of course, the private and public ordinations. (Oh yes, I wrote about a dozen picture postcards.) ... Almost before one knew what had happened, the retreat was over, there were two more Upasakas in the Western Buddhist Order/Trailokya Bauddha Mahasangha (I hope to write a note about this for the next issue of *Shabda*), — Upasaka Bakula (Mr. B. Vakil) from Ahmedabad and Upasaka Dharmarakshita (Mr. F. D. R. Maheshkar) from

Poona, — Priyananda and Padmapani were taking photographs of the retreatants in every possible permutation, the 'English Upasakas' and others were leaping down the hillside in the direction of the 'bus, and Lokamitra and I with Mrs. Maheshkar and Dharmarakshita were climbing into the waiting taxi. It had been a historic occasion. Our first 'Upasaka' ordinations had been held on Indian soil. The Movement was really beginning to be established in India.

The next three days passed hardly less swiftly than the retreat. There was the last of my three public lectures to give, lunches to go out to (the one at the Maheshkar home was a particularly lavish affair, with a ceremonial reception by several dozen women, and culminating in eight name-givings), people to see (including the 'Buddhist' politicians, who now started turning up), the AGM and first Council Meeting of the Trailokya Bauddha Mahasangha Sahayak Gana, Pune (FWBO, Poona), to attend, the Ahmedabad people to talk to, important letters to write, and a day of stomach upset — probably due to a sudden change in weather — to put up with as best I could. At length the last-minute visitor had been seen, the final farewells had been exchanged, and Lokamitra, Priyananda and I were in the taxi bound for Bombay.

As we sat back and watched the landscape unrolling in reverse order to our first journey, I had time to think over the events of the past few weeks and to come, however tentatively, to a few conclusions. In the course of the twelve years that had passed since my last visit there had clearly been some improvement in the economic position of the ex-Untouchable Buddhists of Maharashtra, particularly those living in the cities. More of them were living in proper houses, however small; more of them had responsible positions in government service. In at least two homes I saw television sets(!) Whether this improvement in the economic position of the Buddhists of Maharashtra was commensurate with that of the population of the State as a whole it is impossible to say, but modest though it was the improvement had been deeply resented by a section of the orthodox Caste Hindu community, who believed that 'Untouchables' should continue to be treated as they were in the good old days. Sparked off by the government of Maharashtra's proposal to rename the University of

Marathwada after Dr. Ambedkar, in July and August last year numerous atrocities were committed against Buddhists by the Caste Hindus. In villages in the five districts of Maharashtra collectively known as Marathwada 1,500 Buddhist houses had been destroyed, many people killed (some reports said 400), and a number of women raped. (Friends in Poona gave me copies of reports on the atrocities, both official and non-official, and photographs of the havoc wrought.) The police, who were predominantly Caste Hindu, seem to have connived at the atrocities, and so far as I could make out no one had yet been brought to justice. (The Government of India refused Thames Television permission to film the affected villages.) These events had of course alarmed the Buddhists, and revealed the depth of Caste Hindu prejudice. (Buddhists are also concerned by a proposal, said to be coming before Parliament, to make conversion from one religion to another illegal.)

More disturbing than any attack from without, however, was weakness within. It was clear that during the time that I had been away hardly any Dharma work had been done in Maharashtra, certainly not in Poona, and perhaps not elsewhere outside the state. Yet people wanted the Dharma, and responded enthusiastically whenever they had an opportunity of hearing it. 'Buddhist' politicians were unable to propagate the Dharma, it was obvious, as some of them now realised, and the few monks that were in circulation — both Indian and non-Indian — were in the majority of cases either useless or worse than useless, and seen to be such. In these circumstances, and in view of the enthusiastic welcome I received in Poona, and the success with which Lokamitra's work has so far met, it is clear that the FWBO has a part to play. Indeed, it again and again appeared to me that the WBO/FWBO's whole approach, and its methods of working, were exactly suited to the needs of the Indian situation — almost as though they had been designed for it. Lokamitra and I are agreed that the priorities in Poona are: (1) To train up a body of Upasakas/Upasikas, Mitras and Friends (Sahayaks) who will constitute the nucleus of the Spiritual Community and the New Society in Poona, and in India; and (2) to establish a Vihara in Poona that will serve as a centre for Dharma activities in Poona and the surrounding region and, in fact, in Maharashtra generally. For this purpose Lokamitra will need not less than £10,000 (£5,000 within the coming year), most of which will have to be raised in England.

In Bombay we stayed in a second-floor flat in the Income Tax Colony with one of the Ahmedabad Mitras, an income tax inspector, who had been transferred to Bombay, and lived in the flat on his own, having left his family in Ahmedabad. Since he was out all day at the office, another Buddhist friend had come down specially from Ahmedabad to look after us. This was Amritlal, whom I had known very well in the old days, and who had once spent a fortnight with me in Kalimpong, at the Triyana Vardhana Vihara. During the two days, or less, that Lokamitra, Priyananda and I spent in Bombay together we were therefore well looked after. We did not do very much, as I regarded our brief stay in Bombay as more of the nature of a breather between my programme in Poona and my programme in Penang. Lokamitra and Priyananda in any case had to spend a lot of time — fruitlessly, as it turned out — with the Customs and Excise. (Priyananda *did* manage to find a good Buddha image at last, though: made in Jaipur, and of slightly translucent leaf-green stone.) As for me, I went along to Theosophy Hall and had a long talk with my old friend Sophia Wadia, now seventy-seven, who was very glad to see me and overjoyed to hear of the progress of the FWBO; talked with a couple of very active young Buddhists from Worli, and tried to answer some of the rather theoretical questions put to me by our host. Lokamitra and I also had a very good lunch in a very crowded restaurant with one of the leading Buddhist politicians, an old friend of mine with whom I had once toured the Ahmednagar District. Since I had seen him last he had changed his party, been a minister (twice) in the Maharashtra State Government, and was now a possible candidate for the Chief Ministership.

One of the last things Lokamitra and I did was to go through the FWBO Newsletter free mailing list for India together, crossing out five or six names and addresses that were obsolete and adding three or four new ones. (Both in India and Malaysia I was amazed how the Newsletter gets around, and how useful it is.)

In the morning on Wednesday 7th March [1979] we rose at 3.30, and at 4 o'clock the three of us, with Amritlal and our host, were driving through the silent empty streets of

Bombay in the car which my political friend had kindly placed at our disposal during our stay in the city. The next day Lokamitra would be going to Aurangabad and then, after that, to Ahmedabad, there to spend three weeks with Bakula and our Gujerati Mitras and Friends. (Padmavajra would be looking after the centre in Poona, and taking classes, assisted by Virabhadra and Yuvaraj.) Priyananda and I, continuing our journey, were off to Penang. After the usual farewells, — the three of us had spent two and a half weeks together, and it was not easy to part, — and the usual wait in the departure lounge, the flight was called, we were fastening our seat belts, and to the accompaniment of some rather light Mozart were soon soaring above the clouds.

CHAPTER TWO

# SECOND LETTER FROM NEW ZEALAND

Dear Upasakas and Upasikas,

DURING the writing of my last letter, which took me several days, I settled in here at Suvarnaketu and started getting to know the different members of the community. The place is a fairly old, two-storey wooden building, with a verandah and four good-size rooms on each floor, into which the lads moved three months ago and which they are still decorating. As I wrote before, my own rooms were finished just in time for my arrival, but there is still a lot of work to be done on the rest of the house. Front and back there is a bit of garden, with plantain tree, complete with huge 'tree' of bananas enclosed in a plastic bag, leaning across the front steps, and a grape vine, laden with bunches of purple grapes, half covering the shed at the bottom of the garden in a dense mat of green leaves. The house stands in the usual half-acre section, as it is called, in a street consisting for the most part of very similar houses, all separated by the usual beautiful New Zealand trees, in the suburb of Herne Bay, one end of which is quite fashionable, the other not so fashionable (we are at the not so fashionable end). Up the road is a small park, while crossing the road, and going down a lane, and then down a short flight of steps, one finds oneself on a small sandy beach strewn with sea-shells looking across the blue waters of the Waitemata Harbour. 'Downtown' Auckland is only five minutes away by car.

At the moment of writing the community consists of Purna and Udaya, who are known to many of you; Dave Moore, who will soon be going to England (Sukhavati);

Bernie Tisch, also bound for England it seems, in due course; Bruce Henson, from Christchurch, and Trevor Michael. Patrick Burleigh, originally from England, who was here when I left for Wellington, has gone 'on walkabout', no one seems to know where, while Hum Wol, the New Zealand 'Korean' monk who was staying here, is in Australia. Most of the community members seem to spend their time working either on the house itself or on the Centre, where also there is a lot of work to be done. Bernie has a wood-turning business, where Dave too sometimes works. The latest product is a beautifully proportioned wooden stupa, complete in every detail, about sixteen inches in height.

Purna had apparently hinted that I should be allowed two or three days to settle in after my arrival, but as soon as that period was over requests for interviews and invitations to dinner started pouring in. The latter were mostly from the women Mitras and Friends (a force to be reckoned with in Auckland), two or three of whom usually banded together to invite me. Soon I had got into a daily routine not unlike the one I follow at Padmaloka — except for the more active social life. In the morning I wrote letters and edited material for the *FWBO Newsletter*, for *Mitrata*, and for *Buddhayan* (our new Marathi quarterly); in the afternoon I gave interviews, and in the evening I went out for a meal and a chat, sometimes preceded by a short drive, with whoever had invited me.

On Tuesday 20th March [1979] I paid my first visit to the Centre, where I met the Auckland Mitras, and where we had a lively and useful Question and Answer session. Many of the questions were about the Movement in India, which seems to be sparking off a good deal of interest and excitement. The Centre is situated in a building belonging to the Yugoslav Dom Co., and is one of the pleasantest in the whole Movement. The shrine and meditation room is quite large, with an enormous area of waxed wooden floor that is simply crying out to be used for Yoga classes. Unfortunately, we have no Yoga teacher in Auckland. (Any Order Member who is a qualified Yoga teacher, free from emotional hang-ups, and able to pay his own fare to New Zealand, should correspond with Purna. A very positive situation awaits him.) After the Question and Answer session came a cup of tea, after which we returned to the shrine for a session of Metta-Bhavana and the concluding

Sevenfold Puja. Half way through the meditation there came from below a sort of stamping noise, accompanied by the sound of a harmonium. Apparently it was a Yugoslav folk dance which the members of the Yugoslav Club were rehearsing. However, it only lasted a few minutes, and one had the impression of a lot of stout, rather elderly East Europeans getting rather quickly out of breath.

Over the weekend there was a study retreat. This was held at Suvarnaketu, all the non-Order Members except Dave, who was on the retreat, having been sent away to meditate at a scenic spot on the coast. Vijaya came up from Christchurch for the occasion. Other Order Members on the retreat were Purna, Udaya, and Megha. Mitras present, in addition to Dave, were Keith Downer from Wellington, Jim Sharples, Barbara Gill, Ann Gill, and Verne Barrett. The text studied was *The Sutra of Forty-Two Sections*, and in the course of four sessions we were able to get through half of it. The rest we hope to finish in the course of a second retreat, to be held after my return from Christchurch.

On Wednesday 28th March I left for Wellington, which for the benefit of Order Members who don't know their New Zealand geography is about four hundred and twenty miles from Auckland, and twelve hours away by rail and a little less by road. (Wellington is the nearest FWBO centre to Auckland. Order Members who think six miles a long way to be from the nearest centre should reflect on this.) We should have left a day earlier, but the second-hand Rover which had been purchased for my use, and which the lads (and lassies: Ann Gill is a skilled panel-beater and spray-painter) had been doing up, could not be made ready in time. As it was, Purna and Udaya were working on it all night and the following morning and it was not until midday that the three of us left, Purna at the wheel.

Soon we were out of Auckland and driving through green, hilly country with a scattering of sheep. Udaya thought that it looked like Wales, i.e. North Wales, and so it did, up to a point, except that it was less well wooded, while the trees were of a darker, more uniform green. Townships were few and far between, and usually consisted of one broad main street flanked by shopping arcades, but we did not often go many miles without passing a few smart wooden bungalows. These were painted in various pastel colours, usually yellow or green or pink like the icing on cakes, and more often than not were surrounded by well kept flower-beds and lawns. Even the most isolated were apparently equipped with all modern conveniences, and to an English eye at least it seemed strange to see them set down there in the midst of such a 'Welsh' landscape.

Since Purna and Udaya had had hardly any sleep we did not drive much more than a hundred miles that day and stopped at Otorohanga, where Udaya was born and brought up, and spent the night with friends of his at a pleasant bungalow just out of town. How quiet it was! One could not even hear the low rumble of traffic in the distance, as one can even in North Wales. Bernie Tisch too comes from this area, and Udaya could not resist regaling us with stories of their early exploits. In the morning we left immediately after breakfast, all three of us having enjoyed a good night's sleep. It was a fine day, and after passing through a bit more 'Welsh' countryside it was pleasant to start climbing up into the hills. On either side of the road grew clumps of tall pampas grass with biscuit-coloured plumes, while behind them rose tier upon tier the New Zealand bush, with its rich variety of beautiful trees, many of them with exotic-sounding names with which Purna and Udaya seemed quite familiar. Here and there the lighter green of the fern trees, and the grey skeletal shapes of dead trees, — the latter quite numerous, — made a strange contrast. Soon we must have been a thousand or more feet above sea level, the air grew colder, and we were driving through a fine, misty rain. At a bend of the road we saw a segment of rainbow. The sky was now quite overcast, and we were unable to see the mountains ahead, which were swathed in long veils of cloud. By the time we reached Lake Taupo it had cleared, however, and we stopped for a few minutes to look at the beautiful blue sunlit waters. This famous lake, two hundred and fifty square miles in extent, occupies the crater of an extinct (?) volcano, and is situated almost exactly in the middle of North Island, which meant that we were halfway to our destination. According to Udaya, who seemed to know a lot about such things, it had last erupted only a few years B.C.E. and was not expected to erupt again until about the year 20,000.

Not long after leaving Lake Taupo we found ourselves driving along a stretch of very straight road through the 'desert'. This was not so much desert as scrub. Again according to Udaya, we were driving across a vast lava plain which had been formed when the volcano that held Lake Taupo had last erupted, and the soil was so scanty and so poor that very little would grow there. Purna added that farmers had tried to graze sheep there but owing to the lack of certain trace elements the sheep had sickened and had had to be removed. It was certainly a bleak sort of place, predominantly yellow-brown in hue as though scorched by the sun, and reminded me a little of the landscape through which Childe Roland rides on his way to the Dark Tower in Browning's poem. In the distance there were mountains, but we could not see much of them on account of the clouds. The sky was again overcast, and much darker than before, and there was more than a hint of rain in the air.

When we were again among hills, and had not much more than a hundred miles to go, disaster suddenly struck. A lorry passed us, travelling in the opposite direction, a stone flew up from the road, and our windscreen shattered. After all the work Purna and Udaya had put in on the car, — which had been performing very well, — and the difficulty they had had getting spare parts etc., it was the last straw. However, they soon recovered their customary cheerfulness, a hole was made in the windscreen, and two garages, one temporary windscreen, and one hour later we were again on our way, only more slowly than before. By this time it had started raining, and the further south we drove the more heavily the rain fell. Eventually it grew dark. The last thirty miles of our journey was a bit of a nightmare, especially for Udaya, who was driving. The rain was now falling in torrents, and we seemed to be on the coastal road, with a sheer drop on one side. As we entered the suburbs of Wellington, which stretched for about twenty miles, cars travelling in the opposite direction passed us with increasing frequency. Since our temporary windscreen was only a sheet of plastic, held in place with masking tape, and supported by a wooden strut (the work of the second garage) it was not possible to use the windscreen-wipers, with the result that the headlights of approaching cars were refracted from the raindrops that had gathered on the plastic in such a way that Udaya had to drive through a blur of lights without being able to see the road. In this way, following the motorway, and with the blur of amber lights periodically pierced by winking reds and greens, we entered Wellington and at last arrived — safely — at the Old Centre. As I stepped out of the car I saw that the rain had stopped.

Wellington is several degrees colder than Auckland (in New Zealand, the farther south you go the *colder* it gets), and for the first three days of our stay there the weather was not only quite cold but very wet and very windy — Wellington being famous for its winds. (A favourite local joke says that the first prize in a competition is one week's holiday in Wellington, the second prize two weeks holiday in Wellington.) For the second three days, however, the weather was as warm and sunny as one could wish, with the skies so innocently blue that it was as though they had *never* been grey. We stayed at the Old Centre on Tinakori Road, where a room had been got ready for me, complete with desk and typewriter, and where Megha, who had flown down from Auckland to be with us, also stayed. The Old Centre is a six-roomed wooden bungalow, complete with shrine in the loft, situated at the foot of some well-wooded hills not more than fifteen minutes walk from the city centre. Until recently it was both centre and community, all classes being held there. Now that classes are being held at the New Centre it has become simply a community. Members of the community are Achala, Keith Downer, Geoffrey Byng and Jenine Lindsey. Not often having the opportunity of meeting Order Members, Achala was overjoyed to see us. In fact one of the pleasantest features of our visit was the way in which he delighted in, — positively revelled in, — the spiritual fellowship of the Order. At times it seemed as though the presence of *five* Order Members all at once was almost too much for him and he would burst for joy.

Over the weekend the Old Centre was the scene of a study retreat for the members of the community and the visiting Order Members, plus Ian Allan, a local Mitra originally hailing from Liverpool. I had intended that we should study 'The Sutra of the Eight Great Awakenings of the Great Ones', in the same volume as *The Sutra of Forty-Two Sections*, but at the last minute I changed my mind and decided that we should study 'Conditions of the Stability of the Order' instead. Afterwards I was glad that I had done this. Even though the text had been studied before, in England, a number of new points emerged in the course of the discussion, and those participating, the Order Members in particular, felt that the weekend had been well spent. Our only regret was that two Christchurch Mitras who had planned to join us on the retreat had been prevented from doing so by blocked roads and the ferry strike.

On Monday evening the scene of activity shifted to the New Centre, where we had a Question and Answer meeting followed by a meditation and puja. The New Centre is located near the harbour in spacious premises belonging to the City Council. Unfortunately we do not yet know for certain that we have got them, as the building is situated in the non-residential part of Wellington and a Christian bigot on the Council apparently objects to its being used by Buddhists. As usually is the case, the Question and Answer meeting proved to be a lively and useful affair. Though to begin with it was less 'together' than the one in Auckland had been, in the end it became even livelier and lasted much longer. Among the principal questioners were two lively young American women who asked, among other things, questions about logic (one was in favour of inductive logic, the other of deductive: I suggested they should fight it out between them) and an aggressive young man who kept asking hypothetical questions. One of the young women, who is an ardent feminist, and who wants to put me in a novel she is writing, said that she would be coming to England later in the year and looked forward to joining our spiritual community! I said we would be glad to see her.

Other highlights of our six days in Wellington were an Order dinner at a Mexican restaurant on Friday night, and the Order Metta-Bhavana on *Monday morning*. It seemed strange to be doing the Metta-Bhavana in the morning instead of in the evening, and strange that in order to make contact with the Order one had to cut not only through the barrier of space but also through the barrier of time. All the same, behind the double barrier, the Order was *there*. The rest of my time was for the most part spent getting on with editorial work and giving interviews (two more young men want to go to England), but towards the end of our stay I was able to get out in the sunshine and wander around the Botanical Gardens, with their rose garden, begonia house, and large acreage of pine-scented New

Zealand bush, as well as explore the well-stocked local bookshops. I also had a visit from Indrajala, who was in town for the weekend. Almost before we had time to realise the fact, our six days in Wellington were up and having said goodbye to Achala and the rest of the community Purna, Udaya and I, — equipped with a new windscreen, — were again on the road.

It was a perfect day, all brilliant blue skies and hot sunshine, and with little variation it stayed like that. From the coastal road we could look across the jade-green waters to the sombre purple mass of an island where a Maori chief made a last stand at the turn of the century, and which is now a bird sanctuary. Later, driving up across the lava plain, we could see on our left the mountains that, on our way down, had been covered with cloud. The flanks of the nearest of them were streaked with snow. I also noticed that the poplar trees, said to have been introduced from England, unlike the rest of the vegetation were beginning to assume a tinge of 'sober gold'. By midday we had made such good progress that it was obvious that, if we stopped only at Taihape, for lunch, and at Otorahanga, for a cup of tea and a snack, we would be able to reach Auckland that night, instead of having to stay overnight at Otorahanga and finish our journey in the morning. We therefore decided to do this, and arrived at Suvarnaketu at 9.15, exactly eleven hours after leaving Wellington. The lads, who were not expecting us, were all out at the Centre. We had a meal, and I read my mail. That was three days ago. Since then I have spent most of my time writing and seeing people. Tonight there is an important Order meeting, to try to assess the readiness of the nineteen people who have asked for ordination. On Tuesday April 10th the Ordination Retreat begins, led by Priyananda (I shall be joining it halfway through). — But I am running on too fast. When I began this letter it was my intention to tell you, very briefly, what I had been doing in New Zealand since my arrival before continuing the story of my trip and telling you what happened to Priyananda and myself after we left Bombay. At the end of my last Letter, you may remember, we were in the air and on our way to Penang via Bangkok.

Rather to our disappointment, we didn't see much of Bangkok, where we had to change planes: only a few neat paddy-fields and brown oblong huts and none of the turquoise roofs and gilded pinnacles that we had hoped to see. The airport building was, however, most impressive. After the noise and congestion of Santa Cruz, — not to speak of the squalor and inefficiency, — it was extraordinarily calm, spacious, and well kept, while the uniformed young airport official who greeted us as we stepped off the plane, and the little lady in mauve behind the transit desk who confirmed our forward booking, were alike strikingly courteous and efficient. What a pleasure it was to be in a country where, as it seemed, everything functioned smoothly. I was quite happy to spend the two hours that we had to wait just sitting in the transit lounge contemplating the orderliness of everything. Priyananda wandered off to investigate the very luxurious souvenir shops, returning half an hour later to report that things were as expensive as they looked. One had the impression, indeed, that a glittering net had been suavely spread to catch as many passing Yankee dollars as possible.

If the five-hour journey from Bombay to Bangkok had been pleasant, that from Bangkok to Penang was even pleasanter, and lasted only an hour and a half. The interior of the plane was decorated with lavish good taste (we had transferred from Alitalia to the Malaysian Airline System, and been presented with a cerise-coloured orchid each), and the cabin service was the friendliest and most relaxed that we had so far encountered. There was champagne before lunch, red and white wine with it (Priyananda and I stuck to apple juice), and extra helpings of everything. We were hardly surprised, therefore, when the Penang airport building turned out to be even quieter and more spacious than that in Bangkok, and with even fewer people. Priyananda and I subsequently agreed that it was the most beautiful airport building we had seen in our whole journey. Built in semi-traditional style, with a great deal of magnificent timber-work, and predominently brown-and-white in colour scheme, it seemed more like a temple than an airport building. Hardly had we had time to admire it, however, than after an unusually quick and painless transit through Immigration and Customs we emerged to be greeted by Shin Yueng and two other members of the Young Buddhist Association of Malaysia.

It was 5 o'clock local time and we at once noticed how hot and humid it was. We were driven straight to the premises of the Malaysian Buddhist Association (to which the YBAM is affiliated), and after a wash and brush-up were whisked off to the town's best vegetarian restaurant. As we entered the restaurant, a dozen people who had been sitting round a table near the door rose to receive us: the members of the National Council of the YBAM. They were introduced to us, the meal appeared as if by magic, and we were soon sampling various delicacies and being engaged in conversation. Everybody was evidently very pleased to see us. As soon as the meal was over, and the bill quietly settled, we were again whisked off, this time to the premises of the Buddhist Cultural Service in downtown Penang. Here the members of the YBAM, who seem to have been inspired by the accounts of team-based Right Livelihood projects which they had read in the *FWBO Newsletter*, have set up a Chinese Typing Service. This is not so simple a matter as one might think. The Chinese typewriter contains four thousand characters, and not surprisingly it is so difficult to operate that typists are quite hard to come by. There are two or three of them among the members of the Association, however: hence the Typing Service, proceeds from which help finance other activities. Proudly we were shown the massive machines, which were made in Taiwan. We were also shown the Buddhist Bookstall, which was well stocked with Chinese and English Buddhist books, — among them our own Windhorse Publications, — as well as with images and devotional pictures, rosaries etc. With wonderful kindness and generosity, we were each presented with various English publications, two or three rosaries, and a marble compound figure of Kshitigarbha. Priyananda also got a YBAM T-shirt. The proceedings were far from over, however. Once again we found ourselves sitting round a table, this time for a different kind of feast. Rising to his feet, the Chairman, Mr. Leong, welcomed us on behalf of the Council and proceeded to give a long and detailed account of the numerous activities of the YBAM. Not to be outdone, I rose and responded with what I hoped was an equally long and detailed account of the activities of the FWBO. I think that I can say that I was more eloquent than he was, but he beat me on the facts and figures (he was reading his report, of course, while mine was impromptu). Meanwhile, a round of cold drinks had been brought, and after they had been consumed and we had said goodbye to everybody Shin Yueng drove us back to the Malaysian Buddhist Association. Thus ended our first day in South-East Asia, which had passed with the smoothness and efficiency of well-oiled clockwork. We were most impressed.

Promptly at 8 o'clock the next morning Shin Yueng appeared with a large flask of hot cocoa and a plastic container filled with sandwiches. This apparently was the standard breakfast in Chinese Buddhist circles in Penang. At any rate, we had it all four mornings of our stay in Malaysia, though it may have been that our kind hosts were under the impression that it was the standard breakfast in Western Buddhist circles in England. After all, if one doesn't have bacon and eggs what *does* one have? Over breakfast Shin Yueng outlined the programme that the YBAM had drawn up for us. Shin Yueng was, of course, — as perhaps I should have mentioned before, — none other than our old friend Kah Tong, who had lived for several years in New Zealand, who had been a regular frequenter of the Christchurch Centre, and whom I had met during my own stay there four years ago. On his return to Penang he had taken the Upasaka precepts from a Chinese teacher and was now playing an active part in the affairs of the YBAM. At my suggestion, Priyananda had corresponded with him before our departure from England and in this way the visit, and the programme, had been arranged. (Members of the YBAM had, in fact, been listening to the tapes of my lectures for some time past, and had even transcribed the lectures on 'the Buddha's Noble Eightfold Path' and serialised them in their magazine. Last year they offered to bring out these lectures in book form, properly edited, and I was able to finalise the arrangements for this during my visit.) During our stay in Malaysia Shin Yueng was our constant companion, bringing us our breakfast, taking us out to lunch (the Chinese seem to do their entertaining at restaurants, rather than at home like the Indians), and chauffeuring us, or at least accompanying us, — from place to place. Quiet and considerate, and deeply devoted to the Dharma, he was in many ways a model of the traditional Chinese type of upasaka and, as such, nearer to our own conception of the upasaka than anyone whom I have met — outside FWBO circles — for a long time.

The programme that he outlined was in some ways an alarming one. We would be motoring to Alor Star that afternoon, staying overnight, and returning to Penang in the morning. The following day we would be flying to Ipoh, and the day after that flying down from Ipoh to Singapore in time to catch our onward flight to Sydney, instead of returning to Penang and from there flying on to Singapore as we had planned. Since the airfield at Ipoh was not very big, we would be flying in a small — probably unpressurised — propeller-plane. I did not like the idea of this at all. Eventually it was agreed that the journey to Ipoh, too, would be made by road, though the place was more than a hundred miles from Penang, and that we would return the following day to Penang and fly on to Singapore from there. Shin Yueng was concerned lest I should find the long journey by road tiring, but I assured him that I would not, and he left us to make the new arrangements. Since I had a lecture to give that evening, I decided to spend the morning quietly, making notes and getting the feel of the place. Priyananda went off to explore the shops and temples.

The premises of the Malaysian Buddhist Association (not to be confused with the older, even wealthier, and more conservative Penang Buddhist Association) consisted of a large hall surrounded, on the second and third floors, by a number of rooms. Behind the hall, which contained a stage-cum-shrine complete with image, curtains, and piano, was a temple, quarters for monks (only one, Shin Yueng's teacher, seemed to be in residence, in retreat), and a stupa commemorating the greatest Chinese Buddhist of modern times, the Abbot Tai Hsu. The rooms on the left hand side of the second floor were occupied by the Association's Institute, while somewhere behind or below this were the nuns' quarters. Early in the morning, before dawn, I had heard them chanting, though I did not then know that it was nuns chanting and not monks (there does not seem to be such a great difference between men's and women's voices in the Far East as in the West). As was apparently the custom, they chanted very fast, to a strongly marked, regular rhythm, the chanting being periodically punctuated by the sound of very deep drums, very high-pitched bells, and various kinds of wooden clappers. What they chanted I do not know, — it may have been the *Heart Sutra* and the *Diamond Sutra*, — or the *Surangama Sutra*, but they went faster and faster, with the drums and bells becoming more and more staccato and sounding now above, now below, the line of the chanting, until in the end one had the impression of birds skimming along above the waves, — or the clouds, — on and on into infinity, — until at last the deep tolling of a bell suddenly brought it all to a stop and there was silence. It was very beautiful and, in a strange way, very moving.

The entire complex, — hall, temple, monks' quarters and stupa, — was two or three times the size of Sukhavati, the hall itself and all the rooms being very spacious and well-proportioned indeed. My own room was on the second floor, at the front of the building, which was situated on a busy avenue lined with big green trees of a species unfamiliar to me. The noise of the traffic, as it came up from this avenue, was unusually high-pitched and penetrating. Priyananda afterwards explained that the engines of the diminutive cars and motor-bikes were not four-stroke but two-stroke, whatever that might mean. As the morning wore on, it became uncomfortably hot and humid. However, I continued working on my lecture notes. In the distance, at the other end of the hall, a girl was laboriously practising on the piano, and listening carefully I was able to pick out old favourites like 'Sweet and Low' and 'Dancing Cheek to Cheek'.

After lunch we left for Alor Star, driving first into George Town, then down to the harbour, and so through the toll barrier and onto the car ferry. (Penang is of course an island.) On our way we passed impressive public buildings set in the midst of extensive lawns, Chinese temples both Buddhist and non-Buddhist, — all elaborately carved and brightly painted, — and row upon row of well stocked shops. The only exception to the general colourfulness was a large building belonging to the Jesuits, which was neatly painted in two different shades of grey, like a spiritual battleship. From the deck of the car ferry we looked out across the grey-green, slightly oily waters to the mainland, which was fast approaching us through the haze. Once across, we turned north-east and headed for Alor Star, which was forty or fifty miles away. Lorries, some of them piled high with enormous logs of reddish-brown teak, overtook one another recklessly. Before long, however, the traffic thinned out, built-up areas disappeared, and we were driving through mile after mile of the densest, greenest vegetation I had seen for many a year. On either side of the road there were coconut palms, oil palms, jak trees, plantains, and a host of other trees, often thickly interlaced, as well as scarlet hibiscuses and temple-trees covered with masses of milk-white flowers. We passed dainty wooden Malay houses perched upon stilts among the trees, some of them scarcely visible. We passed enormous plantations of beautiful rubber-trees, each with a little coconutshell cup against its heart, and paddy-fields of vivid emerald green, Keddah, the State through which we were passing, being known as the rice bowl of Malaysia. Occasionally we passed little townships, where Chinese Tong temples and little wooden mosques with tiny green onion domes stood almost cheek by jowl, but the jungle soon swallowed them up and once again we were driving between walls of vibrant green. It was a long time since I had felt the presence of so much vegetable life around me, — not since I was in the New Zealand bush four years earlier, or perhaps since I was in North Wales the Spring before last, — and I found the experience indescribably pleasant and invigorating. How wonderful it was to feel oneself alive in a world of living things! When, three hours after leaving, we entered the outskirts of Alor Star, I was almost sorry to be among bricks and mortar, concrete and steel, once again.

Alor Star was a town of (I believe) some 30,000 people, and we were put up in a guest house situated in between a really beautiful Thai temple, all turquoise tiles and gilded finials, and a more contemporary building belonging to the Malaysian Buddhist Association. Across the way there was a traffic roundabout, in the middle of the roundabout an island, and on the island an enormous piece of abstract sculpture, all sharp edges and acute angles. The meeting, which had been organised by the Young Buddhist Association of Malaysia, did not begin until 7.30. First, presumably in order to make sure of a good audience, there was an American film 'Buddhism in China'. It was a documentary, with an informative and quite reliable commentary, and dealt mainly with the history of Buddhism in China. Though it was at times visually naive, some of the shots were very beautiful in a 'psychedelic' sort of way that the cognoscente of filmic art might consider hackneyed. Anyway, it set me thinking about films (Siddhiratna, Devaraja, Padmaraja, and

Nagabodhi please note), and regretting that such a wonderful medium of communication was so often so badly misused, and wondering when we would have our own Buddhist Film Co-operative and produce films that people would find even more enthralling and inspiring than books and lectures. After the film came my lecture. A hundred or more people had assembled by this time, and I spoke on 'Buddhism in England', giving first a short autobiographical sketch and then a quite detailed and comprehensive account of the WBO and FWBO. This seemed to go down quite well (Shin Yeong interpreted into Mandarin), especially with some of the keener members of the YBAM, including National Council members who had come from Penang, though a few of the people present seemed a bit lost.

The next day, Friday 9th March [1979], was spent mainly in Penang. After breakfasting in Alor Star (cocoa and sandwiches, of course), we left at 8 o'clock and by 11 I was back in my room at the premises of the Malaysian Buddhist Association, whence I sent off a shower of tantalizing picture postcards of sunny beaches and swaying palm trees in the direction of snow-bound Britain. The afternoon was spent preparing another lecture, though I was not feeling very well, partly on account of the extreme heat and humidity, partly because of the change of diet (mainly soya-bean preparations of various kinds). This time I spoke on 'Buddhism in India'. Penang being generally regarded as the headquarters of Malayasian Buddhism, it was a slightly grander meeting than the one at Alor Star, there was a good audience, and Mr. Leong delivered a speech of welcome and presented me with a marble compound image of the Buddha in a transparent plastic shrine backed with green velvet. The inscription on the brass plate read: TO VEN. MAHA STHAVIRA SANGHARAKSHITA, / PRESIDENT, FRIENDS OF WESTERN BUDDHIST ORDER / WITH BEST COMPLIMENTS / FROM / YOUNG BUDDHIST ASSOCIATION OF MALAYSIA. First, however, Priyananda showed the slides of the FWBO in England taken by Roger Jones for the opening of the LBC and gave a commentary. Once again, I thought that we tended to overdo the 'Rags to Riches' image, and regretted that the series did not include some really good shots of the *completed* main shrine. All the same, both slides and commentary aroused quite a lot of interest, perhaps more among some people than among others, though I could not be sure that everyone really grasped the fact that the carpenters etc. were all *committed* Buddhists who were doing the work as an integral part of the process of their own personal development in free association with others similarly committed. The visual medium is a very powerful one, and we must always make quite sure that the message we convey through it is the kind of message we want to convey. Once or twice I had the uneasy feeling that in the minds of some members of the audience, at least, we might be creating the impression that the FWBO was a rather scruffy, impoverished, unsuccessful sort of movement. After all, there was little in the slides as such, i.e. in the slides considered purely visually, to suggest anything to the contrary . Slides were, in fact, a double-edged weapon; and one which we should, therefore, use with extreme caution. (What I am perhaps trying to say is that we should use slides as a *medium in their own right*, not simply as illustrations.)

Anyway, from the slides to the lecture, from England to India. Despite the lack of time, I had prepared my lecture quite thoroughly, and with Shin Yueng interpreting, this time into Cantonese, gave a full account of the three yanas, the disappearance of Buddhism from India, the revival of Buddhism in India, the caste system, Dr. Ambedkar's life and work, my own association with the ex-Untouchables, and Lokamitra's work in Poona and Ahmedabad. Most, if not all, of what I said, was quite new to the audience, but although they seemed interested, — some of them very much so, — I could not help wondering how deep an impression my words had made and whether these affluent, rather middle-class 'born Buddhists', sincerely devoted though many of them undoubtedly were, really had any idea what it was like to be an ex-Untouchable, and whether they even really cared. Still, I had done my best, and hoped that in the hearts of some of them, at least, there was now a feeling of sympathy for their (materially) less fortunate brothers and sisters in the Dharma in India. As I well knew, it was not always possible to gauge the effect of what was said in a lecture and seeds were sometimes sown which started sprouting very many years afterwards.

Ipoh, in the State of Perak, where our final meeting had been arranged, was a thriving industrial town a hundred miles to the south. It was to this town that we were originally supposed to be flying by propeller-plane. Since it would take three or four hours to get there by road, and we wanted to arrive in good time, we planned to leave Penang soon after lunch. I therefore spent the morning of Saturday 10th March, our last full day in Malaysia, preparing my lecture, which I had decided should be a 'Dharma lecture'. This work did not take me more than a couple of hours, which was fortunate, as we were expected for lunch at a nearby Chinese temple. The incumbent of this temple, an English-speaking young monk, with his even younger English-speaking disciple, had attended the previous evening's lecture and had been among the most appreciative members of the audience. Hence the invitation. Indeed, he had been very insistent that we should come, and on our arrival at the temple greeted us with every manifestation of friendliness and delight. About thirty years of age, shaven-headed, and in the usual blue-grey pyjama suit, over which was worn a loose black gown and russet-coloured robe, he was very thin, very intense, and very voluble. (Chinese monks, I could not help noticing, seemed to be of only two types. They were either plump, placid and taciturn, or, like our host, thin, intense, and voluble.) He was extremely interested in the FWBO, and offered to send his disciple to 'Sukhavati' immediately. The only difficulty, he confessed laughingly, was that the boy, who was about twenty, had rather a hot temper. Laughingly, the boy admitted that this was the case. When he became angry he became really angry. I told him the story of Buddharakshita, news of whom I had received in Poona, and warned him that unless he learned to control his temper he would never be able to keep any disciples with him and never become a famous teacher. This boy, incidentally, had been born and brought up as a Roman Catholic, had become a Buddhist of his own accord, and had entered the temple as a monk — I was not sure whether as a sramanera or bhikshu — only a month before.

As for the temple itself, round which we were shown after lunch, it was fairly old, and consisted mainly of a central shrine surrounded by living quarters. Slightly dilapidated, and in need of a coat of paint both within and without, it had a 'lived in' sort of look. Our host was clearly not one to bother much about creature comforts, and seemed to regard the place simply as a base for his activities — or rather, for his activity. His sole mission in life, — in fact his greatest joy, — he told us, was simply visiting people who were in any sort of trouble or distress and giving them whatever consolation he could. Hospitals, orphanages, mental hospitals, prisons, homes for 'naughty boys', he visited them all, and spoke to people regardless of whether they were Buddhist or not. He spoke to everybody, he said. He wanted to help everybody. From the frank and joyous way in which he said this it was clear that he had more than a touch of the Bodhisattva spirit, with no nonsense about it whatever. He was, in fact, very much an individual, with a genuine capacity for communication. While we were still talking, and Priyananda and I still looking at the various images, four or five young men arrived on motor-bikes. Their faces were familiar to us, as they had been present at the meetings both at Alor Star and in Penang. From the way in which they greeted the two monks it was clear that a very good understanding existed between them all. One of the young men, in fact, was about to become a monk himself. (I could not help thinking that he would be one of the plump and placid ones.) Indeed, it was clear that, thanks to our friendly and communicative host, there existed at the temple the nearest thing to a men's community, — in fact, the nearest thing to a spiritual community, — that we had yet encountered in Malaysia. It was a pity that we had to go so soon! At 3 o'clock, however, we were due to leave for Ipoh, and so, after addresses had been exchanged and photographs taken, with many warm expressions of friendship and much waving of goodbyes we parted.

Taking the ferry to the mainland, and turning right onto the south-bound highway, we were soon cruising through much the same kind of countryside as when we had gone north to Alor Star. There was the same abundance of vivid green vegetation, the same dainty Malay houses perched shyly among the trees, the same opulant Chinese villas fronting, — not to say confronting, — the road. The main difference was that there were fewer paddy-fields and more rubber plantations, some of them very extensive indeed, the neat rows of slender grey trunks stretching back from the road as far as eye could see. I also saw a pineapple field or two. Presently, we started winding our way up through some hills, which now rose range upon range before us; the vegetation became more intensely green, more thickly interlaced, and matted with great creepers. In the distance strangely shaped masses of limestone, — one could hardly call them peaks, — rose out of the thin grey wreaths of mist, some with the vertical rock-faces that one sees in Chinese landscape paintings and attributes to the imagination of the artist. On emerging from the hills we saw two or three more such masses rising almost directly from the plain. The countryside was now much less green, built-up areas appeared, and we started to see signs of industrial development. Here and there the landscape had been disfigured by the ravages of open-cast mining, and one of the huge limestone masses, the size of a hill, had been half eaten away. The finger of Mordor had touched even this truly green and pleasant land. Industry had not had things all its own way, however.

Four or five miles outside Ipoh we pulled up in front of another hill, where there was a flight of steps leading up to a kind of lean-to portico and a cleft in the rock that was closed by a grille-like gate such as one sees in prisons. The gate having been opened we found ourselves inside a vast limestone cave temple, which, as the electric lights were switched on one by one, seemed to go farther and farther back, and higher and higher up, into the very heart of the hill. It was more like a series of faery, — indeed of paradisaical, — almost of transcendental, — grottoes rather than a cave temple, if by cave temple one means the ponderous excavations in dark sandstone such as one sees in India. The walls of the grottoes were all greyish-white in colour, and so smooth as to give the impression of chalk rather than of stone. Here and there they bulged out in to boulders and small foothills. Clusters of stalactites hung from ceiling to floor. Flights of steps, like those in some architectural fantasy, ran from level to level, through arches, round corners, and even up into a kind of chimney which we did not venture to explore. In all the halls and chambers of the grottoes there stood, or were seated, enormous painted images of Buddhas and Bodhisattvas, Arahants, and Guardian Kings, while on the surrounding walls were painted figures of gods and goddesses, both Indian and Chinese, enormous flowers, and various religious symbols. Like the images, the paintings were of varying degrees of artistic merit. Most of them were in traditional style, but in others there was an attempt at naturalism. It was just the sort of place that — in its pristine state — I would like to let Chintamani loose on for a few years, with an army of assistants. He would probably make an even better job of it. One of the images, though, was of quite superlative quality. This was a gigantic figure of Samantabhadra, standing alone in one of the grottoes towards the back of the cave, higher up. How long ago it was made, and whether it had been cut out of the limestone or made from plaster, I do not know, but the whole attitude of the figure, and the expression of its face, was one of mysterious dignity and spirituality such as I had hardly ever seen in an image before. It was worth visiting the cave just to have seen it, — worth visiting Ipoh just to have seen it, — worth visiting Malaysia. Even Chintamani, I thought, would hardly be able to do better than that.

As soon as we entered Ipoh I felt it was a different sort of place from either Penang or Alor Star. In some ways it was better, in some ways worse. It was brighter and more bustling; many of the young people wore jeans, and had the rebellious look that one sees in so many young people in the big cities of the West; there was even a hint of aggressiveness, — perhaps even of violence, — in the air. But I did not have much time for reflection or analysis, or even for observation. This was simply what I felt as, losing our way two or three times, we drove to the Kuan Yin Temple, where the four of us, — Priyananda and myself, Shin Yueng, and the taciturn friend who had taken his place at the wheel that day, — were to spend the night.

The place was situated on a busy street, and like the temple at which we had had lunch consisted mainly of a shrine and adjacent living quarters. Here, however, there were three or four storeys, instead of one, and the whole place was built and furnished in much more modern style, — there was an abundance of white tiles, bathroom mirrors, and fluorescent lighting, — and was apparently a fairly recent construction. Whether or not it was officially a nunnery I do not know, but both that evening and the following morning I saw only women there. Women of thirty or forty received us. Teenage nuns, shaven-headed and in blue-grey pyjama suits, showed us to our room on the third floor, where the Tripitaka was kept, and in the most animated fashion took sheets and pillowcases out of cupboards, made my bed, and in short did everything they could to make us comfortable. As soon as we had washed the organisers of the meeting took us to the local vegetarian restaurant. This was quite a fashionable place, with waitresses in red silk trouser-suits and elaborately dressed black hair who looked the very antithesis of the laughing little nuns of the Kuan Yin Temple. Perhaps they were all the same at heart, though, if only one looked deep enough. Among the numerous exotic dishes that appeared before us on the red tablecloth were 'roast duck' and 'shark's fin soup' and 'fish'. These were, of course, soya-bean preparations made to look, and taste, like meat, fish etc. All this was explained to me by a very lively, friendly young man who spoke excellent English and was, I gathered, the secretary of the local YBAM Youth Circle. Soon it was time to go to the meeting, which started at 8 o'clock. After Priyananda had shown the slides, I spoke on 'The Importance of Change in the Buddhist Spiritual Life'. Since Shin Yueng did not speak Hokkien as fluently as Cantonese (or was it the other way round?), a local man interpreted, with Shin Yueng helping out with Buddhist technical terms whenever necessary. The main theme of my talk was that radical change was the essence of spiritual life. After distinguishing change of mental state from change of position in space, and warning that the former was not to be really thought of in terms of the latter, — and incidentally saying something about the FWBO, — I dealt with the change or transformation of the individual first in terms of Stream-entry and then in terms of the Arising of the Bodhicitta, explaining the one as consisting in the breaking of the first three fetters, and the other as occurring in the four different ways described by Vasubandhu, and stressing that they were different aspects of the same process.

The lecture aroused considerably more interest than the other two I had given. This may have been due to the fact that it was a 'Dharma lecture', and therefore more directly relevant to people's lives. On the other hand, it may have been due to the fact that the meeting was held in an ordinary room, which meant that the speaker was close to the audience, instead of being held in an enormous hall, with a hundred people sitting in the midst of a space that could have accommodated two thousand, and the speaker addressing them from the far end, as had been the case in

Penang — *or* due to the fact that there was not a great deal of noise coming in at the windows, as had been the case in Alor Star. Whatever the reason may have been, from the serious and intent expressions with which they followed the lecture, it was clear that there were quite a few aspiring individuals in the audience and that the idea of radical change struck a sympathetic chord in many hearts. It was even more clear from the questions that poured in when the chairman called for them. (Questions had been called for at Alor Star, but none had been forthcoming, and in Penang they had not even been called for.) Some of the questions were about meditation, several of them being put by two eighty year old men who had obviously been trying to practise it. Not everybody was eighty, though. All ages were represented, and both sexes, as well as several social groups. As the questions continued to come in, and the discussion grew more animated, I became conscious of the same kind of genuine spiritual interest that one encounters at FWBO beginners meetings. People had come to the meeting, I felt, not because Buddhism was part of their ethnic cultural heritage and as such had to be supported, but out of genuine spiritual need, however dimly conscious of that need they might be; they had responded positively, even enthusiastically, to what I had said, and a genuine rapport had been established between us. One young man enquired if we planned to establish a branch of the FWBO in Ipoh! On our way to the town Shin Yueng had told Priyananda and me that many Chinese Buddhists in Ipoh were deeply interested in Tantric Buddhism, and very keen on getting Tantric initiations, which they understood, apparently, in terms of the acquisition of *power*, and for which they were prepared to pay handsomely. In recent years, he said, Tibetan lamas had been flocking to the place, from the Karmapa downwards, and of course there had been lots of initiations. (Once again I found myself reflecting that Tibetan lamas always went where there was money: they positively had a nose for the stuff.) There was no trace of any interest in Tantric Buddhism, or of desire for power, in our audience that night. Comparing notes afterwards, Priyananda and I agreed that, probably because it was an industrial town, the people of Ipoh seemed less culturally and socially conditioned than those we had met elsewhere. We also agreed that, if the FWBO was introduced into Malaysia, Ipoh rather than Penang or Alor Star would probably be the best place to start.

CHAPTER THREE

# THIRD LETTER FROM NEW ZEALAND

Dear Upasakas and Upasikas,

CHRISTCHURCH, which shares with Wellington the distinction of being the second biggest city in New Zealand, has the reputation of being 'very English'. Suburbs bear such names as Richmond, Beckenham, Bexley, and New Brighton; there is a Gloucester Street and a Hereford Street; the river that winds through the city is known as the River Avon, while a very English cathedral — designed by Sir Gilbert Scott — stands in a very English square complete with pigeons that strut about as though they had been specially imported from London. The only un-English thing about Christchurch is that it is built on a sort of grid plan, which makes the map of the city look as though it had been designed to display as many English place names as possible.

Purna and I arrived here the day before yesterday, after two days of travel by road, ferry, and again road, and are now staying at the FWBO Centre/Community at Ratnaloka, in a quite large, very English house that would look perfectly at home in Purley, or in fact anywhere in the Home Counties, and which faces onto a very English-looking park. Members of the community are Vijaya, Murray, Brian, John, and Lesley, the last named being a woman. All except Vijaya and Lesley are relatively new, and with Vijaya and Murray travelling to England later in the year the community may not be able to continue in its present form. All that will, I hope, be sorted out next weekend at the AGM.

Since we arrived not much has happened. I have talked to a few people, and been out for a walk. On Sunday we go to Dunedin, where I shall be meeting Padmasiddhi, the only New Zealand Order Member I have not yet seen. Let me therefore take this opportunity of telling you about the Ordination Retreat and our journey down to Christchurch, thus bringing the account of my New Zealand experiences up to date, after which I shall go back and tell you how Priyananda and I spent our last day in Malaysia. There may also be time to tell you about our visit to Australia.

The Ordination Retreat was held at Camp Sladdin, Clevedon, a place about thirty miles south-east of Auckland, not far from the sea. After a pleasant drive through countryside where darkly wooded hills alternated with emerald green pasture, Udaya and I arrived at about 5 o'clock on the afternoon of Friday 13th April, when the retreat had already been in progress for four days and when, under the leadership of Priyananda, a fair degree of spiritual momentum had been built up. Camp Sladdin was situated on the outskirts of the town (I would call it a village, except that the term is not used in New Zealand, and everything was so new), just inside the Clevedon Scenic Reserve, on a strip of very green, rather waterlogged paddock at the foot of a thickly wooded hill, and being a scout camp consisted of little more than a single frame building with one or two extentions and a few primitive facilities. The air was clean and fresh, and despite the sound of cars passing along the highway and the drone of helicopters and biplanes overhead the place was remarkably quiet.

I was accommodated in a caravan which Udaya had borrowed from the friend with whom we had stayed at Otorohanga on our way down to Wellington. This was no ordinary caravan. Udaya's friend had built it himself, of wood, and from the outside it looked like a chalet, or small wooden cottage, on wheels, with windows on either side, a gable-ended roof, a chimney, and with the 'bunk-storey' projecting over the driver's cabin. There was even a railed-in verandah at the back, complete with armchair. Inside, it was fitted up in gypsy caravan style crossed with mock Tudor. There was a dinerette, a sink unit, two armchairs, a barrel-shaped iron stove, complete with iron kettle (both neatly blacked), a bookcase, a stereo set, pictures on the wall, a carpet on the floor, and panes of red and blue stained glass in the leaded windows. Panelling and furniture were all of one of the beautiful reddish-brown New

Zealand woods and finished to a standard that would, I think, have satisfied even Atula. In this delightful hermitage-on-wheels — which seemed just the thing to drive away in for a solitary retreat, parking now on the side of the mountain, now in the midst of a moor, just as the fancy took one — I passed three days and four nights.

My mornings, of course, I had to myself. In the afternoon I saw people, especially those who were *not* being ordained. In the evening, after having dinner with Priyananda and the others (breakfast and lunch were brought to me in the caravan), I attended the Order meeting and led the meditation and concluding Sevenfold Puja. On the shrine, I noticed, there were not only familiar 'English' flowers but also more exotic blooms, among them enormous pink, white and mauve water-lilies, with great curving stems, that closed at night and opened again in the morning. For once, I felt, we were able to recite 'With mandarava, blue lotus, and jasmine' with some degree of approximation to the literal truth. (Vajrabodhi, I remembered, had once told me about Finnish Friends who were not happy reciting the Sevenfold Puja because they were not actually offering mandarava flowers, lamps encrusted with jewels etc.) The weather was very changeable. Sometimes it rained heavily and was as cold and wet and miserable as ever it is in England. At other times it was bright and sunny, and even hot. When it was sunny, if there were no interviews, I usually sat on the verandah, which looked out onto the steep green hillside. Sometimes I went for a walk and explored the town and the surrounding countryside.

Clevedon lay in the middle of a broad green valley almost entirely surrounded by low hills, and consisted of little more than a section of highway flanked with a few shops and other buildings. There was a school, with extensive playing fields, a petrol pump, a butcher's, a baker's, *two* craft shops, a brick church the size of a small house, with a square tower at one corner hardly bigger than a chimney stack, and that was about all. Further down the road there were a few score detached bungalows, each one standing in its own half-acre of lawn, flower beds, and shrubs. In the middle of one front garden a cement seal, painted black, balanced a glass ball on his nose. Some of the bungalows were separated by strips of green pasture which, with their sheep and cows, extended from the fields behind right down to the sidewalk. Everything was very new and very well maintained. A mile or so up the road, however, I found a small wooden church. This was the Selwyn Church, built in 1861. Next door was the vicarage, which according to a notice stood on the site of the Galloway Redoubt, Maori Wars, 1863. In another direction, on the banks of the River Wairoa, beside the road, I came across a truncated pyramid. This was a monument to the first white settlers, a married couple with three children, who landed there in 1852, presumably after sailing upstream from the coast. Clevedon, it seemed, had its ancient history. As I walked along the road in the sunshine, noticing now a huge orange butterfly with bright blue wingtips, now a pair of fantails fluttering in the bushes, I wondered what it would be like to be born and grow up in a place like this, where there was so much space, so much pure air, so much silence, and so much modest prosperity. There seemed little doubt that one would grow up a healthy, happy human being, — as most young New Zealanders seemed to be, — but that one's horizons would be very limited and that, if one wanted to develop as an individual, one would have to leave.

Monday 16th April [1979], the day of the public ordinations, was a day of glorious sunshine, as was only appropriate, and despite the silence that had been observed since the previous day, — perhaps because of it, — a festive mood seemed to prevail, perhaps with an undercurrent of expectation. The private ordinations had, of course, taken place the previous evening, and now, at eleven in the morning, Barbara Gill, Jim Sharples, Keith Downer, Ann Gill, and Dave Moore, having committed themselves with body, speech and mind to The Three Jewels, found themselves, spiritually reborn, appearing in the midst of the Spiritual Community as, respectively, Aniketa, Vipula, Dharmadhara, Suvajri, and Ratnaketu. In the course of the ceremony I looked every now and then at the water-lilies on the shrine, especially the mauve ones, which had opened to their fullest extent, — they were as broad as small plates, — and running over with nectar. Including myself, and not counting Gunaprabha who was in England, there were now altogether sixteen Order Members in New Zealand, the largest number that there had ever been. With this second wave of ordinations on the soil of New Zealand, I hoped, the whole Movement, and the Order in particular, would be more firmly established there.

In the afternoon, after the usual photographs had been taken, I continued seeing the Mitras individually. Among others, I saw — separately — Bonnie and Bill Quirk, Megha's parents, who had come over from Australia for a few weeks and had taken advantage of the opportunity of coming on the retreat. They will be in Australia for two and a half years, it seems, — Bonnie was born there, — before returning to New Zealand for good, and are looking forward to an FWBO being established in Sydney, even though it will be six hundred miles from where they are living. Bonnie is, in any case, hoping to pay a visit to England before long (she is an art teacher), partly for the sake of contact with the Movement, partly in order to see something of European art and architecture at first hand. 'I have never seen a Gothic cathedral!' she exclaimed. Incidentally, quite a number of signs have been pointing to the desirability of our setting up a centre in Australia as soon as possible, and it would seem that we already have more friends and contacts there than we realise. More of this, perhaps, on my return to England. I shall, in any case, be writing about my own visit to Australia shortly. Meanwhile, the Ordination Retreat in New Zealand came to an end, and Purna and I, this time with Achala and Dharmadhara, were once again on the road to Wellington.

Once again it was a day of glorious sunshine. At Hamilton we turned east, and for part of the way pursued a different route from before, which eventually took us down the eastern side of Lake Taupo. On the way we passed through countryside of a type I had not seen before in New Zealand. Hills which had once been ruthlessly and thoughtlessly deforested to make way for the 'white death', sheep, had now been afforested, being covered with plantations of conifers such as one sees in many parts of England, Scotland, and Wales, wherever the industrious but rather unimaginative Forestry Commission has been at work. Here, as elsewhere, the trees grew in straight rows, and seemed to be uncomfortably close together. I could not help contrasting their dark green regimentedness with the wildness and diversity of the native New Zealand bush. For the rest of the journey I saw nothing remarkable, though I enjoyed the trip as much as before. We saw a little more of the snow peaks, and had a better view of the sea as we approached Wellington.

Next morning, having spent the night at the Centre, we caught the car ferry to the South Island. Dawn broke as we were queuing to drive on board, gradually suffusing the sky with pale, clear primrose. It was another glorious day, bright but a little colder than before, and in less than two hours we had crossed the Cook Strait, where we saw three or four dolphins sporting astern in the calm blue sunlit sea, and were making our way through the dark green waters of the Queen Charlotte Sound, steering between thinly wooded hills, and past little islands, up to the town of Picton. South Island, where I now set foot for the first time since my last visit to New Zealand, four years ago, has very few inhabitants, most of them sheep, and is generally considered a sort of poor relation of North Island. Though about the same size as North Island, its mountains are higher, its plains wider, and its rivers broader and deeper, than those in its sister island. Townships are smaller and farther apart, with very few isolated bungalows in between, and there is hardly any traffic. Even more than North Island, South Island is a land of space and solitude, of pure air and silence. Perhaps the most interesting part of our journey was the middle part. Emerging from a range of hills we saw below us, between two foothills, a triangle of brilliant blue — the Pacific. Thereafter we followed the coastal road for fifty or sixty miles, with ocean — now blue, now green, — on our left, and the hills on our right. Sometimes there was barely room for the road to pass between the water and the bare rock. Sometimes, indeed, it led through short tunnels. Eventually we started climbing up into more hills. (I am not sure whether to call them hills or mountains. By Kalimpong standards they were certainly hills, but by Norfolk standards they were mountains.) These seemed barer than those in North Island, with what trees there were more extensively tinged with autumnal gold. Before long the hills (or mountains) started falling away and soon we were driving across a vast plain, here and there thickly dotted with sheep. Apart from the grass, which was lusciously thick and green, there was not much vegetation. I noticed, though, that here and there rows of conifers had been hacked and trimmed into hedges, apparently to act as wind breaks, which made them look even more uncomfortable than their regimented brethren in the plantations of the north. At 4 o'clock in the afternoon, when the sun was quite low in the sky, we started passing signposts to places like Oxford and I knew we must be approaching Christchurch. Soon after 5 o'clock, an hour earlier than expected, we reached Ratnaloka, having taken six hours to cover the two hundred odd miles from Picton. That was now *three* days ago.

Since I started writing this letter yesterday I have talked to a few more people and read, last night, Emerson's 'Thoreau', which is one of the most inspiring things I have read for a long time. Thoreau seems to have been very much an individual, and reading Emerson's very vigorously and vividly written account of him I could not help thinking that his way of life in some respects recalled that of Milarepa, minus the Tantric and magical elements, of course — though come to think of it there was just a hint of the magical in Thoreau's life too. Anyway, I heartily recommend Emerson's lecture or essay (I am not sure which it was) to the notice of all Order Members, or at least to those who don't already know it. It originally appeared in his *Lectures and Biographical Sketches*, and has been included in the *Selected Writings of Ralph Waldo Emerson* (Signet Classics, New American Library, 1965), where I read it.

(While I was writing these lines some mail came, redirected from Auckland. There were letters from Lokamitra, Marichi, and Kulananda. Lokamitra's letter brought me up to date with regard to events in Ahmedabad, where there are now three more Mitras 'and others well on their way', and where they had forty-six people on retreat. Marichi, also writing from India, was disappointed that her visit to Poona had not turned out as she had hoped, and wrote 'with disappointed affection'. I was sorry for the disappointment (though grateful for the continued affection), while acknowledging that the situation in Poona was more complex than she — or I — had realised. As for Kulananda's letter, it contained news of the weather (nothing very cheerful to report from that quarter!), of various letters that had arrived for me, of reactions of different Buddhist groups to this and that, of the Blasphemy press release, of Nicholas Walters' review of 'Buddhism and Blasphemy' in *The New Humanist*, of business activities at

Padmaloka, of the Vinehall Retreat, of a foundation for the purpose of transferring cash from Holland to England, etc., and in short was the positive, news-filled sort of letter that one likes to receive when one is away on tour and has no other means of knowing what is going on 'back home'.) Mention of my reading 'Thoreau' last night, however, brings this account of my experiences in New Zealand right down to the present day (with the arrival of the mail down to the present minute), and it is now time for me to go back and tell you how Priyananda and I spent our last day in Malaysia.

Our last day in Malaysia was a busy one. So busy that we did not have time for any lunch. In fact, I did not even want any lunch. (I suspect, though, that Priyananda did.) We had left Ipoh that morning at 7, and had been back in Penang by 11. As soon as we had finished packing we were taken for our last 'official' engagement, which was a tour of the Malaysian Buddhist Institute and a reception by the staff and students. The Institute conducts three classes in Buddhist studies, elementary, middle, and advanced, besides holding examinations and awarding certificates, and has about sixty students, most of whom, I gathered, attended in the evening. It also has its own Buddhist library and reading room. At the reception the Dean of Studies, who had shown us round, made a speech of welcome, to which I replied in suitable terms, Shin Yueng interpreting. On the whole it had been my impression, during the four days of our visit, that the practical Chinese Buddhists preferred facts and figures to emotional appeals, and that they tended to be a bit sober and humourless in their approach. Since it was my last day, however, and since my audience consisted mainly of teenagers, I decided to unbutton a little and speak in a more relaxed style, make a few jokes etc. The result was that the students enjoyed the talk immensely and responded much as their counterparts in England or in India would have done. In the front row I noticed six or seven little nuns. (Priyananda afterwards said that one of them was a little monk, but I am not so sure.) Several of these nuns went off into fits of giggles at some of the things I said. After the reception they all came crowding round. It was a pleasure to see their cheerful faces, their liveliness, and their frank, friendly curiosity. One of the things they wanted to know was why I did not shave my head in the traditional manner. I explained that, in the West, shaven heads tended to get in the way of communication with non-Buddhists. 'Robes get in the way too,' agreed one little nun. With as little unceremoniousness as was compatible with a speedy departure we left.

During our stay I had been so busy preparing my lectures that I had had no time for sightseeing. In fact I had not really had the inclination either. However, in the hour or so that was left to us before check-in I wanted to see at least one of the more famous temples of Penang. Shin Yueng therefore drove us up into the nearby hills. Here, in the midst of gardens and grottoes, on several different levels, and commanding a fine view of the town, the harbour, the sea, and the mainland, stood the Pure Land Zen Temple (there was a lesson in the name, I thought) and the Pagoda of Ten Thousand Buddhas. Above, on an even higher level, a site had been cleared for the erection of a pure white standing image of Kuan Yin which would be visible from the mainland, Shin Yueng told us, and which would be the biggest statue in the world. The monk in charge of the temple, who had attended my lectures, showed us round the place, escorting us through red-pillared halls and pavilions in which Buddhas and Bodhisattvas sat in gilden splendour beneath pearl-fringed canopies, together with brightly painted Guardian Kings and other deities, and unlocking doors that were not usually opened and showing us some of the temple's treasures, among them a complete set of the great Ming Tripitaka. He also accompanied us up the Pagoda, a multi-storeyed structure with successive sections in the Chinese, Burmese and Thai architectural styles. Climbing flight after flight of steps we found ourselves, on each floor, in a shrine with Buddha and Bodhisattva images of varied provenance. In the shrine at the very top we found, rather disappointingly, an image of a — to me — obscure indigenous Chinese deity in what appeared to be the dress of a government official. The view, however, made up for all disappointments ... But time was getting short and we had to be off.

In the bazaar at the foot of the hill Shin Yueng bought us some of the less familiar local fruits, neatly sliced and in sealed polythene bags, and Priyananda and I ate them on the way to the airport in lieu of lunch. The formalities were soon completed, though Priyananda had a little trouble unfastening and again fastening his pack. After saying goodbye to Shin Yueng, whose care and forethought had contributed so much to the success of our visit, we passed through into the departure lounge and soon found ourselves in the friendly hands of the Malaysian Airline System and, having left at 3.30, on our way to Singapore.

In Singapore we spent six hours waiting for the Royal Thai Airways plane that was to take us to Sydney, and went through Customs and Immigration twice, on arrival and on departure. We could have gone and had a look at the city instead of waiting in the airport but I did not feel like doing this. In any case, I was not very favourably impressed by what we had already seen of Singapore. It was not just that the airport was busier and more crowded than the ones at Bangkok and Penang but that security was so much stricter that one had the feeling of being in a police state. Priyananda and I therefore passed the time talking, drinking cups of coffee, and looking at the souvenir shops. At about 10.30 we left.

A few hours later, after I had dozed for perhaps half an hour, the dawn broke, and looking out of the window I saw that we were passing over a virtually featureless desert. We continued to pass over that desert for the next five hours, during which time it did not seem to change at all. Reddish-brown it stretched, its surface ribbed as though by the wind and with tiny turquoise-coloured lakes lying in the midst of much larger areas of what seemed to be salt — at any rate something white and glistening. There was little or no vegetation and no sign of any human habitation. Only when we were within half an hour of our destination did the scene change. Mountains appeared beneath us, there was a glimpse of the sea, then the usual urban sprawl, and soon we were once again passing through Immigration and Customs. Here I experienced a little difficulty. I was still wearing my robes, and for this reason was an object of suspicion to the authorities. Friends afterwards explained that yellow-robed followers of the Harekrishna movement had been caught smuggling drugs, and that even apart from that members of 'fringe cults' had a bad reputation in Australia. In any case, the Customs official searched my luggage very thoroughly — more thoroughly, I think, than it has ever been searched. At least, he searched my hand luggage very thoroughly. On opening my suitcase he found my album of photographs of Padmaloka and since he seemed interested in them I took the opportunity of informing him that this was where I lived and that I was the Head of the Western Buddhist Order. This disconcerted him a little, and he completed his search in a very perfunctory manner, evidently realising I wasn't quite what they had thought I was, whatever that may have been.

Outside we found my old friends Sten and Rie von Krusenstierna waiting for us — and Mark Lane. After the usual greetings had passed, and very glad indeed we were to see one another, Sten and Rie drove off with me to their house at Ryde, a suburb of Sydney, while Mark drove off with Priyananda to another suburb, where he was sharing a bungalow with three other people including Dipankara's sister. Sten and Rie, I should explain, are the two ardent Theosophists with whom I became friends in Singapore in 1946, as described in *The Thousand-Petalled Lotus*. Rie it was, in fact, who 'converted' me to vegetarianism. At any rate, she pointed out to me one day that being a Buddhist I ought logically to be a vegetarian, I agreed with her, at once gave up eating meat, and from that day to this have been a vegetarian. Since then we had not met, or indeed had any news of each other for many years, though I knew that not long after my own departure from Singapore they had settled in Australia. Last year, however, Rie had seen a copy of *The Thousand-Petalled Lotus* in a Sydney bookshop and exclaimed to Sten 'That's Dennis!' She wrote to me soon afterwards, I wrote back saying that I was thinking of stopping over in Sydney on my way to New Zealand towards the end of the year, she invited me to stay with them, and now here the three of us were together again more than thirty-two years after we had last met in Singapore, when I was still in the Army, and giving my first lectures on Buddhism, and they were struggling to keep alive the Malayan Vegetarian Society. I was now fifty-three, while they were both sixty-nine. Sten had been ordained into the Liberal Catholic Church, of which he is currently Presiding Bishop, while I had become a Buddhist monk in India and eventually started the FWBO and WBO. Naturally we had a lot to talk about in the course of the next two or three days. Meanwhile, however, all I wanted when we reached their comfortable home in Ryde was an early lunch and a few hours sleep, since the Secretary of the local Buddhist

Society, Malcolm Pearce, not knowing how long I would be staying had arranged a Question and Answer meeting for that very evening, and I wanted to be reasonably fresh for the occasion. When I had slept my fill, therefore, and we had had tea together and exchanged more news, off the three of us went to the meeting.

The Buddhist Society of New South Wales is one of the six small Buddhist groups in Sydney, and was founded quite a number of years ago. Their founder, Charles Knight, kept up friendly contact with me when I was in Kalimpong, but when the FWBO was started his attitude changed and he wrote us — influenced, apparently, by letters he had received from certain people in London — a very unpleasant letter. After his death Mrs. Natasha Jackson, the formidable old lady who had edited their journal *Metta* for many years, took over, and was more friendly towards us, though the Society continued to be rather strictly Theravadin. At any rate, when she was in London two years ago she 'phoned me at Padmaloka and, in the course of a forty-minute conversation, gave me a detailed account of all six of the Buddhist groups of Sydney and warned me against Malcolm Pearce who, she said, had ousted her from the Society, with which she now had nothing to do. Meanwhile, Malcolm himself had established contact with me, and I gathered that since Mrs. Jackson's departure the basis of the Society had been broadened and that they were now regularly listening to the tapes of my lectures.

When he heard that I was to visit Sydney he wrote offering me the hospitality of the Society and inviting me to give a lecture under its auspices. Since I had already agreed to stay with Sten and Rie I declined the hospitality and suggested that, instead of a lecture, he should arrange a Question and Answer meeting for the regular members of the Society, as this would set up a better communication between us and enable me to gauge what was the state of Buddhism in Sydney, at least so far as the Society was concerned. This he had done. Hence the meeting which I was now attending. It was held in the Society's shrine and meeting room, which was situated in Malcolm's house, which in turn belonged to the Society — a situation in which I foresee possible complications. About three dozen people were present, including Priyananda, Mark, and Dipankara's sister. Most of them had listened to the tapes of my lectures, with which they indeed seemed very familiar. After Malcolm had introduced me I suggested that to begin with, at least, questions should be confined to the Dharma, the practice of meditation, and the FWBO. Questions then came thick and fast. Since the session was tape-recorded and since Priyananda has a copy of the tape, which he hopes to transcribe, I refrain from giving any details. Suffice it to say that the questions were very much to the point, that they were quite wide-ranging, and evinced a keen interest in the FWBO, and that a very friendly atmosphere prevailed. (Some time later, when similar meetings had been held in New Zealand too, it occurred to me that it would be a good idea to transcribe and edit the tapes of all six Question and Answer meetings of my present tour and bring them out in book form, since many of the questions asked — whether in India, Malaysia, Australia or New Zealand — were of general interest and the answers, if I may say so, quite useful in clearing up misunderstandings and clarifying various aspects of Buddhism, the spiritual life and the FWBO.)

From what I saw at this meeting I concluded that there were already people in Sydney who were sympathetic to the 'FWBO approach' and that, as and when a centre is established there, we would not have much difficulty in enlisting support. This is of course not to underestimate the difficulty that such people might well experience in making the transition from sympathy with the FWBO approach, however genuine, to actually committing themselves to The Three Jewels and transforming their whole life in accordance with that commitment in the sort of way that has been pioneered by the FWBO in England.

Next morning Sten took me shopping in the car, after which we picked up Priyananda and spent two or three hours driving around Sydney. Among other places he showed us The Manor, a large 'English' type building which had been put up by C. W. Leadbeater, the Theosophist leader, at the beginning of the century, and which still belonged to the Theosophical Society. Sten and Rie had lived there for a while on their arrival in Australia, as members of the community, but it was now little more than a sort of Theosophical old folks' home. Situated on the edge of a cliff in what was evidently a select residential area, and surrounded by trees and shrubs, it commanded a magnificent view of yellow sandy beaches and blue seas.

On the whole my impressions of Sydney, as we drove around that morning, were not quite what I had expected. It was much more 'English' than I had thought it would be, which is to say, much less Americanised. Indeed, it struck me as less Americanised than Auckland, as I remembered that city from my last visit. This impression of 'Englishness' may have been reinforced by the fact that there were hardly any coloured people about, especially blacks. In some respects Sydney compared favourably with London and the other big conurbations in Britain. Buildings were very well maintained, — many were quite new, — and the streets were invariably clean and tidy. In the suburbs there were a number of detached wooden bungalows, smartly painted and surrounded by gardens, though they did not seem quite so common, proportionately, as in Auckland. There were no slums anywhere, and no derelict buildings. What made Sydney even more attractive was the fact that it was distributed over a number of hills which, together with the abundance of vegetation in the form of trees and shrubs, diversified the landscape — or rather cityscape — in a most agreeable manner, especially as one went from the city centre out into the suburbs. Then, of course, there was the fact that Sydney was situated on the coast, that the coast was full of sandy beaches, and that these beaches — and the whole city — were for much of the year bathed in sunshine. Yes, on the whole my impressions of Sydney were rather different from what I had expected, and very favourable. As for the 'atmosphere' of the place, it felt charged with energy and very alive. How much of that energy went into cultural activities, — what to speak of spiritual activities, — it would be difficult to say. Probably not very much: Australia has the reputation of being a very philistine sort of place — despite the famous Sydney Opera House, which we saw as we passed over the bridge. But where there is energy there is always the possibility of the refinement of energy. The real problem is when there is no energy, i.e. when energy is blocked, and unable to find an outlet in any direction, or at any level. Sydney certainly had the energy, and since it also had the size, i.e. the people, I felt convinced that it was an ideal place for an FWBO centre, and that, given three or four Order Members of the right type, within four or five years the Movement there could be as big as it at present is in London.

The rest of the day passed more quietly, or at any rate more sedentarily. After dropping Priyananda off at Mark's place, Sten and I returned to Ryde for lunch with Rie, who had spent the morning doing voluntary work in a local hospital. With us at lunch were a brother-bishop of Sten's and a woman secretary, both of whom were at the house for the day working in the office. It was years since I had rubbed shoulders with so many Christians, though these were not Christians in the ordinary sense, and perhaps would not have been recognised as such by orthodox Christians at all. Rie was in fact still strongly inclined to Buddhism, and her — and Sten's — twenty-five year old son and his wife, whom I also met, were actually Buddhists, and had spent some months in a Tibetan monastery in Nepal.

After lunch Sten, Rie and I sat in Sten's pleasant, book-lined study overlooking the garden and simply talked. It transpired that without knowing it we had, during the past year, been just missing each other. The pair of them had been in London in May, just after I had been there, while I had been in Sweden at the beginning of August, just before they had arrived there to collect some furniture and a few heirlooms from Sten's old home, which was not far from Smorland, the very place where I had been staying. On their return from the first of these journeys Rie had discovered *The Thousand-Petalled Lotus* in a bookshop. It seemed inevitable that sooner or later we should meet.

Among other things we discussed different religious groups and movements, and compared notes about our own 'organisations'. (They knew more about the WBO and FWBO than I did about the LCC, having seen copies of the *Newsletter*.) Sten was particularly interested in the way in which we supported our 'full time' Order Members and others, i.e. those who devoted all their time and energy to the work of the Movement. Even though he was a bishop, until his retirement four years earlier he had had to work full time (in a bookshop) in the usual way, as did all their priests, which rather limited their usefulness. (I got the impression that, in this respect, the Liberal Catholic Church was much more like the Arya Maitreya Mandala than the Western Buddhist Order.) They had nothing corresponding to our team-based Right Livelihood projects, and of course they all had (nuclear) families. Rie was particularly interested in our communities, having lived in communities herself in her younger days. Rather to my surprise, she had considerable doubts about the desirability of women's communities, but was strongly in favour of communities for men. Women, she said, had a natural tendency to form strong emotional attachments, and if they were unable to attach themselves to men they attached themselves to other women, which created a very unhealthy situation. Women, she thought, should live only in mixed communities. For men, however, single-sex communities were ideal. She also warned me, though not more than half seriously, that we would have problems when our community members started getting old! (I could not help feeling that she was thinking of the time when she and Sten had lived at The Manor.) According to her, as people grew older they became more and more preoccupied with their own bodily ailments, and their own needs, and therefore more and more selfish and less and less capable of living as members of a community. This might well be true of people not committed to the spiritual life, but not, I hoped, of those who were so committed, whose spiritual development, — and capacity for spiritual fellowship, — could be expected to continue right up to the time of death, despite the infirmities, and even the sufferings, of old age. All the same, we would have to be careful.

While we sat chatting in this way, talking now about the FWBO and the LCC, now about the Gnostics and the Cathars, now about Tibetan Buddhism and a hundred other things, the hours passed, tea-time came and went, the clock struck 7, and Malcolm Pearce arrived to take me to dinner at his place. Priyananda was also there. It was, of course, a vegetarian meal, but Nara, Malcolm's charming Japanese wife, was under the impression that prawns were vegetables, and they unfortunately formed the principal ingredient in the main dish. However, there were several other dishes, and I did not go hungry. All the same, Nara was quite surprised, and a little disconcerted, to find that I did not regard prawns as vegetables, as apparently all good Japanese Buddhists did. But this little misunderstanding was soon forgotten, and we were deep in a discussion on the previous evening's meeting.

Nara had been very much struck by the way in which, in response to several questions, I had stressed the importance of devotion. Western (i.e. Australian) Buddhists, she complained, were very much lacking in devotion. Their approach to the Dharma tended to be coldly intellectual. She seemed, in fact, highly delighted with what she had so far understood — from tapes, the *Newsletter*, and the Question and Answer meeting itself — of the FWBO's more genuinely traditional approach. There were many resemblances, she declared, between the FWBO and the Risshō Kosei-kai, or Buddhist Laymen's Association, with which she appeared to be in some way connected. Both stressed the importance of devotion, both emphasised the role of spiritual fellowship, and both maintained that it was not necessary to be a monk. Resemblances there undoubtedly were, I agreed. Yet there were also differences. So far as I could make out, members of the Association all had jobs and families just like everyone else, and followed much the same sort of 'middle-class' lifestyle — and of course, there were no single-sex communities. However, since there *were* resemblances, even though only up to a point, and since these had clearly impressed and pleased Nara, I let the matter rest there.

Our second — and last — full day in Australia was spent in a completely different manner. Mark took us to the National Park. Though the weather was not so fine as it had been, this did not really matter, as getting to the Park involved a fairly long walk, and it was clearly better for us not to have to do it in the blazing sunshine that had been the rule for the last two days. After Mark had collected me from Ryde in a borrowed car, and I had had a cup of tea at his place and talked to Dipankara's sister, the three of us, — Mark, Priyananda and I, — caught a bus to the Central Station, and from there a train out into the suburbs, changing once on the way. The trains, I noticed, were double-deckers, like buses. As for the passengers, many of them seemed to be office workers, and most were women. The women in particular, both the younger and the older ones, looked exactly like the people one sees at 9 o'clock any weekday morning on the Southern Region commuter trains and the London Underground. The only difference was that everyone was white. The train journey lasted an hour or more, during which time the suburbs thinned out and very nearly disappeared, and we alighted at a very small station opposite a few shops. From here the walk began.

At first it was not very interesting. We walked along the edge of the highway for a bit (it was very busy, with cars zooming past at tremendous speed), then got onto the grass, followed a track past a sort of plantation, and so eventually reached a spot from which we started descending to the river, which was our destination. From here it was much more interesting. The path was steep and winding, with flights of stone steps at intervals, and as we went lower the vegetation became denser, though we occasionally caught a glimpse of the river far below. Many trees had decayed and fallen, and lay covered with moss. There were also great masses of curiously weathered sandstone, some of it projecting over the path, or forming shelves and even caves. In one of these caves, a little away from the path, we stopped for a rest and ate the sandwiches that Mark had brought. It was now past noon, and the sun was shining down through the trees from almost directly above our heads. When we had refreshed ourselves we continued our descent and before long came to a road, on the other side of which was a stretch of parkland, beyond which was the river. Keeping the river on our left, we walked a short distance to where, the river making a confluence with two others, there was a lake. Here there were enormous trees growing right down to the water's edge, some of them dead and with only leafless branches, and in the topmost branches of the trees there were scores of sulphur-crested white cockatoos, such as I had previously seen only in zoos. Here, I thought, was the real primeval Australia at last! Every now and then two or three of the birds, with loud screeches, would take flight across the lake, their plumage dazzlingly white against the blue sky, and alight clumsily in the branches of a tree on the other side. Once or twice there were twenty or thirty of them in flight at the same time — perhaps the most beautiful sight I saw in Australia.

At the jetty we hired a rowing boat. Mark was the first to take the oars, and with vigorous strokes propelled us round the corner and up into another river on our right. The clamour of cockatoos died away. Tree-clad slopes rose on either side, though every few hundred yards the rocky cliff was so steep that no tree could grow on it and it came straight down to the water's edge. The farther we went, the river making such sharp bends that despite its width we could not see either very far ahead or very far behind, the water became clearer and clearer and, in the end, completely translucent. To our surprise we saw that it was hardly more than a foot deep. Rising out of the river were a number of black rocks, some of them just below the surface, which Priyananda, who had taken the oars from Mark, did not always manage to avoid. Eventually, when we had gone more than a mile, rocks and rapids made it difficult to continue, and we therefore beached the boat, and made our way along the narrow sandy bank of the river for a few hundred yards, occasionally clambering over rocks and jumping across rivulets. When we could go no farther, we sat down on a great slab of stone beside the water. High in the trees opposite there were two parrots, busily stripping fruit from the branches, their gaudy red and blue plumage just visible through the thick foliage. Presently, with a scream, they flew over the river to the tops of the trees just behind us. By that time it was beginning to get a little chilly, so we rose and retraced our steps, found the boat, and so gradually returned to the haunts of men. The walk back did not take us so long as I thought it would and soon, feeling pleasantly tired, we were striding along beside the highway in the direction of the station. Since Mark had to go and see a friend in hospital that evening, Priyananda and I said goodbye to him one stop before Central Station, changed trains, and made our own way to Ryde. Sten came and picked us up from the station. Priyananda having been invited to dinner, we both spent the evening with Sten and Rie, who were as kind and hospitable to Priyananda as they were to me, after which Sten gave him a lift back to Mark's place while I continued talking with Rie.

At breakfast the next morning Sten and Rie and I still had a lot to say to each other, but soon it was time for us to collect Priyananda and go on to the airport. This time I experienced no difficulty when passing through Immigration and Customs. I was in civvies, and after scrutinising my passport the official enquired, with a respectful air, 'Are you a bishop, Sir?' 'No,' I replied, 'not quite'. Evidently something episcopal had rubbed off onto me from the company I had been keeping for the last few days! Be that as it may, I was glad that I had met Sten and Rie again after so many years, and we had parted in the mutual hope — and belief — that now that we had re-established contact we would be meeting again before long. But now there was the friendly sound of New Zealand accents in my ears as the stewards and stewardesses walked up and down the aisles talking to the passengers before take-off, Priyananda was becoming visibly excited at the prospect of New Zealand, home and beauty (or was it duty?), while I myself was looking forward to seeing Order Members, Mitras and Friends who, in some cases, I had not seen for four years. Soon we were in the air and on our way.

CHAPTER FOUR

# LETTER FROM ENGLAND

Dear Upasakas and Upasikas,

IT is now six weeks since, on June 12th [1979], the British Airways plane on which I had left Bombay dived beneath a layer of cloud that seemingly stretched from horizon to horizon and emerged above the unsightly sprawl and congestion of Heathrow. After four months in India, Malaysia, Australia and New Zealand I was back in Britain. Kovida and Kulananda — all smiles — were waiting for me at the barrier. Within an hour and twenty minutes I was back in my quarters at Sukhavati looking at the reproduction of Holman Hunt's 'The Scapegoat' which, in my absence, Chintamani had hung above the fireplace in the study. After the noise and bustle of India, London seemed preternaturally quiet and still. A strange hush hung over Bethnal Green. It was as though the layer of cloud through which we had dived — a layer which had begun on the other side of the Channel — had covered the whole country and, like a great blanket of cottonwool, stifled all sound and movement.

The following afternoon Kovida and I drove up to Norfolk (Kulananda was due to leave for Isreal in a couple of days time, and so stayed behind in London). The countryside was very green, most of the trees being in their full summer leaf, though I thought that already I could detect, here and there, a hint of yellow. Padmaloka was looking very beautiful, though the flower garden was sadly overgrown with weeds, and I received a warm welcome from Sona, Mahamati and Andy, as well as from Abhaya, who had joined the community during my absence. It was strange to be back, and for a few days I did not do very much. There was a sort of silence in my mind, like that which one experiences at the end of a symphony concert, when the last notes of the orchestra have died away and one has not yet adjusted to other sounds. Only too soon I had to turn my attention to correspondence and other matters — including retreats, ordinations, and interviews. It was like returning to waking consciousness after a particularly vivid dream, in which one did not experience the limitations of physical existence. The sunshine helped. Shortly after my return there began a series of warm (the others said hot), hazy, indolent summer days that have continued with very little interruption ever since, and I had the satisfaction of seeing the petals of the red waterlilies opening on the dark, sunlit surface of the pond.

At this moment I am sitting at my desk at Sukhavati, looking out of the window. Opposite, there is a plot of bleached grass half surrounded by blocks of flats and the backside of a row of houses. In the middle of the plot, about twenty yards from my window, which is on the first floor, grows a single tree, probably some kind of cherry. Since I started staying at my flat nearly three years ago I have seen this tree covered with snow, covered with blossom, and standing completely bare. At the moment its graceful, spreading branches are thickly covered with green leaves, many of them edged with yellow owing to the lack of rain. I came down to London nearly three weeks ago, and since then have been extremely busy — though once again the sunshine has helped. Most mornings I spend editing the transcript of the tape-recording of *The Threefold Refuge*, in the afternoon I give interviews, and in the evening I do more editing, read, or get on with other work. There have also been various meetings to attend, among them the Chairmen's meeting and the Mitra Convenors' meeting, as well as various Order meetings and meetings of the Sukhavati community — the latter including a community evening at which Vajradaka put on an excellent mime entitled 'Everyman and His Shadow', the shadow in question being not the one cast by the sun but the Jungian archetype of that name, i.e. the more 'negative' side of oneself that we would prefer not to acknowledge.

Life at Sukhavati is not all work and no play, though — not that the two need be too sharply separated, or indeed separated at all. The Saturday afternoon before last I took Yuvaraj and Ratnaketu to Kew Gardens, and a few evenings later the three of us, with Chintamani, went to see the newly released film of *The Lord of the Rings*. (Ratnaketu had of course left Auckland with me, but had had to make the journey from Bombay by a different flight.) Towards the end of the week I shall be going down to the Brighton Centre to take part in a poetry reading, on the way visiting Aryatara, Kalpadruma and Khadiravani. Next week, after participating in the Padmasambhava Day celebrations and in Order Day, I shall be paying visits to Gridhrakuta, Tyn-y-ddol and Heruka. After that I shall be returning to Padmaloka for the second half of the men's Summer Retreat and for the study retreats which will follow in September. If I want to complete the story of my four months abroad — or at least get another instalment written in time for the September *Shabda* — I shall have to do it now, when I have a few days 'spare', i.e. days when there is no really urgent work to be finished and not too many interviews.

In 'Third Letter from New Zealand' I brought the story of my travels down to the point where, three days after my arrival in Christchurch, that rather 'English' city, I received a batch of mail, redirected from Auckland, that brought me news of happenings in India and in England. According to my Diary, that was on Wednesday 18th April. Three months ago! Three months ago I was in Christchurch, New Zealand, and thinking of leaving for Dunedin, two hundred miles farther south! So much has happened since, so many layers of experience intervene, — so many layers of memory, — that it is difficult to recapture the feeling, calm and relaxed, of those golden, early Autumn days in the sedate queen city of the South Island, and the gentle, friendly atmosphere of Ratnaloka, where a lot was happening, but where on certain warm, sunlit afternoons time seemed to stand still and the Timeless to come down and hover above our heads. Apart from writing my Third Letter, and sending off yet another shower of picture postcards in the direction of England, I spent most of my time during those first three days in Christchurch simply talking individually to friends old and new and trying to get the 'feel' of the situation there.

At mid-day on Sunday 22nd I left for Dunedin. Purna, who of course had driven me all the way down from

Clevedon, was once more at the wheel. As we left the suburb of Merivale, and started making our way south, I saw that the foliage overhanging the garden walls was already a mass of vivid orange, with here and there a patch of pure scarlet. Once we were clear of the outermost suburbs, which at last petered out in isolated factories and bungalows, the road was straight (for the first fifty or sixty miles it hardly swerved) and the scenery monotonous. Low on the horizon to the west, perhaps thirty or forty miles inland, were the mountains (I think I can call them that), while to the east — though we did not see it until we approached Timaru — was the sea. We were, in fact, driving down through the great coastal plain that lies between the Pacific Ocean and the Southern Alps. The landscape was practically featureless. Nothing but mile after mile of grass, much of it burnt yellow by the sun, with here and there a few sheep. Beside the road, for part of the way, ran a row of ragged pine trees, and here and there were the same sort of wind breaks that I had seen on the way down from Picton to Christchurch: rows of conifers hacked and trimmed into shape like a garden hedge. There was very little traffic of any kind about, which seemed to be the usual state of affairs, though a surprising number of rabbits, opossums and other wild creatures had been knocked down and killed — rather like the pheasants in Norfolk. Every few miles there would be a small body lying in the road, usually with a harrier hawk in attendance. These birds seemed to have developed an 'ecological' relation to the highway and even to regard it as their territory. At any rate, more often than not they refused to get out of the way of the car, which had to swerve to avoid them, and glared up at us with fierce yellow eyes as we passed. (Like the sheep, the rabbit, the opossum, the gorse bush, and many other specimens of present day New Zealand flora and fauna, the hawk is not native to the country, having been introduced from abroad — probably from Scotland.) Between Christchurch and Timaru there were only one or two townships, and hardly any isolated bungalows. Once, however, we saw standing incongruously in the midst of the flat deserted landscape, a few yards back from the road, a genuine mock Tudor guest house, all black half-timbering and white plaster, such as one might encounter almost anywhere in the Home Counties. At frequent intervals we passed over bridges half a mile or more in length, beneath which a thin trickle of clear water flowed down the middle of a broad bed of dove-grey pebbles. Later on in the year, when the glaciers of the Southern Alps melted, the trickle would grow to a raging torrent. For part of the way between Timaru and Oamaru the sea showed like a strip of indigo on the horizon, while as we drove through Oamaru, a town with a very 'seaside' sort of atmosphere, we could see it, — broader and bluer than ever, — lying at the end of the broad streets of what looked like holiday bungalows, but probably were not, on our left.

A few miles from Oamaru we stopped to see the famous Moeraki Boulders. In order to reach these we had to walk a mile or more up the beach. This was the first bit of real exercise I had had for weeks, and what with the sound and smell of the sea, the feel of the shell-strewn sand beneath my feet, and the breeze in my face, I enjoyed it very much. The Boulders certainly looked strange. It was high tide, and there were forty or more of them visible, some in the water, some out of it and lying half buried in the sand. Some were five or more feet in diameter, others not much more than one foot. All were spherical in shape, though quite a few had split open, so to speak, and lay revealing jagged crystalline interiors. In surface configuration the Boulders resembled nothing so much as gigantic footballs, i.e. they were made up of rectangular 'sections', the 'seams' in between which consisted of a kind of white marble. Probably because it had weathered less easily than the grey stone of which the rest of the surface was composed, in the case of some Boulders the marble of the 'seams' stood out in ridges, as though it had been squeezed out as a result of tremendous pressures. Pressures of some kind had certainly gone into the making of the Boulders. According to what I learned later, they were formed many millions of years ago by the accumulation of lime salts round a tiny core. Erik (*Chariot of the Gods*) Von Dainiken, however, thought that they had come from outer space, and had something to do with flying saucers. A few years ago, Purna told me, he had paid a visit to New Zealand especially to see them. Behind the Boulders there was a sort of clay bank, rising steeply to something more than the height of a man. From the top of the bank, strangely mingled with the salt smell of the sea, came a breath of unearthly sweetness — the scent of millions of gorse-flowers in bloom. At the foot of the bank, and continuous with it, there were some extraordinary formations of what appeared to be grey-green rock. Touching the 'rock', I found it soft and cold. In fact, I was able to break off a piece. It was of the texture and consistency of plasticine, and with a little effort I was able to mould it with my hands. Higher up, the clay of the bank was of a tawny colour. Breaking a piece of this off too, I found it was loose and friable, and contained hundreds of tiny threads, which could be pulled out. I had no idea what, geologically speaking, it might be — any more than I had any idea what the grey-green plasticine was or how the Boulders had come into existence. As Purna and I walked down the beach back to the car, with the rising tide swirling close to our feet, I found myself wishing — not for the first time in my life — that I knew a little more about the mysteries of nature.

We had not gone many more miles before the mountains started coming nearer to the coast. From time to time we saw more of the sea. Once or twice, indeed, the road ran directly beside it, and our eyes searched the grey rocks below for the seals which are sometimes seen there in large numbers; but apparently it was too early — or too late — for them, and we saw nothing. All we saw were a few black shag standing sentinel on the rocks. Soon we were driving through quite hilly country, where there were more sheep and more trees, the poplar being particularly conspicuous. There were also more townships, some of them with squat stone churches crouching beside the road. (Elsewhere in New Zealand, outside the major cities, the churches are nearly always built of wood.) As we approached one such township we saw a signboard which announced, beneath the name of the place, 'Population 500', but whether this was meant as a boast or as an apology we were unable to tell.

When we were a few miles from Palmerstone, the road having turned inland, I saw something that almost made me rub my eyes with astonishment. There in front of us, only three or four miles away, was Glastonbury Tor, complete with tower! As we passed by it, I saw that it was in fact smaller than its Somerset original, but exactly the same in shape, while the tower stood exactly the same distance to one side of the actual summit. Had some immigrant ley line freak, seeing the resemblance between this hill and the Tor, built the tower to make himself feel more at home in these southern latitudes? (On the way back to Christchurch we took a closer look at the tower, though without getting out of the car, and seeing that it was slightly bulbous towards the top concluded that it was either a water tower or a war memorial — which seemed to make the resemblance between this unknown hill and its 'tower' and Glastonbury Tor and *its* all the more of a coincidence and all the more remarkable.)

Before long the weather, which so far had been all blue skies and brilliant sunshine, started to change. Ahead brooded a low bank of black cloud, and as we passed beneath it, as beneath a dark canopy, it started to rain. It was still raining, though not very heavily, when we emerged from the foothills and started entering the suburbs of Dunedin, the fourth largest city in New Zealand (population 120,000, or somewhat less than that of Norwich), which stands on low hills at the head of an inlet. Plunging into the city centre, we passed the 'John Knox' Church, narrow and spiky, passed the Octagon, with its Anglican cathedral and its seated statue of Robert Burns, climbed a rather steep hill, skirted a meat factory (the stench was sickening), climbed more hills, and eventually drew up outside the hillside bungalow that was the house of Padmasiddhi and his wife Jane, with whom we were to stay.

As we were short of time, and had in any case come simply to see Padmasiddhi and Jane — though I was of course always on the lookout for suitable locations for new centres — we did not spend much more than a day and a half in Dunedin. Part of this time was spent sightseeing. On the morning following our arrival Padmasiddhi took us for a drive up the Otago Peninsular, the well-wooded, rather hilly piece of land that bounds the inlet at the head of which Dunedin is situated on its seaward side. We followed the coastal road. The early mist had nearly dispersed in the hot, bright sunshine, and looking back across the grey waters of the Otago Harbour, as the inlet is called, we could see Dunedin spread out over its hills, 'All bright and glittering in the smokeless air.' Bobbing up and down on the wavelets, or sunning themselves on the line of grey rocks that separated the inlet from the road, were aquatic birds of various kinds, mostly gulls, brown ducks and shag. As we drove slowly on, turning with the frequent winding of the road, the vistas of hill and wood and water that opened before us became more and more entrancing and houses and gardens more and more rare. A signpost pointed the way inland to Lanarch Castle, a grand 'Scottish Baronial' mansion built in the 1870's and said to be the most expensive ever built in the Southern Hemisphere, but none of us particularly wanted to see it.

At length, having left the main coastal road, we emerged at the top of a bare, silent, grassy headland and after driving a short distance stopped outside the gates of the Royal Albatross Colony, i.e. the Colony of the Royal Albatross, which Padmasiddhi had hoped to show us. Unfortunately the place was closed, and we had to content ourselves with exploring the cliffs, where there were extensive beds of red- and yellow-flowered succulents, and with looking down at the surges some fifty or sixty feet below, where we saw a seal swimming. Standing alone on the deserted headland, — the others had left me for a few minutes to climb further along the cliffs, — with nothing between headland and horizon but the heaving blue of the sea, and nothing above but the motionless blue of the sky, it was not difficult for me to feel stealing upon me, from far away in the south, a breath of the utter silence and utter solitude of those unimaginable Antarctic wastes. As though in confirmation of my feeling, there appeared high above the Colony, rising and falling in the depths of the blue sky, a tiny white speck — the Royal Albatross.

On the way back to Dunedin we stopped to see the Glenfallen Woodland Gardens, some twenty acres of hillside thickly planted with ornamental trees and shrubs of every kind, both indigenous and imported, as well as with flowers, and intersected by a maze of little paths. In the middle of the garden, half hidden by trees, there was a kind of rustic cottage, complete with dove-cote, that dispensed morning coffee and afternoon teas. Sitting out in the garden amidst the roses and fuchsias, and sipping our coffee (actually it was long past noon, but we had got off to a late start that morning), and munching our 'scones with strawberry jam and fresh cream', it was difficult to believe that England was twelve thousand miles away. Peacocks sunned their magnificent trains on the balcony of the cottage, or dragged them along behind them through the bushes. Families of exotic fowl explored the ground at our feet. Sparrows, —

the ubiquitous, democratic sparrows, — came and perched on the backs of the chairs for crumbs. In short, Glenfallen Woodland Gardens was one those places that arouse intimations of the archetype of the Primeval Garden, wherein man lived at peace with himself and with nature, and it was with a degree of reluctance that I for one left it.

Our next stop was a small holiday resort on the other side of Dunedin, a few miles up the coast. On the way we saw thirty or forty black swans paddling in a lagoon. The scenery of the resort, indeed of this part of the coast generally, was not to be compared with that of the Otago Peninsular, the dream-like 'Mediterranean' beauty of which was quite exceptional, but we walked for a while on the broad, flat sands, and once again I enjoyed the fresh sea air and the exercise.

In the evening I had a long discussion with Jane, who had been at work during the day (Padmasiddhi had taken the day off), on the subject of feminism. Jane, a teacher in a local high school (Padmasiddhi I think is a remand officer), was herself an ardent feminist, though not an extreme one, and since she was moreover an intelligent and articulate person we were able to have a quite worthwhile exchange. What Jane got out of it I do not know (she said afterwards that she would think about some of the points I had made), but so far as I was concerned the discussion was useful in that it clarified two points that had not been very clear in my mind. I saw that (1) the feminist reading of history as the story of Woman's oppression and exploitation by Man belongs not to history but to mythology, and can be compared with the anti-Semitic reading of history as the story of the world-wide conspiracy on the part of the Jews to concentrate wealth and power in their own hands so as to be able to enslave the Gentiles (Cf. the spurious 'Protocols of the Elders of Zion'). Men have of course sometimes oppressed women (and women, men), just as Jews have sometimes enslaved Gentiles (and Gentiles, Jews!), but in neither case are the facts sufficient to justify a reading of history either in feminist, or in anti-Semitic, terms: such interpretations are not history but myth. Why the myth should have arisen, and why anyone should *want* to believe it, is of course another question. I also saw that (2) the FWBO and WBO offer the individual woman incomparably more freedom and scope for personal development than the Women's Movement (i.e. Feminism, Women's Lib. etc.) can possibly do. The FWBO and WBO in fact make the Women's Movement unnecessary.

Next morning Purna and I spent some time in Dunedin (we had already walked round the Octagon the day before, after our outing with Padmasiddhi), admired the parti-coloured stone buildings of the Otago University, and visited the Art Gallery, which contained the best collection of pictures I had yet seen in New Zealand, and where I particularly noticed a painting by G. F. Watts. Although Dunedin has the reputation of being a rather 'Scottish' city, just as Christchurch is supposed to be a rather 'English' one, my own impression was that despite the statue of Robert Burns and the Scottish names above a number of shop fronts, it was not so much Scottish as English — or rather British. In any case, what with its Octagon, its city centre, and its numerous stone buildings, the place had an air of compactness and solidity about it, so that it seemed much more definitely a city than either Auckland or Wellington, or even than Christchurch, and when we left — precisely at noon — I had little doubt that Dunedin would be able to support an FWBO centre.

Back in Christchurch a busy six days awaited me. Purna had originally planned that, with Padmasiddhi for guide and companion, we should return to Christchurch via Queenstown, which would enable me to see more of the South Island, particularly the Otago region, then at its most beautiful. Owing to lack of time this project had to be abandoned, and we therefore drove back the way we had come, Padmasiddhi promising to follow the next day and spend more time with us in Christchurch.

Apart from getting to know people better, particularly Lesley and Murray, who were members of the community, and Greg, who lived on his own outside, I talked with Vijaya, Purna and others about the future of the centre, and took part in some of the activities. The problem confronting Ratnaloka, which of course housed both the centre and the community, was that with the departure of Vijaya and Murray for England (Murray wanted to 'get trained' as he put it, and return to Christchurch at a later date) there would just not be enough people left to pay the rent of the place or run a regular programme of activities. What, then, would happen to the Christchurch FWBO, into which a lot of energy had been put over the years, particularly by Vijaya, who for long stretches had been the only Order Member connected with it?

Quite a lot of people had thought that with my arrival all problems would be solved. When it dawned on them that this would not be the case, and that Bhante was not going to wave his magic wand and conjure Order Members out of thin air, so that everybody could live happily ever after, some of them felt quite resentful. (As I said, I had no magic wand, but it was as though they thought that I *did* have one hidden away somewhere and that for some obscure reason or other — perhaps out of failure to understand the situation, perhaps out of sheer perversity — I refused to use it.) They also felt resentful, — and puzzled, — when I insisted on having part of the day 'to myself', instead of being available to them all the time, as they seemed to think I ought to be. They were quite unable to appreciate the fact that work in connection with the Movement as a whole (e.g. correspondence, checking and editing for the *Newsletter*, for *Mitrata*, and for *Buddhayan*) followed me around all the time and had to be attended to — or that I might want to be alone occasionally. Only Purna, I sometimes thought, really understood my position. Whenever I stayed anywhere for more than a couple of days he made sure that I had my mornings to myself and could get on with my 'own' work. Had it not been for his thoughtfulness and efficiency I probably would have experienced, at times, more difficulty than I actually did. As it happened, the question of the future of the Christchurch FWBO was settled, at least for the time being, at the AGM held the day before my departure, which was attended not only by Vijaya, Purna and myself, but also by Indrajala, Padmasiddhi, Priyananda and Dharmadhara, besides Greg and Murray. At this meeting Order Members based on Auckland and Wellington agreed that, in collaboration with local Mitras and Friends, they would keep the Christchurch FWBO going with a skeleton programme of quarterly weekend retreats and other activities. (As I was writing the previous paragraph of this Letter I received from Achala the welcome news that this arrangement was working satisfactorily, and that he had just led a weekend retreat near Christchurch for thirteen people.)

A few evenings earlier in the week I had conducted a Question and Answer meeting. This was quite well attended by regular Friends and Mitras, as well as by a few comparatively new people. Among the latter were an older man who arrived slightly drunk and who, though he had been born and brought up in China, seemed to have some difficultly in distinguishing between Buddhism and Islam, and a young man who went out of his way to be as hostile and aggressive as possible. On the whole, though, the evening — which ended with a puja and meditation — was a success. Some good questions were asked, and soon a lively and positive atmosphere prevailed. Eventually, even the hostile young man relaxed and allowed himself to be a bit friendly. All the same, I wondered once or twice whether it was really any part of my work for the Dharma to allow myself to be used as an Aunt Sally by people who simply wanted to indulge their negativity.

When I was not busy with my 'own' work or concerning myself, in one way or another, with centre affairs, I went out walking. Ratnaloka was situated right on the edge of the north-eastern corner of Hagley Park, in the centre of the city, so that I could either go downtown in the direction of the bookshops, or else wander on the banks of the Avon, among the beautiful trees and shrubs of the botanic garden, where Vajrakumara and I had spent more than one pleasant hour on my first visit to New Zealand. This time I took no photographs, but simply enjoyed the renewed contact with nature.

Contact with nature was to be, in many ways, the keynote of the next three or four days. Though lack of time had prevented me from seeing the Otago region, Purna had so arranged things as to make it possible for me to see the West Coast which I had more than once been told, was like no other part of New Zealand. My busy six days in Christchurch having come to an end, the morning of April 1st therefore saw us speeding across the Canterbury Plain in the direction of the foothills of the Southern Alps. With us was Vijaya, who had decided to take a few days off. Once again we were blessed with blue skies and brilliant sunshine, which not only stayed with us throughout our trip to the West Coast but even accompanied us to Wellington and all the way back to Auckland. Though the landscape was flat and uninteresting, being diversified only by the occasional wind break or a few sheep, I noticed running beside the road a line of low bushes which, though leafless, were covered with masses of scarlet berries. Before long the foothills rose before us with increased rapidity, we crossed a river and, the foothills having opened to receive us, not much more than an hour after leaving Christchurch we were making our way up a steep series of hairpin bends through a more rugged landscape. On our right, a glacier had gashed a mountain almost from top to bottom. I had of course been this way before, on my first visit to New Zealand, when an ordination retreat had been held on the banks of Lake Lyndon. Soon we passed Lake Lyndon. There it lay, blue and unruffled in the midst of its sand-coloured hills, with the chalet in which we had stayed a tiny dot at the far end. Further on there were more sand-coloured hills, some of them with fantastically shaped outcroppings of black rock that looked for all the world like ruined castles, and further on still, and higher up, green valleys covered with flocks of white sheep — but hardly a human habitation. At one point the landscape rose before us in three distinct tiers and three contrasting bands of colour. First came the sand-coloured hills through which we were actually driving, then the dark green of mountains covered with pine, and finally, above them all, the ethereal pinks and greys of the highest ranges yet visible.

When we had been driving for perhaps two hours I noticed that the character of the vegetation had changed, and that growing by the roadside were tiny Alpine plants of various kinds. I also noticed that many of the rocks and boulders were streaked with what appeared to be rose-red paint, not unlike the vermilion with which, in India, Hindu villages daub the Shiva lingam and other sacred stones. Closer inspection revealed that this was not paint but a red lichen so tiny that it could be brushed off like powder. By this time we had passed Lake Pearson, which was several times bigger than Lake Lyndon, and had come as far as Arthur's Pass, which was just below the snow line and the highest point of our journey. Here we stopped at a sort of Alpine village for a cup of tea.

As we did so, four or five olive brown parrots with rose-coloured patches under their wings, alighted heavily on the bonnet of the car and started gnawing vigorously at the windscreen wipers. These were kias, inquisitive and sociable birds that have little fear of man and are even said to attack newly born lambs, though they normally live on fruits, buds and leaves. On getting out of the car we were surprised to find how cold it was, despite the sunshine, and we were glad of our cup of tea. A few miles further on we got out for a second time, to look up at the snow-covered peak that rose (Purna said) three thousand feet above our heads to a height of seven thousand feet above sea level. After that we started to descend, very steeply. For several miles we zigzagged down a series of hairpin bends, dropping deeper and deeper into a narrow gorge, the perpendicular walls of which, densely covered in New Zealand evergreens, rose higher and higher on either side. At length we reached the bottom, where the turquoise-coloured waters of a river pursued their rocky, boulder-strewn course. The gorge gradually widened out, its green walls becoming less and less steep, the river widened out too, and after a few more miles we were driving through low foothills and so into more open country. On our right was the river, at this time of year more shingle-bank than water, on our left the regenerated native bush, where thousands of graceful tree palms, rising up out of the black-and-gold gorse bushes like so many green umbrellas, stood sheltering the young evergreens from the heat. The landscape on this side of the Alps presented a very different appearance from the landscape on the other side, through which we had passed only a few hours before. On that side, the eastern side, it was yellow, barren, and dry. On this side, the western side, it was green, lush, and humid — and there were even fewer people. Eventually, however, we saw some sheep, then an isolated homestead or two, and finally the little township of Kumara. From Kumara it was only a few miles to Kumara Junction, where shining beyond the reed-beds we saw the blue-grey waters of the Tasman Sea.

Shantytown was situated a few miles farther up the coast, and inland. Purna had thought that this relic of the old pioneering days would interest me, which indeed it did. It stood in a clearing in the forest and consisted, for the most part, of two or three rows of wooden buildings, some belonging to the original settlement, others brought from elsewhere in the region. The first building into which we looked was the coaching station, where a tall coach with four enormous, rather frail-looking wheels stood beneath a high arch the walls of which were hung with sets of leather harness. This was the passenger coach that had plied between Christchurch and Shantytown. In those days the journey took four days, whereas we had done it in five hours. Earlier in the week I had been reading Dickens' *American Notes*, and it occurred to me that he must have travelled in much the same kind of coach as I saw now, and that some of the American settlements through which he passed must have resembled Shantytown, even though he made his journey in 1842 and Shantytown sprang into existence two decades later. Next we saw a demonstration of gold-panning. Dirt from the bed of a stream was shaken in a pan of water in such a way as to wash out the grains of soil and rock and leave a few tiny pieces of gold gleaming in the bottom of the pan. It was to the gold rush of the mid 1860's, of course, which had brought development to the West Coast, that Shantytown had owed its brief existence. Among the shops and other establishments, many of which contained articles belonging to the period, were a dry goods store, a barber's (which was also the tobacconist's), a press and newspaper office, a bank where the gold dust was weighed, a saloon with wing doors and stage, and a carpenter's shop (here there was a magnificent collection of tools of every kind). Next to the carpenter's shop stood a one-roomed square hut with a pointed roof: the Chinaman's House. Chinese labour had also contributed to the development of the West Coast! At the other end of the social scale, so to speak, was a first-floor apartment filled with mid-Victorian English furniture, crockery and pictures, probably the residence of the settlement's leading citizen. At any rate, the ground floor had apparently been occupied by civic offices of some kind. There was also a schoolroom (now a museum, with many mineral specimens), a neat little hospital complete with surgical instruments and other hospital equipment, and a small whitewashed church. At the centre of the settlement there stood, side by side, a lockup just big enough to contain one man, a pillory –– and a gallows. Altogether Shantytown was a fascinating place, and like the old wooden quarter of Turku (Abo), which I had seen on my last visit to Finland, it gave one a very vivid impression of how people had lived and worked in the days before the introduction of modern technology. In some of the shops the characteristic smell still lingered. In the barber's shop, for instance, I distinctly perceived the smell of soap.

Down the road from Shantytown, as it were, was a small wildlife park, which also seemed worth a visit. On the way we stopped at a souvenir shop, where I found some quite magnificent specimens of New Zealand greenstone, both varieties of which — the semi-translucent and the opaque — come from this part of the West Coast. Though they were cheap enough, they were also rather heavy, and in the end I regretfully decided that their combined weight would be too much for my limited baggage allowance. Instead, I bought small pieces of rhodonite and arragonite to add to my 'collection'.

The wildlife park consisted of fifteen or twenty acres of rather nondescript, marshy land situated beside a bit of rather stagnant river and contained various enclosures with deer, goats, wild pigs etc. On entering we were greeted by a very friendly fallow deer who insisted on following us around and nuzzling us in the ribs until she was perfectly satisfied that the small bags of animal food we had bought were quite empty. In the house for birds and small mammals two opossums stared at us from a hole in a tree-trunk with sad, bulging eyes. With their soft, dense fur and air of general helplessness they looked the embodiment of all that was most innocent and lovable in the animal world, but they were officially classed as 'noxious animals' and I knew that farmers hated them for their depredations. The fence had not been built, it was said, that could keep an opossum out, and whenever they broke into an orchard they had the distinctly unlovable habit of taking *one* bite out of every fruit they plucked and throwing it away. Eating in this manner they could in a single night spoil quite a lot of fruit.

At the next place at which we stopped and looked the interest was again mineral, or mineral and vegetable, rather than animal. After passing through Greymouth, the chief town of the West Coast as well as its principal port, we followed the coastal road north for about thirty miles, and so came to Punakaiki and the famous Pancake Rocks. For much of the way the green-clad hills fell directly into the sea, so that it had been necessary to cut the road out of the hillside about a hundred feet above sea level. At Punakaiki itself there was a strip of sweet-smelling native bush between the road and the sea and through this we had to make our way in order to reach the rocks. First came a mass of sub-tropical vegetation so dense that one could hardly see the blue sky, where the moisture dripped from rotting tree-trunks and where one plant battened on another in a grim struggle for existence. Emerging from this Darwinian nightmare, the path ran between enormous clumps of what in New Zealand is called flax — the Maoris make cloth from it — but which seemed to be a kind of sisal. Beyond the silvery spikes of the 'flax', stretching for several hundred yards along the coast, rose the fantastic grey shapes of the Rocks.

These were stratified flat-rock formations which had been created by the action of wind and sea water on the limestone cliffs over a period of many thousand, perhaps millions, of years, and they did in fact look like piles of hundreds of grey pancakes — or chapattis — of different shapes and sizes. In the midst of the Pancake Rocks was a sort of cistern, about a hundred feet square and sixty deep, which although almost perfectly rectangular seemed to be of natural origin. Every time the tide forced its way through the subterranean inlets that connected it with the sea the water in the cistern raged and boiled with a hollow booming sound so loud that we could hardly hear ourselves speak. More remarkable still was the Blowhole. This was a vent in the Rocks from which shot, at regular intervals, a great jet of spray that, before drifting away, hung against the blue sky in a great white plume nearly a hundred feet high. With each jet of spray came a harsh, panting sound. One could well imagine the Maoris who first discovered the place thinking that a great monster lay imprisoned beneath the Pancake Rocks and that the harsh, panting sound was the sound of his breathing. Standing there with the spray falling on my hair, and listening to that unearthly respiration, I almost thought there was a monster imprisoned there myself.

The scenery between Punakaiki and Westport, thirty or so miles up the coast, was at first even more beautiful than that between Greymouth and Punakaiki. Hills — perhaps I should say mountains — covered even more densely with even greener vegetation swept down to yellower sands and bluer seas, while in between them the ribbon of coastal road wound its way round spurs and across rivers, now several hundred feet above sea level, now running level with the sands. Houses of any kind were rare. I noticed, though, that a good deal of work was being done to improve the road, which was part of the national highway system, and from time to time friendly workmen waved to us as we passed. According to Purna, the improvements were being carried out in the interests of tourism, which not everybody was agreed was a good thing, even though the region was economically backward and needed the money that a more vigorous tourist trade would undoubtedly bring. For my part, in my usual unprogressive fashion I heartily wished that the West Coast might remain 'backward' for ever!

I also noticed that quite a lot of timber milling was going on. There had been signs of this all the way along the coast, but now the signs were unmistakable. Great stretches of forest had been thinned, and even cleared. Gradually the character of the landscape changed. It became wilder and more rugged, while the vegetation assumed a darker hue. By the time we reached Westport the change was complete. Both timber milling and coal mining were much in evidence, and the whole countryside had a ravaged look.

There had even been a change in the weather, the sky now being overcast, and — was it my imagination? — there seemed to be a touch of something brooding and sinister in the atmosphere. At the same time, the impression I received was not that man had selfishly imposed the ugly demands of industry upon an innocent and unspoiled nature, thus degrading and defacing it. Rather was it that there was something in the nature of the region itself which corresponded to the industrial activity of man, and had called that activity forth. I remembered that according to the Maha-Parinibbana Sutta the Buddha had said that wherever ground is occupied by powerful devatas or spirits, they bend the hearts of the most powerful kings and ministers to build dwelling-places there, and devatas or spirits of middling and inferior power bend in a similar way the hearts of middling and inferior kings and ministers. In much the same way, might not the spirits of coal and iron, and even timber, bend the hearts of men to exploit them industrially?

From Westport we continued further north to the small coal mining settlement of Granity, and from Granity inland up into the hills to the even smaller settlement of Millerton, about two thousand feet above sea level, which was our destination. At each stage of our journey the people seemed to grow poorer and shabbier and more of the old pioneering type, while the buildings became increasingly more ramshackle. By the time we reached Millerton there were no people at all to be seen, and few buildings that were not in an advanced state of dilapidation. The view, though, as we looked down towards the sea, was magnificent.

Passing a derelict hotel where Don Marshall, a Mitra now in Brighton, had once worked, and driving for a few dozen yards along the track that curved round the hillside, we at length stopped outside the tiny batch where we were to spend the night. It stood on a small concrete plinth fifteen or twenty yards back from the road in the midst of gorse bushes, long grass, and weeds. On either side, also surrounded by gorse bushes, were two other batches, from the chimney of one of which came a whisp of smoke. As we stepped out of the car, we felt how cold it was, and how quiet! The batch had been bought by Dexter a couple of years ago, and Vijaya had already made use of it for a solitary retreat. A more suitable place for such a purpose could hardly be imagined. It consisted of three tiny rooms, one of which was the kitchen; there was no electricity, and for water one had to rely on rain water stored in two large drums. Before long Vijaya had a fire burning in the stove (local wood and local coal, heaps of which we had seen in a number of front gardens) and was preparing a meal from the provisions we had brought with us from Christchurch. The meal consisted principally of a kind of vegetable stew, which he made in a blackened saucepan, followed by cups of tea. The remainder of the evening we spent quietly talking. Before going to bed I went outside for a few minutes. The air was cold, but very clear, and looking up I saw that the indigo depths of the sky were ablaze with millions of stars. How flashingly alive they were, as though indeed 'Still quiring to the young-ey'd cherubins'. Then, as my eyes wandered towards the southern quarter of the heavens, I saw blazing there the four brightest stars of a constellation I had not seen before: the Southern Cross.

The second day of our trip was not so eventful as the first. I rose early, and was walking up and down the track in time to see the dawn breaking above the mountains. An angry flush of crimson it came — a crimson that crept, streak by streak, along the underside of the lowering grey clouds and eventually changed to a sullen primrose. Looking obliquely up the coast, I could see green hills running down into little sandy bays, the wavering white line of tide-edge along the beach and, further out, vast stretches of motionless grey water as yet untouched by the sun. Purna and Vijaya also rose early. It did not take us long to finish our simple breakfast, and by 9 o'clock we were off.

As we were loading the car I heard a gentle, high-pitched *pee-pee* coming from quite close at hand. A family of weckers was foraging in the gorse bushes and bracken at the edge of the track. At least, Purna said they were weckers, and having never seen a wecker before I was not in a position to contradict him. Indeed, it was the first time I had even heard of this small brown fowl, which like the better known kiwi is one of New Zealand's flightless birds. As we watched, the whole family wandered out onto the track and were soon busily pecking at the ground underneath the car. Though the chicks kept close to the hen bird, while the cock pioneered ahead, none of the weckers seemed to have the slightest fear of man. Unlike Cowper's Alexander Selkirk, I found the tameness of these innocent wild creatures delightful rather than shocking.

Since the coastal road came to a dead end further up, we had to get to Nelson, on the north coast, by way of the Buller Gorge, which meant doubling back on our tracks as far as Westport. We were not many miles out of Granity when I had another lesson in New Zealand ornithology. Out of the long grass at the side of the road there suddenly appeared a pukeho. This is a very handsome bird, metallic blue-green in colour, and about the size of a hen. Its legs are longer than a hen's, though, and it walks with its feet farther apart — probably because it is a marsh bird, and therefore used to wading. Beak and legs are both rose-red in colour.

At Westport, which is situated at the mouth of the Buller River, we turned inland and started going up the Buller Gorge, which cuts its way through the mountains in a north-easterly direction. From the time that we entered the gorge until the time that we left it, or its continuation, some five or six hours later, we were in a veritable wonderland of great sweeps of pebbly river-bed laced with stretches of jade-coloured water, — steep mountain slopes densely covered with native evergreens, — narrow winding roads cut so deeply into the sheer cliff face that there was a roof of rock overhead, — single land bridges lightly suspended between massive walls of living green, — creeks with names that suggested they had been first explored at the time of the great gold rush, — in short a wonderland of green and gold and blue which, as we slowly wound our way through it, was so enchanting that it succeeded in 'Annihilating all that's made / To a green thought in a green shade' much more effectively than Marvell's garden, and on a much grander scale, with the result that of this part of our journey I retain only blurred, very general impressions right up to the time that we reached a spot within a few miles of the small mountain township of Murchison. This spot was the epicentre of the great earthquake of 1929, and signs of the disturbance were still visible.

In Murchison, which is nearly half way between Westport and Nelson, we stopped for a cup of tea. The walls of the teashop were entirely covered with the crudest and most tasteless oil paintings imaginable. They were the work of a local woman, who apparently was hoping to make a few honest New Zealand dollars out of the passing American tourist. Most of these daubs were of the landscape type, but three — the crudest and most tasteless of all — were religious in character. One of them showed a group of people grovelling at the foot of a ladder, with a city consisting entirely of black churches in the background. Well might they grovel! Coming down the ladder towards them was the sinister figure of Jesus, wearing a stiff white sheet, and with what can only be described as a really nasty smile on his face.

From Murchison onwards I became conscious of a change in the character of the scenery. There were the same walls of living green on either hand, the same river bed below, but here and there native bush had started giving way to plantations of conifers. Presently mountains became foothills and the forge a broad valley. In the meadows beside the river — now not the Buller but the Motupiko — poplars and aspens appeared, each one of them a pillar, or a cloud, of pure, luminous gold. At one point evergreens and deciduous trees had been planted in alternate rows in such a way that, now that it was Autumn and all the deciduous trees had changed colour, the entire hillside was covered with green and yellow diagonal stripes, as if nature herself was flaunting the colours of the local football team. Before leaving the foothills we drove up to an observation point, where we were greeted by the pleasing fragrance of the Manuka, or Tea Tree, said to be the commonest of the native New Zealand shrubs. From horizon to horizon the distance from north to south, and from east to west, must have been forty or even fifty miles. Nothing but green hills and valleys and purple mountains with, towards the far south, a hint of pure white that was the northern most end of the Alps! Nothing but cloudless blue sky, pure air, and silence!

As we approached Nelson there was yet another change in the character of the scenery. It became flatter and less wild. There were fields where herds of Jersey cows peacefully grazed, as well as orchards and market gardens interspersed with smart modern villas set amidst green lawns and beds of colourful flowers and with two or three shiny new cars parked outside the door. The contrast with Westland was already striking, and when we reached Nelson I was not surprised to find that it was a prosperous and even fashionable little place. Situated at the head of Tasman Bay, with a population of (I believe) some 20,000, it enjoys one of the highest annual sunshine averages in New Zealand and is therefore known as the 'sunshine city'. Certainly the mid-afternoon sun was bright and warm that day as Purna and I (Vijaya had gone off on his own) walked the broad, straight avenues looking into the windows of shops and observing the stylishly clad passers-by. Apart from the antique shops we were particularly interested in the bookshops, of which there were indeed quite a number for such a small place. There was even a second-hand bookshop. All the bookshops contained at least one shelf of books on the eastern philosophies and religions, most of them published in England. Sitting in the rather 'continental' café-cum-bar where there were wood-carvings hanging on the wall and people playing chess, Purna and I agreed that there was plenty of scope in New Zealand for the wider distribution of Windhorse Publications. Later on, I learned that Nelson had even once had its own tiny Buddhist group.

From Nelson it was less than two hours drive to Canvastown, where Purna had arranged for us to stay overnight with Marion, an English-born Mitra, and her American husband Dermot, both of whom I had first met in Christchurch in 1974/75. Canvastown consisted, so far as I could see, of a hotel, a petrol pump, a post office and two or three shops lined up beside the road at the head of a valley. A short distance up this valley Marion and Dermot lived, in a frame bungalow they had built, or rather rebuilt themselves. When we arrived only Marion was in. Dermot, who does odd jobs for well-to-do farmers in the locality, came an hour or so later. Both of them were extremely glad to see us and made us very welcome. News having been exchanged over a cup of tea, and the thirst of our host and hostess for first-hand information about the progress of the Movement assuaged, Marion set about preparing a meal. Purna talked with Dermot, who played with the children. Vijaya walked in the garden. As for me, I explored the well-stocked bookshelves in the living room. It was strange to find, in this out of the way corner of New Zealand, the same books — including the latest *Mitrata* — and the same records that one would find in an FWBO community in England.

That night I slept in the retreat cabin that Marion and Dermot had built in the far corner of the orchard. Was it an opossum that I heard scuffling on the roof in the early hours or was it only the scraping of an overhanging branch of an apple tree as it swayed in the wind? In the morning, after breakfast, Purna and I went for a walk, first down to the highway, where birds high in a group of big trees were emitting pure bell-like notes, then back along the track past the bungalow and up the narrow, sheltered valley for a couple of miles. It was a fine day, though the sun had not yet risen above the shorn green hills, so steep as to be almost conical in shape. On our right was a thoroughly English hedgerow, with river beyond; on our left, fields and the occasional farmstead. By the time we returned to the bungalow Marion had cut sandwiches and was ready to take us on the picnic she had planned. The place she had chosen was Pelorus Bridge, a well known beauty spot ten or twelve miles back along the road to Nelson. Here we spent an hour walking round the loop of the nature trail through the forest, where Purna and Dermot had a happy time identifying the great trees that rose nearly a hundred feet above our heads, after which, crossing to the other side of the road, we drove down a winding track, through more forest, to the picnic place. This was situated beside a river that foamed along between banks of grey rock. Soon a kettle was boiling on a fire of twigs, and we were sitting round a rustic table in the hot sunshine eating our sandwiches. The only thing that spoiled the otherwise idyllic nature of the scene were the wasps. According to Dermot they were German wasps that had been specially imported to deal with a certain kind of fruit fly but, like other such imports, they had got out of hand and were now a nuisance. Once we had finished eating, however, they left us to enjoy the beauty of the place unmolested. Purna and Vijaya lay in the sun. Marion gathered a kind of silver-grey moss from the trunks of the trees at the edge of the clearing. I strolled along the banks of the river watching the racing waters. All too soon it was time for us to leave. Since Purna, Vijaya and I planned to drive straight on to Picton, without stopping again at Canvastown, we said goodbye to Marion and Dermot and in a few minutes were back on the highway heading north-east.

It was the third afternoon since our departure from Christchurch, and we were now on the last lap of our trip. Since it would take us less than two hours to reach Picton, where we were to catch the Wellington ferry that night, we had plenty of time and could linger on our way. Well might we linger! Once we had left Havelock (where the tiny museum contained mementos of Lord Rutherford of Nelson, the discoverer of radioactivity), the greater part of our short journey took us along the coastal road that skirted first the Mahau Sound and then, when we had crossed the narrow neck of the intervening peninsular, the Queen Charlotte Sound. The scenery was of the same 'Mediterranean' type as that of the Otago Peninsular — and even more beautiful. Emerald green hills ran down into waters of sapphire blue, and every turning of the road revealed vistas more enchanting than the last. Sometimes it was difficult to tell whether a pyramid of solid green floating in the midst of the channel was, in fact, an island, or whether it was a headland projecting from the opposite shore of the Sound. At several places, one arm of the Sound ran into another, thus adding to the variety of the scene.

As we approached Picton the luxury villas appeared more and more frequently among the trees, both above and below the road, clustering in such numbers around the beautiful sandy bays that they almost amounted to townships. In Picton there was nothing of special interest to see, and we spent the time we had to wait before driving onto the ferry sitting in cafes or strolling along the waterfront. Vijaya had originally planned to make his way back to Christchurch from here, but he now decided to accompany us to Wellington, so that he could confer personally with Achala — who had been unable to attend the AGM — about the future of the Christchurch Centre. It was together, therefore, that the three of us drove onto the ferry shortly after 7 o'clock, when it was already dusk and the stars had started appearing in the sky.

The voyage from Picton to Wellington lasted nearly four hours. For the greater part of the way there was a heavy swell, and by the time we reached our destination I felt destinctly uneasy. Fifteen minutes after disembarkation we were exchanging greetings with Achala and Dharmadhara in the kitchen of the Old Centre, and ten minutes later I was in bed — but not before I had heard the joyful news that, all obstacles having been overcome, the New Centre was now definitely ours.

At 7.30 next morning Purna and I left for Auckland. With us was Priyananda, who had arrived from Christchurch a couple of days earlier and had been waiting for us. By mutual consent we followed, for part of the way, a more westerly route than the one Purna and I had taken five weeks earlier, on our return from my first visit to Wellington. Diverging from the latter at Bulls, and rejoining it south of Te Kuiti, nearly a hundred and fifty miles farther on, we saw more of the scenic beauties of North Island which, even if they are less spectacular than those of South Island, certainly give the visitor no cause for complaint. By this time, however, I was feeling quite tired. The strain of travel was beginning to tell, and for much of the journey that day I *saw* rather than *felt* how beautiful North Island was. Purna too, I sensed, was tired. He said nothing, but though he was as efficient and reliable as ever I noticed that he was not quite his usual cheerful self.

Among other places, we stopped at Wanganui, a small town on the west coast, as well as at the Mangawhero Falls, a few dozen miles farther on. As we looked round Wanganui, a pleasant place that seemed just big enough to support an

FWBO centre, Purna reminded me that Subhuti had been born there — or perhaps it was his mother. Anyway, Subhuti definitely had *some* connection with this part of the world, so before we left I bought a picture postcard of the town to send him.

By 5.30 we started seeing the lights of Auckland on the horizon, and by 6.30 we were back at Suvarnaketu, having been eleven hours on the road. As I mounted the front steps, I noticed that during the three weeks that I had been away the bananas had ripened inside their plastic bag and were now a bright yellow. Three weeks! It seemed that I had been away much longer than that. Somebody brought me a cup of tea. I started looking through my mail. In another three weeks I would be leaving for India. The fact that I was now back in Auckland meant that I was on the last lap of my New Zealand tour, and tomorrow must start thinking about my lectures.

CHAPTER FIVE

# SECOND LETTER FROM ENGLAND

Dear Upasakas and Upasikas,

I

SOME years ago I read a poem (by Southey, I think) in which, conventionally enough, the poet compares human life to a river. As the river pursues its course, flowing now past sunlit meadows, now between overhanging cliffs, it gathers momentum, so that by the time it approaches the end of its long journey it is flowing much more rapidly than it did at the beginning, and the houses and trees on its banks are fairly racing past. It is the same with life. The older we grow, the more quickly time seems to slide by, so that by the time we reach middle age events are rushing past us at several times their previous velocity, and a year seems hardly longer than a month did when we were young. Yesterday I celebrated, or observed, — or at least noticed, — my fifty-fourth birthday, so that it was not surprising that, in the course of the day, the moralising poem should have floated into my mind and given rise to various reflections appropriate to the occasion. For me, these last few years, time has indeed been passing much more quickly than it did when I was in India, or even than it did during the early days of the 'Friends'. This has never been more so than during the past year, and particularly the last few months, — even the last few weeks, — when increasingly it has seemed that the more there was to do the less time there was in which to do it.

Since writing my last letter I have spent more than a month at Sukhavati, as well as visiting the Brighton Buddhist Centre, Aryatara (Purley, Surrey), Gridhrakuta (Manchester), Tyn-y-ddol (North Wales), and Heruka (Glasgow). At the moment I am again back at Padmaloka, where the men's Summer Retreat is now into its fourth week, having come up from London two weeks ago today. It is mid-afternoon. The bell has just gone, which means that the (Hatha) Yoga class is about to begin. (Since Abhaya is now leading the retreat, and Vimalamitra and Mike Scherk are also on it, Yoga is figuring more prominently in the retreat programme than it usually does.) Once again I am sitting at my desk looking out of the window. The view is very different from the one which I have at Sukhavati. First, immediately below my first-floor study, comes the broad sweep off the gravelled drive, then a flower-bed full of red, yellow and white roses all in bloom, next the ample expanse of the lawn, — back and forth over which the swallows are skimming, presumably in search of flying insects, — while finally, springing up out of the shrubbery comes the encompassing wall of trees beyond which there lies, almost unseen, the road. On a bench to the right of the lawn sit Kovida and Mahamati, enjoying mugs of afternoon tea. Every now and then I can hear, faint in the distance, Kovida's rather high-pitched laugh, as he and Mahamati talk.

Originally, I was going to finish telling you what happened after my return to London six or seven weeks ago, — you see how quickly time is passing, — and *then* carry on from the point at which I had ended my last Letter, but now on second thoughts I think I will go straight back to the beginning of my three weeks in Auckland, which were also my last three weeks in New Zealand, and try to complete the story of my tour in strict chronological sequence. This will have the advantage of ensuring that the impressions of my stay in Auckland, which have become a little blurred already, as well as the impressions of my second visit to India, are not further obliterated by recollections of the events that have piled up since. (The more I think of it, the more the happenings of each day in my life seem to provide the materials for an interesting book!) It will also have the advantage of enabling me to continue following the main narrative thread of my story before, with my return to England, it starts separating out into a whole web of events and activities.

My first day back in Auckland was a busy one. At 10 o'clock I received a visit from Eve Gill, who was about to leave for England and Amaravati, and gave her a few things to take back for me. In the afternoon I sent off a shower of picture postcards, my biggest so far, in the direction of England, and another, a much smaller, shower in the direction of India. In the evening I attended the AGM of the FWBO (Auckland), as well as the Council meeting immediately following, at which Udaya was re-elected Chairman.

Next morning I started work on the first of the three talks I was to give under the general heading 'A New Buddhist Movement: The Meaning of FWBO'. Publicity for these talks was already well advanced. Thanks to the efforts of various members of the community, downtown Auckland was fairly plastered with Vipula's attractive orange posters with the hand-coloured lotus flowers. Patrick Burleigh in particular showed great resourcefulness in putting them up wherever they were most likely to cause displeasure to the 'establishment'. Since I wanted time in which to immerse myself in the subject matter of the talks, I decided to restrict interviews and outings until after I had actually given the second talk, by which time, I hoped, I would be sufficiently into my stride for distractions of this sort not to matter.

For the next two weeks, therefore, I spent the greater part of the day at my desk, or walking up and down the room, reflecting on the ideas and images that came into my mind, arranging them in logical sequence, and making notes. Suvarnaketu was an ideal place in which to do this. Apart from the fact that I had my own quarters, the place was very quiet. During the day the boys were all out working, either down at the centre, where there was still much to be done, or at Bernie's wood-turning factory, then in process of becoming a Friends co-operative. Sometimes they were so busy that they did not come back for lunch. There was always someone around to look after me, though, and see that I got my meals at the proper time. Patrick and Ratnaketu especially were very particular about this. When they were on the premises I could be sure not only of my lunch, but of my morning coffee and afternoon tea as well.

Ratnaketu, in fact, took his duties very seriously, and was so concerned that I should be well looked after that with my morning coffee I got, more often than not, not just one biscuit, but three or four biscuits and two large pieces of cake. Probably he wanted to make quite sure that I had enough energy for the talks. Be that as it may, whether on account of all the cake and biscuits I was getting, or for some other reason, I certainly had enough energy for the talks, which were given at the Pioneer Women's Hall, in downtown Auckland, on three successive Wednesday evenings, and which judged in terms of the audience's response were a modest success. Since Purna has already written about the talks in the FWBO *Newsletter* I shall say no more about them. I enjoyed giving them, and although, as some of you know, I am still dissatisfied with the talk or lecture as a medium of communication, I looked forward to our Wednesday evening gatherings as the highlight of the whole week.

Once I had given my second talk I was able to make myself more available to people, which meant that my last ten days in Auckland, — my last ten days in New Zealand, — were very busy ones. In addition to interviews, and the occasional meal out (I had already had a pleasant evening at a restaurant with Akshobhya) there was an Order Members' Study Retreat at Suvarnaketu, in the course of which we completed our study of *The Sutra of Forty-Two Sections*, and a Question and Answer meeting at the Centre. The Question and Answer meeting was as lively and useful as the one held seven weeks earlier, shortly after my arrival in New Zealand, but on the whole less emotionally-positive. At times I detected a distinct undercurrent of disgruntlement. This was due, no doubt, to the fact that a number of people were present whose request for ordination had not been granted and that *some* of these people felt disappointed, even resentful, that they *had not been given what they wanted*. Even allowing for the fact that their experience of the Order had not been very extensive, or very deep, and for the fact that the Auckland Chapter of the Order had not always succeeded in embodying the ideal of Spiritual Community, — even allowing for the fact that the ideal of individual spiritual commitment to The Three Jewels was difficult to understand, — I found their attitude to 'ordination' quite extraordinary. They really seemed to think that I had come from England with a thing called ordination in my luggage, and that if they could only bring enough pressure to bear on me, or pull the right strings, I could be persuaded or coerced into parting with it. They also seemed to think that a *strong desire* for 'ordination' was the same thing as *genuine commitment* to The Three Jewels — that your *wanting* to be ordained was proof of your *readiness* to be ordained. With *micchāditthis* such as these prevailing it was not surprising that so many of those who had originally asked for ordination (fourteen out of a total of nineteen) could not be ordained or that, when they realised they were not going to get what they wanted, they should feel disappointed, even disgruntled. Some were simply unable to understand why they were not being ordained. Others attributed their failure to secure 'ordination' to the hostility of certain Order Members, for which, of course, they had various explanations. A few realised that they were not, in fact, ready for ordination, and quietly got down to the task of making sure they were ready next time.

So far as I was personally concerned, one of the strangest things about the whole question of ordination, as it had arisen in Auckland, was the fact that so many people seemed to think that ordination had nothing to do with their having any kind of genuine human communication — much less still any kind of real personal relationship — with me. Of me as an individual they were quite unaware. I was simply the possessor of the thing called 'ordination'. (They were also unaware, in some cases, of Order Members as individuals. Order Members were a sort of Praetorian Guard standing between them and Bhante, i.e. between them and the possessor of the much-coveted treasure, and counted only to the extent that they were in a position to vote either 'for' or 'against' him giving it to them.) *Micchāditthis* about ordination were not, of course, peculiar to Auckland. Inasmuch as like all *micchāditthis* they are based, ultimately, on our unawareness of Absolute Reality, such *micchāditthis* lurk below the more illumined surface of our thinking everywhere in the Movement. In Auckland, however, they seemed to be more in evidence than anywhere else, as well as bolder and more aggressive — like dragons which, in the absence of any St. George, have become accustomed to roaming the countryside unchecked and terrorizing everybody. One particularly bizarre incident that occurred only a few days before I left New Zealand illustrates the extent to which this was the case. A rather peripheral Friend whose own request for ordination has not been acceded to, but who still hoped to be ordained, happened to see one of the women Mitras in a bookshop. She was not personally known to him, nor he to her, but apparently he had seen her at the Centre and heard that she too had requested ordination. Without a moment's hesitation (I was told) he marched up to her and said, much to her astonishment, 'Don't worry. *I* shall see that you are ordained.'

Thinking things over at a later date, it appeared to me that the root cause of the Bhante's-come-with-ordination-in-his-luggage *micchāditthi* was our natural propensity to look upon 'ordination', 'Enlightenment' etc. not as levels of being and consciousness towards which the individual can grow but rather as objects which it is possible for him to appropriate *without himself undergoing any change*. The root of this *micchāditthi* in turn, as of others like it, was the great First Fetter, the fetter of *sakkāyadiṭṭhi/-satkayadṛṣṭi* or '(unchanging-) self-view', the view that there exists as the permanent subject of our ever-changing experiences a self that does not change. Here abstraction (from the actual flow of experience), reification (of the self-concept abstracted), alienation (from oneself as part of the flow of experience), and pseudo-identification (with the abstracted, reified self-concept) are all involved. This 'unchanging-self-view' is also at the bottom of more homely misunderstandings, as when we think of happiness, for example, as a 'thing' which it is possible for one person to give another, — a thing which if necessary can be demanded and extorted,— rather than as a quality of the way in which they actually relate to each other and as having no existence apart from that. It is at the bottom, likewise, of the kind of misunderstanding that, three or four years ago, arose (I recalled) among the women connected with the Archway Centre, when they apparently thought that the enhanced spiritual fellowship which the men enjoyed when they were on their own together, without the women, was a 'thing' that the men selfishly wanted to keep to themselves, without sharing it with the women — even going so far as to hide it away somewhere whenever a woman appeared on the scene. Now that they have their own spiritual communities, of course, the women know that such enhanced spiritual fellowship is not a 'thing' at all but simply a development of the way in which individuals relate to one another in a situation free from inter-sex tensions. — But such examples could be multiplied endlessly, and it is time I got back to my last ten days in Auckland. Before doing so perhaps I should add, in fairness to the Auckland Friends and Mitras, that the Bhante's-come-with-ordination-in-his-luggage *micchāditthi* might not have been quite so much in evidence had my stay in New Zealand been a longer one. The fact that I was there for only two and a half months, and probably would not be coming again for several years, if at all, meant that for some people their 'being ordained' assumed an urgent — almost a desperate — 'now or never' character, with the result that despite Purna's and Udaya's best efforts ordination was seen more in terms of *getting* and less in terms of *growing* than might otherwise have been the case. For my own part, I heartily regretted that I could not stay longer in New Zealand, and leave only when more people had been ordained; but time, as usual, was short. I was expected in India (Lokamitra was growing impatient), as well as in England, where I had promised to be back in time for the men's Ordination Retreat at Padmaloka.

As it happened, the Question and Answer meeting (the undercurrent of disgruntlement at which prompted the above reflections) was only the second function I had attended at the Auckland Centre since my return from the South Island. The first was the Wesak Day celebration, held ten days earlier, which I attended only in the evening, the greater part of the day having been spent — most enjoyably — in the preparation of my second talk, which was entitled 'Western Buddhists versus Eastern Buddhism' and which turned out to be the most successful of the series. Since my last visit, which had taken place two days before the Ordination Retreat, a great deal of work had been done on the Centre. There was a new image and a new image-table, the reception area had been extended, and various facilities improved. I particularly admired the restful and harmonious colour scheme, and the way in which the beautiful New Zealand woods had been used to the best advantage. Before the meditation that preceded the Question and Answer meeting, as well as before the dedication ceremony on Wesak Day, there was a slide show, with commentary by Priyananda.

The slides shown on Wesak Day were the same ones that he had shown in Malaysia, i.e. slides of Sukhavati, the LBC and other FWBO centres and communities in England (those shown before the Question and Answer meeting were recent shots of Sukhavati by Kulamitra), but it was noticeable that the response was very different. People were much more keenly appreciative of the fact that all the work on Sukhavati, for instance, had been done by our own 'members' out of a sense of spiritual commitment. On both occasions, indeed, the slides not only gave people a vivid and inspiring picture of FWBO activities in England, but also enabled them to feel that, even though they were twelve thousand miles apart, 'Friends' in England and 'Friends' in New Zealand were all parts of the same current of spiritual energy — all parts of the same 'new Buddhist Movement'.

Though the preparation of the talks took up so much of my time, — so much that I could not spend the whole of Wesak Day at the Centre, — I did manage, even during the last ten days of my stay, to get out of the house occasionally for a short walk. These breaks in routine were all the more enjoyable on account of the fine weather. The rather unsettled conditions that had prevailed for a few days after my return had given way to a virtually uninterrupted spell of mellow, early Autumn sunshine which, continuing day after day, bathed the empty streets, — the white frame houses, — the fragrant evergreens, — in a soothing yet invigorating warmth. On one of these brief outings I discovered, in Herne Bay itself, a small Rudolph Steiner bookshop that contained an unusually interesting selection of literature. So interesting, indeed, that I ended up buying quite a few volumes. Among them was Balzac's 'occult' novel *Séraphita*, for which I had been on the lookout for several years. Written in a highly lyrical style, the story unfolds against a background of Swedenborgian philosophy and culminates in the 'apotheosis' of the author's androgynous hero-heroine in a concluding chapter that is surely among the most extraordinary pieces of writing in all literature.

Not all my outings took place during the day. At least one of them took place quite late at night. After my second talk a friend whom I had known in England, quite a few years ago, took me out for a coffee and then drove me up to the top of Mount Eden, one of the extinct volcanoes with which the landscape of Auckland is dotted. It was a clear, starlit night. Looking down, I could see, in all directions, nothing but street upon street of sparkling yellow and blue lights that stretched, with diminishing brilliance, as far as the environing blackness of the horizon. Since much of the city was laid out on a grid-plan, in several places the criss-cross lines of lights marked the darkness off in squares, much as in Sukhavati, the Buddha Amitabha's Pure Land in the West, the golden cords mark the ground of lapis lazuli off in squares. It was almost as though, here and there, the Pure Land was trying to break through into the Saha World — Sukhavati into the city of Auckland.

With increasing rapidity my visit drew to an end. Almost before I had time to realise what was happening, my last talk had been given, my last day had arrived, and I found myself having a farewell lunch in the Rose Garden Restaurant with (so far as I remember) Purna, Udaya, Megha, Priyananda, Aniketa, Vipula, Dharmadhara, Suvajri and Ratnaketu. (Akshobhya had already left for England by sea.) Situated on a park-like elevation, in the midst of a well kept garden where beds upon beds of late Summer roses were still in bloom, the restaurant certainly deserved its name, and was the ideal venue for the last meal that we would all be having together for some time.

Next morning, soon after 6 o'clock, Ratnaketu and I left Suvarnaketu for the airport, the members of the community all accompanying us. Other Order Members, Mitras and Friends also came to the airport to see us off. Ratnaketu was of course travelling with me, and his parents and younger brother too were there to say goodbye. The last few minutes that we all spent together in the concourse were the most poignant. More than one person shed a few tears. But the flight was being called, soon we were in our seats, the plane had taken off, and after a few minutes New Zealand was nothing but a stretch of green far below us — far behind us.

Now that my visit was over I was sorry to be leaving. In the course of the two and a half months that I had spent in New Zealand I had not only seen more of the country but learned to like it more than ever. I was sorry to be leaving the blue skies, the miles of evergreen bush, the snow-covered mountains, the broad rivers, the sandy beaches, the pleasant little townships, and the general sense of openness and freedom. In particular I was sorry to be leaving Suvarnaketu, where I had spent so many happy days, where I had begun to feel quite at home, where I had found it easy to get on with my work, and where, above all, I had started to make friends. All that was now over for the time being, except to the extent that it could be kept alive in memory, or continued with the help of letters. Still, I had the satisfaction of knowing that I had left the Order not only bigger than before, but stronger, and that whatever misunderstandings might prevail on the subject of 'ordination' the Mitras and Friends were a constantly-expanding group of unusually healthy, positive and devoted people. I had the satisfaction, in short, of knowing that the future of the Movement in New Zealand was assured.

## II

My original idea had been to break the return journey to India by spending a night or two in Hong Kong, where there was a Friend who would have been happy to put me up, but a closer look at the map showed that this would mean going a little out of my way, and in any case time was short. I therefore decided to go via Sydney and Perth and not have any stop over. After an uneventful journey across the Tasman Sea in our friendly Air New Zealand plane, with nothing but blue sky without and filtered golden sunshine within, Ratnaketu and I accordingly found ourselves in Sydney, where we had a three hour wait before catching the Qantas flight that was to take us on to Bombay.

While Ratnaketu collected the duty free camera that Priyananda had bought for Lokamitra in Auckland, I walked up and down the concourse and bought some rather spectacular picture postcards — the Sydney Opera House by moonlight and the Australian desert at dawn — in ye olde Australia shoppe. I did *not* buy any of the horrible souvenirs made from kangaroo skin, which had been cut and twisted and glued to make every conceivable kind of object from handbags to picture frames. Neither did I buy any of the pitiful Aborigine painted spears, which I could imagine being turned out by the thousand at one of those awful missionary-run handicraft settlements that I had seen in the film *Walkabout* a few years ago. The rest of the time we spent sitting in the bar, making each plastic tumbler of coffee last as long as we could, and occasionally emerging for a stroll up and down the concourse. At 1 o'clock in the afternoon we left.

For the greater part of the next hour we flew over mountain ranges covered with forests of dusky green, then halted briefly at Melbourne, after which we started on the long haul across the featureless red waste of the Australian desert. It was evening when we reached Perth. Here we were able to leave the aircraft and spent an hour in the smoke-filled atmosphere of the transit lounge, which was crowded with two or three hundred Western Australians. The place seemed to be awash with money, if not with much else. On the bookstall were rack upon rack of large, magnificently illustrated books on the scenery, the people, the natural resources, and the flora and fauna of the region. Thumbing through some of these glossy volumes, which were much too expensive for me to buy, I got the impression that Western Australia was a fascinating and distinctively thriving place with a life and character of its own quite different from that of Eastern Australia.

We had not been long in the air again when darkness fell. Ratnaketu was soon sound asleep in his window seat beside me. I dozed off for half an hour or so. After five or six hours we started to see spiders' webs of misty lights below us — presumably the towns and cities of Ceylon and South India. At 1 o'clock in the morning, local time, eight hours after leaving Perth, and twenty or more hours after leaving Auckland, we arrived in Santa Cruz. The air felt very warm. In fact, it was rather like being in a mild steam bath, without the steam. The shabby, dilapidated interior of the terminal building was strangely quiet. There were very few people about, apart from police and coolies. Our luggage having emerged onto the primitive delivery belt with unbelievable rapidity, we made our way through the blear-eyed Immigration Control to the Customs. Here we were greeted by an enormous banner reading 'CUSTOMS OFFICERS ARE YOUR FRIENDS. THEY ARE HERE TO HELP YOU.' The rather flashy Indian family immediately in front of us did not seem to be finding the officers either friendly or helpful, but then every member of the family, down to the tiniest tot, was heavily laden with expensive cameras and tape recorders which, so the head of the contingent claimed, they were taking straight to Ceylon and had no intention whatever of selling them en route in India. 'All right,' said the customs man at last, cutting short all the arguments and expostulations, 'you can deposit them under bond and collect them in Madras after producing your forward tickets.' Ratnaketu and I, who in any case had nothing to declare (not that that necessarily always helps), were allowed through after only the briefest of interrogations and some casual scribblings on our luggage in white chalk. However, we were still not free to go. Somewhere along the way Ratnaketu's passport had got caught up in the bureaucratic machinery, and it took him nearly half an hour to retrieve it. Meanwhile, our luggage was waiting with a quite unnecessary coolie, on a quite unnecessary trolley, for the use of which we had to pay five rupees each on our way out. It was with sensations of relief that we saw, standing at the bottom of the ramp, the very welcome figures of Lokamitra and Dharmarakshita, the one in his yellow robes the other in his smart, Western-style shirt and trousers. Lokamitra darted to the rescue. Within minutes he had commandeered a taxi, bundled us in, loaded on the luggage, fought off hordes of coolies and beggars, and steered us past inquisitorial policemen who wanted to know where we were going and made a show of writing the information down in their notebooks. At last we were clear of the airport and rattling over the potholes in the direction of the city. At last we could sit back and relax — or at least sit back. Out of the corner of my eye I could see that Ratnaketu, who had not been out of New Zealand before, was rigid with what appeared to be culture shock and hardly daring to look out of the window. Whenever he did so he closed his eyes for a minute as though unable to believe what he saw. At 2 o'clock in the morning Bombay looked like a ghost city. Great crumbling buildings. Deserted streets. Harsh electric lights. Rows upon rows of white-cocooned figures lying along the pavements, in doorways, on steps. In the air the sickly, inescapable smell of urine. When we had rattled along for a while, and had penetrated deep into the heart of the city, we all found our tongues and Lokamitra and I, in particular, started exchanging news and making enquiries about mutual friends. By 3 o'clock we were at Churchgate, where Lokamitra had arranged for us all to stay at our friend Solanki's flat in the Income Tax Colony, which was vacant. Within minutes of our arrival I, at least, was in bed, or rather, was stretched out *on* the bed (it was too warm for bedclothes), from where I could see through the open window the black fronds of the coconut palms silhouetted against the starry sky.

The next day was mainly one of rest and adjustment. Lokamitra had, however, arranged two appointments for me. After a late breakfast, therefore, we all took a taxi to the Fort area, where Lokamitra and I went to see my old friend Sudhakar Dikshit, the proprietor of the publishing firm of Chetana Ltd., while the others went off hand in hand to buy some white cotton shirts and pyjamas for Ratnaketu. Dikshit was by birth a U.P. brahmin. I had got to know him through my Polish ex-Jesuit friend Maurice Frydmann, whom I had met for the first time in Gangtok, where we were both staying at The Residency with Apa Pant, the then Political Officer (another friend!), and with whom I thereafter sometimes stayed on my visits to Bombay. Both Maurice and Dikshit were ardent admirers of J. Krishnamurti. Both also had a certain sympathy for Buddhism, or what they thought of as Buddhism, and thus it was that Chetana Ltd. had brought out my *Crossing the Stream* in its Buddhist Library series, of which I have been invited to become editor. (The series only ran to four volumes, but that is another story.) Despite his spiritual interests, Dikshit was a very bitter man. The bitterness was largely due to the battles which, in his threefold capacity as publisher, bookseller and restauranteur, he was constantly having to fight with Indian officialdom. To relieve his feelings he had once written a satire entitled *The Story of Pompapur.* In the fifteen years that had passed since our last meeting he had not changed very much, except for the fact that he looked much older. At seventy he was as bitter as ever and out of communication to an appalling degree. Lokamitra had already met him once or twice and discussed with him (as he thought) the possibility of bringing out a new Indian edition of *Crossing the Stream*, and this discussion he now wanted me to follow up. It soon became evident, however, that Dikshit had not understood Lokamitra at all, and that we were talking at cross purposes. I did learn from him, though, that Maurice Frydmann had died two years earlier, and that he had been with him at the time. When we left I, for my part, did so with a feeling of sadness. Though Dikshit had been glad to see me, he had not really emerged from the cave of his own bitterness, but only glared out of it for a few minutes in an uncomprehending sort of way. His lifelong preoccupation with spiritual teachers and spiritual teachings seemed to have done him no good whatever.

Ratnaketu having made his purchases, as a result of which he was attired in loose white garments that made him look younger and more innocent than ever, Lokamitra treated us all to lunch at the Chinese vegetarian restaurant through which one had to pass in order to reach Chetana's bookshop, where we had already browsed for a few minutes before meeting Dikshit. Though the maize soup was not quite so good as that which Priyananda and I had tasted in Malaysia, the meal was a very enjoyable one. By ordinary Indian standards it was also rather expensive, but as Lokamitra remarked, I did not come to India every day. I certainly did not! To me, indeed, it seemed extraordinary that I should be back in India again at all and still more extraordinary that four people with such very different backgrounds should be sitting in a Chinese restaurant in Bombay talking about the FWBO.

As soon as the meal was over, — or rather, as soon as we had finished talking for the time being, — Lokamitra and I went to meet Ardeshir Mehta and Dr. Sundri Vaswani at Stadium House. Dharmarakshita and Ratnaketu went to do a bit of sightseeing. Ardeshir, whom I had met more than once on my previous visit, was of course the son of my old friend Dr. Dinshaw Mehta, of the Society of Servants of God. Sundri was the good Doctor's chief — perhaps his only — disciple. About fifty years of age, she had been the first Indian woman to obtain a degree in statistics at the London School of Economics, and I had known her for as long as I had known Dr. Mehta himself. She came from a Sindhi brahmin family in which holiness was, as it were, hereditary. Her uncle, Sadhu Vaswani, a noted saint, had been the acknowledged spiritual leader of the Sindhi community. There was a statue of him, clad in what appeared to be a nightshirt, and wagging an admonitory finger at the passing cyclists, standing at a crossroads in Poona. One of Sundri's brothers had succeeded their uncle in the saintship, though there was another brother, some of you may be interested to learn, who was the black sheep of the family, and in whom the hereditary holiness appeared to have become extinct. As I mentioned in my 'Letter from New Zealand' though Ardeshir accepted many of his father's ideas, and worked for the NC Corporation (one of the 'earning arms' of the Society) he found it a bit inhibiting to work under the direct control of God's personal representative, as Dr. Mehta believed himself to be. Sundri was made of sterner stuff. She did not find it in the least inhibiting to work under direct control of this sort, and carried out all orders with rigid fidelity. Ardeshir had been greatly impressed by what he had heard of the FWBO, and even seemed to prefer its emphasis on individual freedom and responsibility to his father's strictly authoritarian approach. Sundri, however, soon made it clear that so far as she was concerned no spiritual movement could be taken seriously that did not accept without reservation God's guidance as received through his personal representative Dr. Mehta. All the same, she was glad to see me (we had met frequently in the fifties and early sixties), and I took the opportunity of asking her to convey my best wishes to Dr. Mehta, and to explain that I would not, after all, be spending a few days with him in New Delhi. By this time Dharmarakshita and Ratnaketu had done their sightseeing and were waiting for us outside. We did not have much more to do in the Fort area. A few visits to airline offices trying, without success, to get Ratnaketu onto the same British Airways flight to London as myself, a long wait outside the travel agents while Lokamitra collected our train tickets to Ahmedabad and back, and we were on our way back to Solanki's flat for a quiet evening and an early night. The next two weeks were going to be very busy ones for us all, and it was important that we should get all the rest we could.

At 9 o'clock the following morning we transferred to the Poona-bound taxi at Dadar and were soon making our way through the outlying suburbs of the city. The scene was much as it had been four months earlier, when I had made the same journey with Lokamitra, Priyananda, and Virabhadra, though now the weather was hotter and every scrap of vegetation scorched and withered. There was one difference, however. Lumbering along the road were red antediluvian monsters covered in scales. Closer inspection revealed that the monsters were, in fact, the latest acquisitions of the city transport corporation. What seemed to be the chassis of old red double-decker London buses had been mounted, at a slight angle, on the backs of diesel trucks, the cabins of which projected from underneath them like enormous snouts. As their panelling was a mass of tiny patches the grotesque hybrids actually did seem to be covered with scales — just like real monsters. All that was missing was the tail. It really was strange to see them trundling along the streets, with their passengers all sitting tilted at a slight angle, those in front being higher than those at the rear. An hour or so later, when the tailless red monsters had been left far behind us and we had started climbing up into the hills, we saw something that struck me as being even stranger. It was Sunday, and apparently there was more traffic on the roads than usual, some of it not very high-powered or in very good condition. At any rate, the initial ascent was so steep, and the hairpin bends so sharp and so numerous, that some twenty or thirty vehicles lay strewn like the carcasses of great beasts on either side of the road, their occupants clustering dejectedly around them, or peering into their entrails. Nor was that all. At intervals along the road were Muslim pilgrims, most of them elderly men with white beards. They were on their way, Lokamitra thought, to a celebrated Muslim shrine — probably the tomb of a saint — which was situated a few miles this side of Poona. In this there was nothing strange, of course. What was strange was that, for the most part, they were not actually walking, but standing facing the road, — bowing towards the road, in fact, — with their arms stretched out in a gesture that was either a benediction or an appeal for alms — or both. Their lips were moving, and judging from their attitude, and the intensity of their concentration, they were praying. It was as though they regarded it as part of their duty, as pilgrims, to help the drivers with their prayers, and in fact they did actually seem to be doing that, as though the prayers were a sort of psychic force that was pulling and pushing and lifting the cars and lorries and other vehicles up the steepest part of the ascent and trying — not with complete success, it seemed — to prevent them from having accidents and breakdowns. I was reminded of the closing scenes of the film *Close Encounters of the Third Kind:* there seemed to be the same kind of atmosphere. I was also reminded of the occasion when, in the Cathedral of (I think) Notre Dame in Luxembourg, in 1966, I had actually 'seen' the prayers of the worshippers winging their way through the air towards the figure of the Virgin with Child on the high altar.

In Poona there was not much for me to do. We were to spend only one night at the Vihara, in fact, before going on to Sinhagad for the Ordination Retreat. All that Lokamitra had arranged for me in the way of 'programme' was a meeting with Mitras and regular Friends at the Ahalyashram at 7.30 that evening. Until then I was free. After Ratnaketu had met Padmavajra, and I had had a cup of tea and a hot bath, and we had all had lunch under the hospitable roof of our neighbours the Inamders, whose smiling faces were there to greet us as we stepped over their chalk-decorated threshold, Lokamitra and I therefore took a taxi into the city. Here I bought some colourful Jaipur-ware wall plates and bowls for Padmaloka, as well as a few rosaries. The wall plates were decorated with peacocks, which I thought particularly appropriate for Padmaloka, the abode of the Lotus, of Padmasambhava, and of Amitabha, 'The Infinite Light', the Buddha of the West. Crossing the road from souvenir shop to souvenir shop I noticed, as I had done in the course of the fifteen or twenty yard walk from the Vihara to the Inamders, how different the climate of Poona was from that of Bombay. There was the same intensely blue sky overhead, the same blindingly brilliant sunshine all round; but although the weather was almost as hot as it had been in Bombay, the heat was not oppressive, and there was no humidity. One was not laid prostrate by the heat, but rather was strengthened and invigorated. I felt glad to be in Poona, glad that the strong dry heat was penetrating me to the bone and drawing, as it seemed, all the aches and pains out of my joints, glad that we would be going up to Sinhagad the next day, where there would be nothing but dark blue sky above one's head and nothing but sun-soaked brown earth and rock beneath one's feet. But before we could go to Sinhagad there was the evening meeting to attend.

At about 7 o'clock, therefore, when the air was much cooler, and the sky beginning to grow dark, we went along to the Ahalyashram, which had been the venue of the three public meetings held during my previous visit. On the present occasion we met not outside in the courtyard, under the stars, but inside, in a shabby hall lit by the usual dust-covered electric bulbs. Lokamitra's idea in holding the meeting was to give Mitras and regular Friends the opportunity of asking questions about the Dharma and the FWBO, as well as of having a little personal contact with me. At first it looked as though his good intentions might be frustrated. People were slow in coming (though a few turned up who were not Mitras or regular Friends at all), the proceedings started late (partly due to trouble with the tape-recording equipment), and the air of general dullness and listlessness that hung over the gathering was so thick that one could have cut it with the proverbial knife (it may have been that everybody was tired after the day's work). Eventually the atmosphere cleared, positivity emerged, questions started coming in, and by the end of the evening it was clear from the interest and enthusiasm now prevailing that the meeting had been a great success. What questions I was asked I no longer recollect. (After writing the first part of this Letter I was forced to break off for a while, and five months having now elapsed since that evening in Poona impressions have inevitably begun to fade.) From a section of the transcript which Padmavajra has sent to me for editing I see that one of the questions asked was about the origins of the division between the Hinayana and the Mahayana, and whether we were followers of the one or of the other. In reply I said that the division had come about mainly for historical reasons, and that we were simply Buddhists, and as such free to take from any form of Buddhism whatever we found was helpful to us in our personal spiritual development.

The Ordination Retreat lasted five days (including the days of arrival and departure) and was confined to the six Order Members and the nine people being ordained, plus the two girls doing the cooking. This simplified the logistics of the operation considerably — quite an important point in a place like Maharashtra, where public transport is both infrequent and unreliable and private transport — apart from the ubiquitous bicycle — unthinkable so far as ordinary people are concerned. It meant, in short, that Lokamitra could hire a small bus that would take all seventeen of us, together with our cooking pots, our bags of rice and flour,

our bedding, and our shrine equipment, — not to mention our suitcases, — all the way from the crowded by-lanes of Poona to the comparatively unfrequented heights of Sinhagad, without the danger of anyone getting lost, or missing the bus, or forgetting which day of the week it was. It also meant that instead of occupying two bungalows, as we had done last time, we could all get into one, the PWD bungalow, which was bigger and more comfortable than the Tilak Bungalow. We did not get into it without a struggle, though. There had been a case of double booking, it seemed, for on our arrival we found it already occupied by a touring government official and his minions, and it took Lokamitra and Dharmarakshita some time to establish our own prior claim. Eventually they did so, and we could settle in.

Before long the shrine was set up, the evening puja and meditation began (we had not arrived until 6.30), and the whole retreat plunged into a sea of silence from which it would not emerge — except for study, and apart from individual lapses, which were severely rebuked by Lokamitra — for what some people must have felt was quite a long time. As for me, after the events of the last few months I was not sorry to be on my own again, in the same room that I had occupied the last time, from where I could hear Lokamitra's voice raised in exhortation and the occasional tinkle of the meditation bell. It was very pleasant to be able to sit there knowing that the retreat was going on perfectly well without me, and that all I had to do was to get ready for the ordinations and think of nine new names for nine new members of the Order. It was very pleasant, in fact, to know that the Movement itself now had, to a great extent, a vigorous life of its own, and that in Britain, Finland, and New Zealand, it was able to function without me, at least for a while. This time I did not even write any picture postcards at Sinhagad. Nor did I look out of the window very often at the hills, which were of a yellower, dustier brown than they had been on the occasion of my first visit, three and a half months earlier. The hot weather had, in fact, now reached its peak, and the monsoon was expected to break within a few days. The whole of the surrounding countryside, and the great bare rock of a mountain on which we ourselves were encamped, lay exposed all day to the hot, dry, brilliant sunshine.

On the second day of the retreat, however, there was a change of atmospheric conditions which, I assumed, presaged the coming of the monsoon. Suddenly, out of a sky that, only minutes before, had been one uninterrupted expanse of cloudless blue, there burst a shower of hailstones. At first they were as large as peas, but after a few minutes they were coming down as big as marbles, banging and thundering on the corrugated iron roof, and bouncing up from the ground with the force of their impact. Soon rain started coming in through the roof at several points, and I had to shift my bed. Within a couple of hours it was all over. The thunder, which had rolled and crackled alarmingly, accompanied by repeated flashes of lightning, died away grumblingly in the distance. Looking outside, I saw the virtually unbroken arch of a rainbow — no, two rainbows! — shining brilliantly against a background of silver-grey mist and cloud. All this while, the retreatants continued with their afternoon meditation, apparently without moving a muscle, even though they could not hear Lokamitra's bell on account of the uproar, and though the hailstones came bouncing in among them through the open doors. The only other occasions on which I was disturbed, if that is the right word, was when Mrs. Maheshkar brought in my meals, or when Padmavajra brought me a cup of tea, and when Lokamitra, Padmavajra, Dharmarakshita, Ratnaketu and I had our evening Order meetings, which were held in my room. Order meetings while on retreat in India, with Order Members of both English and Indian origin attending! It was another sign of progress.

By mid-morning of the fifth and last day of the retreat Mitras and Friends started arriving from Poona in good time for the public ordinations, the women wearing the usual colourful saris, the men dressed in more nondescript, not to say hybrid, fashion. Our young bhikkhu friend Khemadhammo was also there, in his brilliant orange robe, having turned up two days earlier, with an elderly bhikkhu friend, and been sent away by Lokamitra until the proper time. He was now back again, beaming at everybody in his usual friendly manner. By this time the private ordinations were of course all over, four of them having been conducted on the Wednesday evening, and five on the Thursday evening (the public ordinations were held on Saturday 1st June). At both the private and the public ordinations I was touched to see that all the ordinees (some of whom did not speak English) had learned by heart not only the Pali formulae to be recited but the English verses as well, and that they were all word perfect. After the public ceremony, which was not only an occasion of deep spiritual significance, but also one of great festivity and rejoicing, everybody streamed outside for the usual group photographs, the saris of the women giving them a distinct advantage. As I had noticed earlier, some new Order Members were wearing special shirts, sarongs, and even suits. Dharmaditya, the oldest Indian Order Member, was smartly dressed in a salmon pink denim suit, exactly the same as Suvrata sometimes wears in England, which gave him a distinctly 'ministerial' look — not inappropriately so, in view of the fact that he conducts most of the name-giving, marriage-blessing, and death-condoling ceremonies that are held in Buddhist Poona. Dharmalochana (Mrs. Maheshkar), for her part, was wearing a saffron-coloured blouse beneath her white silk sari and looked, if not quite so ministerial, even more business-like. Looking round at the new Order Members, some of whom (like Dharmalochana, Dharmaditya and Silananda), I had known for twenty years and more, I felt very happy that, even though we had been separated for the greater part of that time, we were able to come together at last in this way.

After partaking of the final meal, for which the women — hitherto restrained in the interests of austerity, and to save time for extra meditation — were allowed to give free rein to their natural urge to feed everybody as richly and generously as possible, the retreat struck camp, people made their way down the flights of stone steps to the car park just outside the main gate of the fort, and Lokamitra, Padmavajra and I, with Dharmarakshita and (I think) one or two others, squeezed into the taxi which had come for us, the bus not being available. When we were only a mile from Parnakuti, having proceeded so far without mishap, the taxi broke down. Or rather, the engine stopped because there was no more fuel in the tank. Ensued the type of situation so common in India. Lokamitra had already paid the driver's mate, who was apparently the owner of the taxi, but he had got out on our way through the city, taking the money with him, and not leaving anything with the driver for petrol. Lokamitra roundly refused to part with any more money (as the driver demanded), the cost of petrol having been included in the taxi hire. The driver maintained that he had no money for petrol. Stalemate. Frustration. Eventually, as time was short, Padmavajra and I, carrying some of the luggage, started walking, while Lokamitra remained in the taxi guarding the rest of the luggage, and Dharmarakshita went looking for a cycle rickshaw. We had not gone very far along the road, and were already beginning to feel quite hot (it was mid-afternoon) when we were overtaken by Dharmarakshita, who had succeeded in commandeering a cycle rickshaw more quickly than we had expected. Soon Lokamitra came bowling along in another cycle rickshaw, and before many minutes had passed we were all back at the Vihara and Padmavajra was putting the kettle on for a cup of tea.

At the Vihara there was quite a lot to be done, and we had only an hour in which to do it, before leaving for Bombay and from there, catching the night train, travelling on to Ahmedabad. Besides the usual packing, there were last minute interviews with people who wanted to see me before my departure. Among the latter were our good old retired friend Mr. Kadam, who somehow managed to combine an intensely rationalistic attitude towards Buddhism with a strong devotion to Lokamitra, and whose generosity it was that had placed the Vihara building at the disposal of the FWBO for so long, and our bluff, jovial railway engineer friend Mr. Ramteke, who had more than once lent his car, and whom I had first encountered as a student in Jabalpur some seventeen or eighteen years ago. Another visitor was the newly ordained Vimalakirti (formerly Mr. Gangawane), from whom we had parted only a couple of hours earlier, who came bringing his wife, a trained nurse, and their two small children. They had not yet had the opportunity of meeting me, and he was very keen that they should do so before I left Poona.

At last we were ready to start. Lokamitra gave some final instructions to Padmavajra, who with Ratnaketu and other Order Members and Mitras, was to follow the next day, Ramteke drove us to the taxi terminus, our luggage was transferred, and for the second time in three months Lokamitra and I were driving down through the hills to Bombay. With us (I think) was Dharmarakshita, who had (I think) some work to do for Lokamitra in Bombay before catching the train to Ahmedabad the following night with the rest of the party. (So much happened so quickly, — and so many months ago, — that the impressions left were rather faint, and I cannot always recollect exactly what occurred.)

It was very pleasant to drive through the luminous blue of the evening, with the stars coming out, and the temperature gradually decreasing. At 9 o'clock we reached Dadar, where we changed to a local taxi, arriving about an hour later at Bombay Central Station. This was the first time I had been inside an Indian railway station for about twelve years. Nothing had changed very much. There were the same concrete platforms, broader and even dirtier than those in England, the same unhygienic refreshment kiosks, the same heavy wooden benches, the same hawkers of hot savouries, the same red-shirted licensed porters, the same crowds (though our platform was comparatively empty), the same glaring contrast between rich and poor. If there had been any change at all, it was simply that everything looked older and shabbier than before, as though it had not been cleaned, or repaired, or repainted, in all the twelve years that I had been away. This applied particularly to the rolling stock. As it came trundling along the platforms, it looked so dirty, and so antiquated, that I wondered how much longer it could possibly last. These impressions were confirmed when, at about 11.30, our own train arrived, and Lokamitra and I climbed on board and took our places. Our first class carriage had clearly been promoted from second class status, once green upholstery was showing signs of wear and tear, and the paint and varnish were scarred and chipped in a hundred places. Still, we had two reserved sleeping berths, there was a battery of electric ceiling fans, all of which worked, and only two other passengers to share the four-berth compartment with us, so that by Indian standards we were very comfortable indeed. I did not sleep much that night. Even if I did manage to doze off, I would soon be woken up by the noise and glare of one of the many big stations through which the line passed, and at which we invariably stopped. At dawn I got up, and Lokamitra soon followed suit. Luckily, there was water in the toilet, and we were able to wash off some of the grime that had come seeping in through the windows during the night — and was still seeping in. A couple of hours later we had breakfast —

at least I think we had breakfast (impressions are again rather vague). Perhaps we only had a cup of tea — or a cold drink. At length, after a long, slow, tedious haul through a sort of semi-industrialised hinterland, at 10.30 we drew up at the biggest station we had so far seen, I saw two ancient minarets rising above the roofs of the tumbledown buildings at the side of the track, and knew that we had reached Ahmedabad. Bakula and Jayawardhana were on the platform waiting for us, and were soon inside the compartment, joyfully greeting us, and pressing into our hands sweet-smelling nosegays made up of small red roses with very sharp thorns. Within minutes we had emerged from the station, had made our way through the jostling mass of pedestrians, taxis, and cycle rickshaws, and were sitting in a cycle rickshaw ready — as we thought — to move off. We were stuck there for fifteen minutes. Probably because he saw that we were Europeans, and knowing that taxis would not ply within the city limits, the cycle rickshaw man was insisting on adding an extra rupee to the three or four rupee fare. Bakula and Jayawardhana were strenuously resisting the imposition. It seemed that our visit to Ahmedabad was not getting off to a very good start.

After a great deal of haggling, and when Lokamitra and I were growing rather weary of it all, the cycle rickshaw man consented to start peddling, — on what terms I do not know, — and with our two friends leading the way we left the station precinct and were caught up in a jostling, horn-hooting stream of traffic that included not only buses, taxis and handcarts, but little trolleys drawn — at their own sedate pace — by supercilious-looking camels. I was reminded that on my last visit, twelve years earlier, I had once looked out from under the hood of my cycle rickshaw to find myself right up behind an elephant. Soon the streets became narrower, and before long we were making our way through a veritable maze of by-lanes, where there was hardly room for us to pass between the earthenware pots, stringbeds, trays of red peppers, and little knots of squatting women on either side. At length we stopped. As soon as we dismounted, people gathered round us with a curiosity that was not altogether friendly. Negotiating a short passageway, and passing through a low door, we found ourselves inside the Vihara. This consisted of one small room only, with attached bathroom, but it was quiet, and there was a ceiling fan which our friends immediately turned on full blast. Bakula's aged aunt, who lived next door, brought us some tea, two or three old friends dropped in to pay their respects, but apart from that not much happened. The whole area seemed rather dead. (It was not a Buddhist locality, of course, as many of the localities in Poona were.) At about midday, we were taken for lunch to Bakula's house, where I had been before, and which was so narrow that it seemed to consist entirely of stairs and landings. After lunch we returned to the Vihara, the two places being only a hundred or so yards apart. By this time it was about 12.30. At 1 o'clock, by arrangement with Lokamitra, Bakula was to come and take us to Sarspara (?), where we were to stay for a few days before going to Gandhinagar. At 5 o'clock, however, he had still not come. Either there had been a misunderstanding or, what seemed more likely, a crises had occurred within the family, or in connection with his work, which demanded his immediate attention. In the event it was not until early evening that we were able to make the move, nor did we learn the reason for the mysterious delay.

Sarspara, if that was the name of the place, seemed to be one of the more outlying suburbs of the city. Scattered round a sort of sandy maidan stood several dozen new bungalows. One of these had been placed at our disposal. Apart from the bed, table and chair in my room, there was no furniture, neither was there any glass in the windows, which were protected by iron bars and wooden shutters. There was, however, an electric table fan, which the inhabitants of Ahmedabad themselves were beginning to regard as a necessity rather than a luxury, especially at that time of year. The next day Padmavajra, Ratnaketu, Dharmarakshita, Dharmalochana, and the rest of our Poona friends arrived, having caught the night train from Bombay as we had done. They had travelled third class, however, under much more crowded and much less comfortable conditions, and the train had reached Ahmedabad an hour late. Distributing themselves between the two other rooms they made up for at least some of the sleep they had lost, before going out to 'do' the sights of Ahmedabad, which some of them were visiting for the first time.

That night I slept very badly indeed. In fact I hardly slept at all, and got up feeling distinctly unwell. The weather in Ahmedabad was very hot — much hotter than it had been in Poona, or even Bombay. It had been the hottest day of the year, with the thermometer standing at 120° Centigrade, which is quite hot, even for India. Eventually I realised that the heat was coming not only from outside me, but from inside me as well: I had fever. Expecting that it would subside, I said nothing to anybody, — indeed for an hour or two I did feel a little better, — and after lunch made a few notes for the first of my two lectures, which I was due to give that same evening. By 3 o'clock I had a very high fever indeed: it seemed to be centred in my head. As soon as the others became aware of what was going on, they did whatever they could to help. (Fortunately or unfortunately, people usually cannot tell when I am ill, and know about it only if I inform them.) Dharmalochana at once sent out for some ice, and started applying cold compresses to my forehead. Strange to say, a handkerchief soaked in ice water, and folded into eight thicknesses, would be quite hot and dry after being laid across my forehead for less than half a minute. I was reminded of the Kagyupa yogis of Tibet, as described by Mme. David-Neal, who as a test of proficiency in the *tumo* or 'psychic heat' meditation dry off sheet after sheet of cloth that has been dipped in icy water and wrapped round their naked body. As soon as one compress was dry, Dharmalochana applied another. Jayawardhana, who was staying with us at the bungalow and looking after us, massaged my feet, while Dharmarakshita fanned me. Somebody else soused the rough straw matting that hung outside the window in water, and sprinkled water on the ground round about. The application of cold compresses, the massage, and the fanning, were kept up without intermission for more than four hours, Dharmalochana in particular being untiring in her exertions. As a result of these ministrations I felt a little better, though the fever was still quite high, and I felt very weak. By this time it had become obvious to everyone that I would not be able to give my lecture, and that my place would have to be taken by Lokamitra, who of course had had no time to prepare anything. Off he therefore went with Bakula, leaving Dharmalochana and the others to look after me. Two hours later he returned in triumph, having risen to the occasion magnificently, and given a stirring address to an audience of about five hundred people. He had also arranged to move me to an air-conditioned room in a hotel, where I could be quieter and more comfortable. Dharmalochana in particular was not at all happy with this arrangement, thinking that I would not be properly looked after in a hotel. At 10 o'clock, however, we left Sarspara by taxi, accompanied by Jayawardhana and another friend. As soon as I saw the hotel I was glad we had come. It occupied two adjoining sides of a spacious compound in which stood lofty coconut palms and other trees, while just over the wall on a third side flowed the river Sabarmati. The low, whitewashed buildings were in the 'colonial' style, and probably belonged to the last century. I had a large, lofty room at the far end of one wing, near the river, Lokamitra one at the far end of the other wing, diagonally across the compound from mine.

For the greater part of the three days that we stayed at the hotel I did practically nothing. I ate very little, spoke very little, and for the first two days at least saw very few people, with the result that the fever abated slightly. Among those who came to see me was an Ayurvedic physician, a youngish man who had studied in one of the 'modern' Ayurvedic colleges in Ahmedabad itself. (Ayurveda or 'The Science of Life' is the traditional system of Indian medicine, which treats physical illness mainly by means of herbal remedies.) An allopathic doctor had come to see me at Sarspara, and I had allowed him to examine me, but he had only advised me to take curds and said that there was nothing much wrong with me and that I would soon be better. The Ayurvedic physician countermanded the curds, and prescribed pills for the fever and the high blood pressure, as well as a preparation of conch shell ash and cinnamon as a tonic. According to his diagnosis, owing to all the lecturing and talking I had been doing I was suffering from an excess of *raja-guna*, the passionate or fiery element, and it was this that had brought on the fever and other symptoms. Much of what he told me about my constitution agreed with my own observations, and I therefore felt more confidence in him than in the allopathic doctor, and followed his direction implicitly. Most of my other visitors were old friends and disciples who wanted to renew their contact with me. They included Yashodhara, the ex-brahmin teacher who had sometimes interpreted for me, Rahula, now a police officer, who had already been to see me in Poona, and Amritlal, who had looked after me in Bombay on my first visit, and who now came bringing his family.

When there were no visitors, and when it was not too hot, I sat out on my verandah, watching as the gardener saturated every inch of the compound in bucketfuls of water that immediately soaked into the dry earth. The trees were full of birds, mostly Indian crows in their smart, pearl-grey cravats; but there were plenty of small song-birds as well, and it was very pleasant to see them darting in and out of the greenery, and to hear them calling and whistling to each other. Striped tree-rats crouched motionless on the ground, or raced up and down the trunks of the trees. Looking up and over the wall, I could see the city's principal bridge, across which there flowed in both directions a constant stream of traffic. From whatever reflections these sights might have suggested I was recalled, on our second full day at the hotel, by the realisation that I was due that evening to give the second of my two lectures, and that a certain amount of pressure was being brought to bear on me not to disappoint the people who would be coming to hear me, who had already been disappointed once, and who in all likelihood would not have another opportunity of hearing me for several years. With reluctance, I resisted the pressure. The fever had gone down hardly at all, I still felt very weak, and clearly it would be wiser for me not to exert myself in the way that giving a lecture would require — not even to the extent of giving the 'two words' that, it was suggested, I might give instead. Lokamitra therefore deputised for me again. It was just as well that he did. Although he rose to the occasion more magnificently than ever, and gave an even more stirring address than before, it was not without having to surmount difficulties. While he was speaking the electric power supply failed, all the lights in the hall went out, and the electric fans stopped working. For much of the time, therefore, he had to speak by the light of a few candles, while the atmosphere grew more and more stifling.

By the afternoon of our third full day at the hotel my condition had not really changed very much, but as a result of the comparative rest and quiet I was feeling better, and at 5 o'clock we therefore left for Gandhinagar as planned. Gandhinagar is the new, administrative capital of Gujerat, and is situated about twenty miles from Ahmedabad. It consists of an enormous expanse of what must once have been desert, but which is now dotted with trees, over which are distributed huge blocks of flats and blocks of offices at such wide intervals that sometimes they seemed to disappear over the horizon. In one of these blocks the retreat was to be held. It seemed to have been built specially for conferences and camps of various kinds, though it was more like a caravanserai than a conference centre in the Western sense. However, it was clean and spacious, and we were received by the staff with unusual courtesy. Unfortunately, there had been some hitch, or misunderstanding, in connection with the booking, and in the end we had less space at our disposal than we had expected. Altogether upwards of forty people came on the retreat, most of them being from Ahmedabad, with smaller contingents from Poona and Gandhinagar — not to mention England and New Zealand. Some of our Friends, I noticed, were present *en famille*, several married couples having brought their children, all of whom behaved beautifully. (The married couples, needless to say, did not behave in the way that married couples tend to behave in England, even on retreat. Husbands and wives treated each other in a natural, friendly manner, and there was a marked absence of emotional tension and sexual 'game-playing' between them.)

I was given a room on the second floor, overlooking the garden at the back, and from this room I could hear at intervals the sound of chanting in the distance as the retreat, led by Lokamitra, got under way. Though the room was quite pleasant, the thermometer was still hovering very near the 120° mark, and at times I had to choose between putting on the ceiling fan, which gave me a sore throat, and enduring the heat. Generally I opted for the sore throat as the lesser of the two evils. The fever continued, my temperature rising and falling slightly for no apparent reason, but never rising as high as it had done in Ahmedabad. After a day or two my appetite returned, and I felt a little stronger, from which I concluded that I was getting better. The fever left me completely, though, only after I had returned to England. Whenever there was a breeze, I sat on the balcony, from which I could survey the garden, a square expanse of well-watered lawn at the far end of which stood a row of fine eucalyptus trees, with silvery trunks, and feathery, drifting foliage. Running behind the trees, as well as to the right of the lawn, was a low hedge. On this hedge I more than once saw a magnificent, blue-green bird cautiously creeping along. It was over a foot in length, and may have been some kind of Indian cuckoo. Across the hedge to the right, beyond a clump of flowering trees, a block of flats or offices was in process of construction, the work having only just started. The coolies were mostly women, — tribal women, probably, judging by their colourful, bedraggled costume, — who lived, with their children, on the site, in tiny shelters made of bits of cloth stretched over ropes. In the evening they would fill their brass pots with water and then, with the pots balanced on their heads, go back to the shelters and prepare a meal on a fire of sticks out in the open air. The children, I noticed, all seemed quite healthy and happy, and to be getting on quite well without very much in the way of education or clothing.

On the third and last day of the retreat, at 10 o'clock in the morning, our Friend Ratnakar received his public ordination, the private ordination having taken place the previous evening. It was fortunate that I had started feeling stronger. People came flocking from Ahmedabad and Gandhinagar for the occasion, and in addition to conducting the ordination ceremony, — as well as three Mitra ceremonies, — and giving a talk, I had to devote some time to the new arrivals, many of whom wanted to see me, especially as this was to be my last day in Ahmedabad. As in the case of the ordinations which had been held at Sinhagad, only ten days earlier, the occasion was a colourful and festive one, culminating in the taking of group photographs in the scanty shade of the eucalyptus trees. Indeed, it was one of those rare occasions when positive emotion is deeply imbued with spiritual awareness, — when feelings of devotion rise up like a fountain, and *kalyana-mitrata* overflows in all directions, — so that while giving my talk, especially, I forgot the fever and felt, as I looked round at the joyful faces of all the people crowded into our improvised shrine room, that I was in the Pure Land.

But it was soon time to come down to earth. At 2 o'clock we left for Ahmedabad, where I spent the afternoon in a quiet room in Bakula's house looking at some of his books. Then there were people to see, including my old friend Bhikkhu Sivalibodhi, who had come specially from Bombay, farewells to be said, some light refreshment to be taken, and at about 10 o'clock Lokamitra, Ratnaketu and I left for the station accompanied by Bakula, Amritlal, and all the other friends who wanted to see us off. The platform was packed with people, and it looked as though the train was going to be full. Luckily, we had secured reserved berths in the first class again, and as there was only one other person to share the compartment with us the three of us were quite comfortable. Soon the last farewells had been said, and the last waving, white-clad figures on the platform had disappeared as the train gathered speed. I was glad that I had been able to see Ahmedabad again, glad that I had been able to meet so many old friends, and only sorry that owing to the fever I had been able to do so little for them.

On reaching Bombay the following morning we debated whether to have a late breakfast at the station restaurant or whether to go straight to Solanki's flat, at which Lokamitra had arranged for us to spend the day before moving out to the hotel at Juhu Beach for the night. We decided to go straight to the flat. Solanki had left the key with a neighbour, Lokamitra said. On arrival we found that the key was not with the neighbour, who indeed knew nothing about the matter. It seemed as though our visit to Bombay was not getting off to a very good start either. Thinking that the key might be with the manager of the Japanese Temple at Worli, with whom Solanki sometimes left it, Lokamitra took a taxi there to investigate, but meeting with no better success with the manager than with the neighbour he was obliged to return empty-handed. We now began to wish we had had breakfast at the station restaurant. It was still only 11 o'clock, and we could not move into our room at the hotel until 5. How were we to pass the time until then? We did not relish the prospect of spending six hours sitting on our luggage on the landing outside the door of Solanki's flat, where it was too dark to read and where there was nothing to be had to eat. In the end Lokamitra and I decided to go out shopping. We went out twice, in fact, leaving Ratnaketu to guard the luggage and promising to bring him back something to eat. On returning from our first expedition we found that the neighbour's wife had provided him with a folding chair, and given him a cup of tea, besides allowing him to use her toilet. What she thought of so unorthodox a request as that he should be allowed inside her flat for this purpose I cannot imagine. But no doubt New Zealand innocence and charm as usual worked wonders.

The Juhu Beach Hotel was situated near the Santa Cruz airport, and was convenient for catching the early morning flight to London. We arrived at about 5 o'clock, and after the rather tiring — and unexpected — events of the day it was a relief to be able to settle into our small room in the bungalow-like annexe, even though it was to be only for a few hours. Soon, recovered and refreshed, the three of us were sitting at a small table in the open-sided dining-room extension — actually no more than a roof of coconut palm thatch supported on poles — enjoying our last meal together. Looking out from under the thatch we could see the broad terrace of the hotel, with its iron tables surmounted by multi-coloured umbrellas, below the terrace a vast expanse of yellow sand, and beyond the sand the deep blue, quivering waters of the Arabian Sea. Lokamitra had apparently thought that we would have the beach to ourselves, and that after experiencing the crowded conditions of Ahmedabad and Bombay I would be able to commune with nature in solitude for a few hours; but whatever it may have been a few years ago Juhu was now a fashionable seaside resort, rather like a smaller and flashier Bournemouth, and popular in the evening, as we could see, with the Bombay film-making set. After our meal we went for a walk along the beach, then sat on the terrace for a while before going to bed. Despite the crowds (really very small by English Bank Holiday standards), and the cluster of refreshment stalls, it was very pleasant to see the sun set, and the light gradually fade, and to feel the stillness of the night descending all along the coast and over the land.

We did not have many hours sleep. Lokamitra and I had to be up soon after 3 o'clock, and at the airport by 4.30, in order that I could catch the 6.30 plane (Ratnaketu was to leave by a later flight). In the event the plane left about two hours late, so that after saying goodbye to Lokamitra (who thereupon returned to the hotel for Ratnaketu!), and negotiating the passport control desks, the police guards, the security check, and another lot of police guards, I had quite a long wait in the crowded departure lounge. Not that I minded the wait. The tiresome departure formalities were behind me, — the squalor and inefficiency of India were behind me, — it was a fine morning, there would be friends waiting for me on my arrival at Heathrow, and all that I now had before me was a pleasant, nine hour flight in the company of BA air hostesses who, even if the advertisements *did* make them look like policewomen, were really angels in disguise. Alas, I had under-estimated the resourcefulness of Indian officialdom, which was capable of dragging a soul back from the gates of Hades, let alone an airline passenger from the exit door of the departure lounge. Before I could leave the shores of India there was an unpleasant experience in store for me.

I had been sitting in the departure lounge for about an hour, when I heard my name called out over the loudspeaker system. Would I contact the airline desk at the end of the lounge. On my doing this, I was told that I was wanted for a spot baggage check. In this there was nothing unusual, though I had never had the experience before. The airline courier whom I had contacted steered me out past the second lot of police guards, and pointed me down a flight of steps and along a dark tunnel. First, however, he took charge of my ticket and passport, which made me a little uneasy. The baggage check turned out to be a mere formality, and within a matter of minutes I returned through the tunnel and up the steps into the area behind the passport control desks. Here I was met by the courier, who attempted to lead me back to the departure lounge by the same way that I had come, i.e. past the second lot of police guards *without* going through the security check, which I had of course already gone through. The police, however, barred my way, and despite the explanations and expostulations of the courier insisted that I go through the whole departure procedure a second time, starting with the passport control, where there were long, slowly moving queues at all the desks. Throwing up his hands in despair, the courier handed me — and my ticket and passport — over to an airport official. This personage eventually managed to find a desk where the emigration officer was willing to stamp my passport out of turn, so that I could proceed without delay to the next stage of departure (this is a highly condensed account of what actually happened), but at this point the worst hitch of all occurred. It was discovered that I had left India eighteen days earlier, on May 26th, the same day on which I had arrived. There the two stamps were on the same page of my passport, one directly beneath the other. *Where had I been in the meantime? What had I been doing?* That was the sixty-four thousand million rupee question. I could feel the suspicion thickening around me. Obviously, I could be some kind of spy. In vain I tried to explain that I had *not* left India on May 26th, and that I had been occupying myself in a perfectly lawful manner in Poona and Ahmedabad. Suspicion only thickened further. In fact, it positively congealed. The airport official abandoned me to my fate. Obviously, if I had left India on May 26th, as my passport clearly stated, and had not re-entered it since, I was not there now, and since I was not there now there was no question of my going through any departure formalities. It was a truly Kafkaesque situation, and for a moment I realised what it must be like to live under a totalitarian regime, and be caught up in the bureaucratic machinery. I realised what it must be like for the individual *when nothing he says is believed*, and when he has no power to determine his own fate. Fortunately, my plight was observed by a bright, efficient young airport official, a South Indian, senior in rank to the first one, and apparently entrusted with the special responsibility — possibly unique in India — of cutting through red tape. Tapping one of the passport control officers vigorously on the shoulder, he insisted that he stamp my passport forthwith, which he did with an ill grace, and an air of, 'Well, if you insist on such a blatantly irregular procedure,' after which I was free to go through the security check again and so back into the departure lounge, where my flight was being called. Thinking the matter over afterwards, I recalled that the passport control officer who had stamped my passport the first time had gone off duty immediately after doing so (I remembered the protests of those behind me in the queue, for there was no one to take his place). Perhaps he had been on duty all night. Though the passport was stamped with a rubber stamp, the *date* of arrival or departure had to be written in by hand. Perhaps the officer, tired and sleepy after his spell of duty, had simply copied the date in the stamp above without realising what he was doing. Be that as it may, I was heartily glad that it was all over, and that barring accidents I was now well and truly on my way back to the UK.

## III

The flight was one of the smoothest and pleasantest I have ever experienced. For the greater part of the way there was no cloud, so that there was nothing between the rich blue sky above and the sunlit earth below and nothing, therefore, to obstruct our view of the countries over which we passed. Pakistan, Iran, Turkey, Bulgaria, Yugoslavia — I was surprised how dry and barren they all were, with nothing to relieve the vast expanses of pinkish ochre other than the faint corrugations of mountains and the grey and white smudges that might have been towns. Had it not been for the captain's periodic announcements (British Air seemed to be making a point of keeping its passengers well informed) we would not have known where we were. Thanks to these announcements, however, we knew that we were passing practically over Mount Ararat, on which Noah's Ark came to rest after the Flood (the wreckage was not visible), and that the line of silver shining on the horizon was the Caspian Sea. What was of greater interest to me, we also knew that the city on the western of two promontories that almost touched each other between the blue of the Bosphorus to the north and the blue of the Sea of Marmora to the south was the city of Istambul or rather, as I still thought of it, the city of Constantinople or Byzantium. My imagination was deeply stirred. Looking down, I could see three or four tiny domes in the midst of the grey indistinctness of the city but we were too high up for me to be able to tell if they were the domes of Santa Sophia. Only when we were well into Eastern Europe, and passing from Yugoslavia to Austria, did the pinkish ochre of desert and seeming desert start giving way to the dark green of forests. Another announcement from the captain told us that we were passing over Salzburg. Once again my imagination was stirred, and I could almost hear the strains of '*Eine Kleine Nachtmusik*' ringing in my ears. Soon after this we started flying above cloud, which by the time we reached France stretched uninterruptedly below us in a grey, mottled mass that lasted for the remainder of the journey. Some time before this I had noticed that we were being accompanied, as it were, by two strands of brilliant white cloud which, for the whole of the time that I observed them, hardly varied in thickness, and which remained — except when they crossed over, which they occasionally did — apparently about a foot apart. Since I observed them for about an hour, and since we were travelling at about five hundred miles an hour the strands must have been at least five hundred miles in length. What the phenomenon was I do not know. Perhaps it was, in fact, a kind of cloud formation. Perhaps it was the exhaust of some artificial satellite. Whatever it was, it was very beautiful, streaming against the blue sky like the narrow gossamer scarf of a Dakini.

After flying above cloud for several hundred miles we started to descend. Under the cloud were London and Heathrow (we did not see anything of the Channel or the countryside), and outside the exit were waiting Kovida and Kulananda, as related at the beginning of 'Letter From England'. A night in London, a drive up to Norfolk with Kovida, three weeks at Padmaloka, and I was back in my flat at Sukhavati for a month, as further related in the same Letter. Since at the beginning of *this* Letter I went back to the beginning of my last three weeks in Auckland and completed the story of my tour in strict chronological sequence, instead of first finishing my account of what happened after my return to London six or seven weeks earlier, as I had originally intended, I now have to go back to the point at which I was sitting at my desk at Sukhavati, looking out of the window. In other words, I have to fill in the gap between the point at which I started writing my last Letter and the point at which I started writing this one. Before I do that, though, there is an incident to be described that occurred just before my departure from Padmaloka and which took me, on 27th June, down to London for the day. This was the funeral of my Uncle Jack.

Uncle Jack was the youngest but one of my mother's five brothers, and he and his first wife were familiar figures of my childhood days. He was my sister's godfather, and had given us our first bibles, a green one for me and a plum-coloured one for her. Ever since his 'conversion', which I believe took place when he was in his twenties, he had been much given to religion and was a regular churchgoer, not once missing Sunday morning service for decades together. Though she disapproved of some of his ways, my mother was very fond of him, and had kept up regular contact with him, as she had always done with all her brothers and sisters. When she wrote telling me of his death she added that she was not well enough to attend the funeral herself and asked if I could go instead. Since it would clearly please her to have someone from her own immediate family present at the funeral, and able to give her a proper account of it afterwards, I decided to go.

Shortly before 12 o'clock, therefore, I was ringing the bell of the tiny terrace house in Tooting Bec where Uncle Jack had lived for nearly fifty years, and where I had often been to see him as a child. The door was opened by a very attractive woman of about forty, in deep mourning. She recognised me at once and led the way to the front room. Here I found Audrey, my Uncle Dick's second wife, and my cousin Peter, Uncle Dick's eldest son by his first wife, who was several years younger than myself but whose thinning hair and sizeable paunch made him look quite a lot older. After a few minutes Uncle Dick himself came in, still quite sprightly despite his eighty years. They were all unaffectedly glad to see me, and at once started enquiring after my mother and sister. Rather to my relief, they seemed to be treating the occasion as a family reunion rather than as a funeral, and laughed and chatted quite uninhibitedly. More than thirty years had passed since we had last met. Readers of *The Thousand-Petalled Lotus* will remember that I had made contact with Uncle Dick and his family in Calcutta in 1945, when I was still in the Army, and that I stayed with them for a month or so at the beginning of 1947, before moving to the Ramakrishna Mission Institute of Culture in Wellington Square. The woman who had opened the door turned out to be my cousin Gillian, Uncle Dick's and Audrey's only child, who was now a grandmother, and whom I remembered as a thin-faced, ringleted little girl of ten or eleven. She was the only one in mourning, Uncle Dick being clad in a light and Peter in a dark grey suit while Audrey wore an ordinary dark frock.

Despite the laughter and the happy, friendly atmosphere, however, it was impossible to forget the nature of the occasion that had brought us together. Wreaths and bouquets lay against the wall, ready to be put on top of the coffin when it arrived, and on the table by the window Audrey had put out the cups, saucers and plates that would be required for tea after our return from the cemetery. Clearly by Jilly Cooper's standards it was going to be a quite working class type of funeral, which I suppose means that the family must be regarded as belonging to the Definitely Disgustings. Though he was taking it all very well, Uncle Dick had clearly been deeply affected by his brother's death, as I knew my mother also had, and I noticed that every now and then Audrey looked at him in a concerned sort of way. Though she and Uncle Dick had been divorced some years before, and though he had since remarried, he and Audrey had remained on amicable terms, and she continued to regard herself as part of the family.

By some misunderstanding the hearse and the accompanying car — both big, black, and shiny — were rather late in arriving, but eventually they turned up, and Uncle Jack's funeral could begin. There was something strangely final about it all. The wreaths and bouquets were placed on top of the coffin (one from my mother had arrived only a few minutes earlier), four of the undertaker's men climbed into the hearse, and the five members of the family squeezed into the second car with the two remaining undertaker's men, including the older man who appeared to be in charge. All six undertaker's men were clad in the customary funereal black, but though they were grave enough in their demeanour they were not unduly so. Slowly the little procession moved off down the street. A couple of right turns, and we were making our way up the Upper Tooting Road, incongruously caught up in the faster-moving stream of traffic. When I was a boy in that part of South London, I remembered, men always raised their hats when a funeral passed by. No hats were raised for Uncle Jack on his last journey. Men didn't wear hats any more, in fact. Times had changed. Turning left out of the main road, we nosed our way through a maze of back streets and at length drew up outside a church somewhere to the north of Clapham Common. To my surprise, it was a Pentecostal church. As far as I had known, Uncle Jack had always been a staunch member of the Church of England, as had the rest of his family (except for Auntie Kate, my mother's eldest sister, who had married a Roman Catholic), but it now transpired that some twelve or so years ago he had stopped going to Trinity Church, Tooting Bec — where he and his first wife had been married and where he had been a Sunday School teacher for nearly forty years — and transferred his allegiance to the Pentecostal church at Clapham. At least it showed an enquiring mind.

The coffin having been borne into the church on the shoulders of the six undertaker's men, and placed on a trestle immediately in front of the Lord's Table, the service began. The Family sat by itself in the middle of the front row. Behind us were scattered two or three dozen other mourners, most of them quite elderly, and most of them members of the church who had known my uncle, though there were also a couple of representatives of the firm for which he had worked for about forty years as cashier and which had at last pensioned him off. The service was conducted by a rosy-cheeked woman minister of about sixty who wore a black hat and black coat. There were, of course, the usual extempore prayers and much singing of hymns, in which the congregation joined quite lustily for their age — and, I thought, quite musically. None of your middle class, Church of England murmuring here! No question of leaving it all to the choir! I did not join in the hymns, of course, though my relations did, especially Audrey, who indeed seemed to be making quite a point of doing so, but it may have been only that as a music teacher she felt herself to be on familiar ground. Or she may have been trying to make up for the lack of participation on my part. Be that as it may, to me the most interesting — and surprising — part of the proceedings was the minister's address. She spoke clearly and confidently, thought not very well. Most of her address was devoted, not unnaturally, to Uncle Jack. Not only had he attended the church regularly for many years, but he had been an Elder. Indeed he had been one of the pillars of the church. He had given it his time, his energy, and his interest. He had identified himself with all its activities. The Sunday evening service and the mid-week prayer-cum-social meeting were the most important things in his life, the very centre of his existence. He was, in fact, the embodiment of all the

Christian virtues, and lived only for God. This certainly did not sound like the Uncle Jack that the Family had known, but nobody so much as raised an eyebrow, and I was left wondering whether a similar — though not, I hoped, a corresponding — difference existed between Order Members as they appeared to the Movement and Order Members as they appeared to their relations. Concluding her address, the minister confidently assured us that Jack, as she called him, was now in heaven, and that his friends — it was not clear if relations were included — would surely meet him there one day.

The coffin was then put back inside the hearse, the minister introduced herself, some of Uncle Jack's Pentecostal friends offered their condolences, and once again the little procession moved off, this time with the minister squeezed in with us in the back of the second car. After the minister and I had discovered that we had acquaintances in common, and she had explained that she was the widow of the previous minister and the sister of the minister before that, and after we had slowly negotiated another maze of back streets, we eventually arrived at the gates of Wandsworth Cemetry. Somewhere among the hundreds of thousands of tombstones, I knew, my father's stepfather and stepsister lay buried. Another misunderstanding having occurred, we had to wait for half an hour before the burial could begin. Only the grave-digger knew where the grave was, and he could not be found. Looking out of the car window, I saw that the part of the cemetery where we had halted was full of headstones to which large photographs of the deceased — some black and white and some coloured — had been affixed either above or below the names, which gave the area a distinctly odd look, as though the heads of the deceased had pushed their way up through the ground and were looking round and grinning at one another. The names on the headstones were all Polish. By the time we gathered round the grave, — more than a dozen people had followed us from the church, — there was a drizzle of rain from the grey sky. The burial did not take long. The coffin was lowered into the grave, which was about six feet deep, the minister read a few verses from the bible, and that was that. I had expected that at least a few token spadefuls — or handfuls — of earth would be thrown onto the coffin, but this was not done. Apparently the grave was to be filled in later. Perhaps there was a union rule to that effect. As we left, I saw that Uncle Jack had been buried in the same grave as his first wife, whom I remembered quite well. She had died as long ago as 1947 (?), and the inscription on the displaced headstone of the grave had already become difficult to read.

The return journey to Tooting Bec was much quicker than the outward one. In less than forty minutes we were all having tea together in the tiny front room, the minister and seven or eight of Uncle Jack's closest friends having been invited back for the occasion. The minister took off her hat, the cups of tea and plates of cakes and sandwiches circulated, and the aged tongues started wagging. (That it was *not* a high tea, and that the sandwiches were cut quite thin, I suppose meant that the family could be regarded as having progressed from the Definitely Disgustings a little in the direction of the Jen Teales.) With one exception, all Uncle Jack's friends were women, most of whom had, apparently, buried their last husband many, many years earlier. On the whole they were a cheerful, friendly, communicative lot, and it was clear that being, as they mostly were, well into their eighties (Uncle Jack had lived to be eighty-seven), they had long come to terms with the fact of death, both their own and other people's, and for all their church membership regarded it in a natural, pagan, fatalistic sort of way. Even the minister, unbending over a second cup of tea, was heard to remark, to general agreement, 'Poor old Jack, we shan't see *him* any more!' — a remark strangely at variance with the pious sentiments to which she had given such confident expression at the close of her address in the church. She was, I think, quite unconscious of the contradiction.

Talk about one death — I learned all the details of my uncle's last illness, which was short but quite unpleasant — naturally led to talk about others. A lively, hearty old woman of eighty-seven related how, three years earlier, she and her husband had been taking the radio for repair when he dropped dead at the bus stop, and how she had not been allowed to get into the ambulance with the body and had had to go back home with the radio by herself. She told the story as a comic episode, to the accompaniment of roars and cackles of laughter from the other old people present, all of whom had evidently heard it before and did not mind hearing it again.

While all this was going on in the front room, Uncle Dick, as executor, was sorting out the family photographs and a few other things he wanted to take away. Among the photographs was one of my great-grandparents which must have been taken a hundred and ten or a hundred and twenty years ago. My great-grandmother's features were very much those of my mother and all her sisters. My great-grandfather, however (my mother's father's father), did not look like any of his descendants, as far as I knew, or rather, they did not look like him. He had a round head, and a small moustache, and looked more Polish than Hungarian. Uncle Dick told me that he had come to England in 1842, at the age of twelve, which meant that he had been born in 1830, which I had not known before.

By four o'clock the cakes and sandwiches were all finished, the general hilarity had died down, and everybody started thinking of going home. Lifts were offered and accepted, Peter and Audrey gave me their addresses and urged me to visit them, and I made my way back to the Tooting Bec tube station with plenty of matter for reflection. Whether because they belonged to an older generation, or because of their 'working class' background (I put the term within inverted commas to emphasise its imprecision) the old people whom I had met were clearly not only unafraid of death but determined to enjoy what remained to them of life as much as they could. There was also a great sense of solidarity amongst them and much mutual sympathy and supportiveness. The minister and two or three of the other women had evidently done a great deal for my uncle during his last illness, not only visiting him constantly but also doing his cooking and cleaning and washing (his second wife had died five or six years earlier), and it was clear that in transferring his allegiance to the Pentecostal church he had found a second family and a second home. It was no less clear, however, that with the possible exception of the minister the significance of their membership of the church was for all of them social rather than spiritual. In its own way, and despite its formally religious character, the church was in fact their 'positive group', giving them companionship in their old age and help in time of trouble. That what is, or what should be, essentially a spiritual community, should instead be only a positive group, and nothing more, is, of course, a pity; but nonetheless it is good that there should at least be a positive group. In the case of our own Movement it is important to remember that though the Spiritual Community, as represented by the Order, is to be clearly distinguished from the positive group, as represented by the FWBO, and though it would be disastrous if the two were ever to be confused, nonetheless the positive group has a definite place in the total economy of the Movement — both in its own right, as it were, and as the organisational basis and 'recruiting ground' for the Spiritual Community.

After my day in London I returned to Padmaloka for the ordinations which were held at the end of the one week men's Ordination Retreat (to attend which I had been in a hurry to get back to England), and after *that* I went down to London — and Sukhavati — for a month. My first three weeks there were described, briefly, in the last Letter. During my fourth week the main events, so far as I was concerned, were the Poetry Reading at Brighton on July 28th and the celebration of Padmasambhava Day at the London Buddhist Centre on August 3rd, in both of which I took part. Although my original intention had been to visit Aryatara, Kalpadruma, and Khadiravani on the way down to Brighton, I had so much to do in London that, in the event, I was able to visit Aryatara only, on the way back. I was glad that I could do at least this much, not only on account of the warm welcome that I received, but because Krister (now Ratnapriya) from Finland was travelling with me and during the short time that he was to be over here I wanted him to see as many of our centres as possible. The Poetry Reading itself was more than a success, as I expect you all have gathered from the report in *Newsletter* 44, and what with Romantic poetry and Baroque music (mainly Paul Simmonds on the harpsichord), we were indeed 'In the Realms of Gold'. For my part, I enjoyed the occasion immensely. Friendliness and enthusiasm reigned supreme, and since I had not taken part in a public poetry reading for some years it was quite exhilarating to be able to experience what had become — unfortunately — an unfamiliar dimension of human communication. By the end of the evening I was convinced that there should be more public poetry readings in the Movement. Among the eighty or so people who were present I was glad to see Akshobhya, who had left New Zealand shortly before I did. As he, also, spent the night at Amitayus, I saw him next morning at breakfast, but these were my only glimpses of him while he was over here, as he did not visit either Padmaloka or Sukhavati.

The celebration of Padmasambhava Day was, if anything, even more enjoyable than the Poetry Reading. Besides the friendliness and enthusiasm, which on this occasion too were present in abundance, there was a touch of what can only be described as the Transcendental. Meditation, and readings from *The Life and Liberation of Padmasambhava*, having gone on in the main shrine room throughout the day, there had built up a truly 'celebratory' atmosphere. This was the first time that I had officiated in the main shrine room since conducting the dedication ceremony there last December, and it was good to be surrounded by the rich, glowing colours again and to see the eager, expectant faces of the hundred or more people who had crowded into what felt like a miniature Pure Land or even, for a few hours at least, a miniature Copper-Coloured 'Island'. Not having had time to prepare a proper lecture, I spoke extemporaneously on the Great Guru for forty or fifty minutes. A prepared lecture has the advantage of a definite plan, a definite structure. It is built up bit by bit, as though with bricks, or great squared stones, and stands solid and complete. It is buttressed with arguments and high-domed with aspirations. An extemporaneous talk grows like a flower, unfolding in accordance with the inner law of its own organic development *and* in accordance with the kind of response which it evokes. The prepared lecture is suited to one kind of occasion, one kind of purpose, the extemporary talk to another. Whatever misgivings I may have felt about having to speak on the subject of Padmasambhava without formal preparation were dissipated by the way in which my words were received. It indeed seemed that the blessing of the Great Guru was on us that night.

Three days later I left for Manchester with Kovida, Kularatna, Anandajyoti, and Ratnaguna. Kovida was at the wheel. He had come down from Padmaloka two days earlier, and in his usual energetic fashion had already been out a number of times, both on his own and with me. On the afternoon of his arrival we had spent a couple of hours on Hampstead Heath with Yuvaraj, Kularatna, and Ratnaguna, walking in the bright afternoon sunshine from the Ponds to

Kenwood, where we had tea and cream cakes, and that morning itself we had done a quick round of the West End bookshops. Now we were driving up the Ml at an ever-increasing speed, having left Sukhavati immediately after lunch. It was a warm, rather oppressive day, and the three 'lads' in the back spent the greater part of the journey dozing. We stopped once, to drink tea from our two flasks, and to eat the cakes, biscuits, crisps, winegums, smarties etc. that we had bought at one of the motorway shops. Kularatna, who had taken over the driving, induced me to try one of his rather primitive boiled sweets, which were as big as marbles, almost completely tasteless, and lasted a very long time. This led, I believe, to a rather inconclusive discussion of the psychology of sweet-sucking in the adult male.

At 6.30 we drew up outside the end-of-terrace house which is Gridhrakuta or 'The Vulture's Peak', which as everyone knows is our Manchester Centre-cum-Community and the abode of (at that time) Sagaramati, Ratnaguna, Suvajra, Virabhadra, Sthiramati, and John. Sagaramati was away at Padmaloka, leading the first two weeks of the men's Summer Retreat, but we were warmly welcomed by Suvajra, who made us tea. I had seen Gridhrakuta more than once before, but it was Kovida's first visit, and he naturally wanted to have a good look round. From the hard look that came into his blue eyes, and the way in which his nose wrinkled slightly, I could tell he was not very impressed by the place. Before long John appeared, having spent the day working — on his own — on the new Centre, and Virabhadra bounced in after a spell of duty at the hospital. Soon the unspoken question that was uppermost in everybody's mind was 'What about supper?' I had been rather taking it for granted that we would be eating at Gridhrakuta, as we were expected there, but it turned out that no meal had been prepared, and apparently there was no money in the house to buy provisions. Eventually, just after Virabhadra's arrival, somebody suggested that we all go out for a meal together. The idea at once met with general acceptance. Two or three voices mentioned the name of a favourite Indian restaurant in the city centre. Within minutes we were all off — all except Ratnaguna, who had a guitar pupil coming for a lesson, and John, who seemed to have disappeared. Since the Cortina was not big enough for six people (in India, I could not help reflecting, it would have been made to hold ten or twelve), Virabhadra took his sports car along as well. Parking where we could in a side street, we set off on foot in search of the Indian restaurant, as nobody knew exactly where it was. Eventually we found it, but it was closed. Where to go now? The next suggestion was an Italian restaurant in Albert Square. (Apart from actual vegetarian restaurants, which are not very common in England, it is only at Indian, Italian, and Chinese restaurants that it is at all easy to get a vegetarian meal.) Soon we were crossing the Square, with its statues of bygone national heroes and civic dignitaries, and looking up at the enormous Victorian Gothic pile of the town hall, probably the largest municipal building in Britain. Luckily, the Italian restaurant *was* open, and after a quick look at the menu we went inside. There followed one of the pleasantest and most positive social evenings that any of us, I think, had enjoyed for a long time. To begin with, the restaurant itself was spacious and attractively furnished and decorated, with a predominance of varnished natural wood, there were no customers except ourselves, the service was good, and the food really excellent. Most important of all, we all knew one another quite well, communication was open and free, we were glad to be together, and we had a lot of worth-while things to talk about. It was two hours before we left. At my suggestion Kovida picked up the bill, but for one reason and another he was in such a jolly mood that he did not mind, and in any case I think there were one or two 'contributions' forthcoming the next day. Back at Gridhrakuta we were soon feeling ready for bed. It was not clear, however, where Kovida and I would be staying. Eventually it transpired that we had a choice and could either stay at Gridhrakuta or enjoy what Kularatna called 'the middle class comfort' of his parents' home, where he himself was then staying, his parents themselves having gone to Wales for a few days for a funeral. Reading, as I thought, Kovida's thoughts, I opted for the middle class comfort. In less than an hour the three of us were distributed round three different rooms in a detached suburban house. I was in Kularatna's parents' room, Kovida was in his brother's room, while Kularatna himself occupied the guest room. When I was in bed Kularatna brought me a mug of cocoa, after which I read for a while, and then slept.

After breakfast the next morning the three of us collected Anandajyoti from Gridhrakuta and set off for North Wales. Anandajyoti was going to work at Tyn-y-ddol for a week, Kovida and I wanted to see what progress had been made with the renovation of the place, while Kularatna was coming along just for the sake of the ride and the company. It was a dull, overcast day, with only fitful gleams of sunshine, and I must admit that after my recent experience of New Zealand's Southern Alps I found the hills of North Wales, especially when seen through the rain, rather unimpressive. More than three years before I had spent two months at Tyddyn Rhydderch, with Andy Friends, and as we drove past Wrexham, and through Llangollen, I recognised many familiar landmarks. At Corwen, the rain having eased up, we spent some time looking for a second-hand bookshop that was no longer there, after which it was only a ten minute drive to Tyn-y-ddol, or rather to our parking place a little further on past Tyddyn Rhydderch. Jyotipala, Kamalashila, Alaya and Jeff were very glad to see us, and soon Jyotipala was proudly showing us all the work that had been done. The place had certainly been greatly transformed since my last visit. I particularly admired the gleaming white walls and bright yellow doors and window-frames of the small outbuilding, which now had quite a Tibetan look. One of the large outbuildings, probably once a barn, had been turned into a spacious shrine room that was Zen-like in its beauty and simplicity. Having seen everything that there was to see we sat down to lunch, which consisted of an excellent soup followed by a fine cake specially baked by Alaya. Not long after Kovida, Kularatna and I left, partly because we did not want to disrupt the community's working day too much, and partly because we wanted to go to the coast.

Heading due north we passed through Denbigh and St. Asaph and so came to the busy seaside town of Rhyl. For the greater part of the journey our way lay through one of the most beautiful parts of North Wales, but all too soon the half-forested green hills, the flocks of sheep, the drystone walls, and the picturesque stone cottages, gave way to an ugly, patchily industrialised urban sprawl. Rhyl was a place of broad esplanades, rows of hotels, and much sea frontage. From my last visit, which I must have made at about the same time the previous Summer, I remembered the magnificent display of flowers I had seen at the Royal Floral Hall, a large glasshouse on the sea front that dated seemingly from Victorian times, and suggested to the others that it was well worth a visit. We were not disappointed. The profusion of bloom was incredible. There were hundreds of different kinds of bedding plants and flowering shrubs, all brilliantly coloured, and all in full bloom. So closely were they massed together, and so narrow were the little winding paths in between, that it was at times quite difficult to squeeze through, especially as there were so many people around, most of them looking incredibly coarse and ugly in comparison with the flowers. Among the few plants that I was able to identify were the fuchsias. There were several dozen different varieties of these, many of them so old that they had grown from shrubs into small trees that now touched the ceiling, from which their red and white and pink and purple flowers hung down in cascades above our heads as in some Persian miniature painting. There were almost more flowers than greenery, in fact, and certainly much of whatever greenery there was in the place was hidden by a cloud of red, or yellow, or white, or blue blossoms. Amidst all this floral splendour, their plumage no less brilliant than the flowers themselves, two or three allegedly vicious macaws sat listlessly on their perches. Once outside again in the open air, we took a quick look at the sea then had a cup of tea at an ice cream parlour-cum-café a few yards further along the front. The weather had been quite changeable all afternoon, but now the sky cleared and the sun shone through the window where we were sitting with an agreeable warmth. For a time we amused ourselves listening to the cacklings of the groups of ancient harpies that came staggering in off a coach, some of them extraordinarily grotesque in appearance. Then, having had enough of Rhyl, we returned to the car, and after following the coastal road for as long as we could, turning off onto the inland road through Cheshire returned to Manchester. On our arrival at Gridhrakuta we found Ratnaguna in the kitchen preparing a meal, with some assistance from Sthiramati, who had turned up at last, having been stranded in Birmingham the previous night on his way back from London. The meal turned out quite well. When it was over, Kovida, Suvajra and Ratnaguna smartened themselves up and went out together for the evening, Kularatna departed for home, while Sthiramati and I retired upstairs for a chat.

The following morning was dedicated to the arts. After breakfast Kovida, Sthiramati and I visited first the Whitworth Gallery, and then the City Art Gallery, in between taking in one or two second-hand bookshops. As on my last visit to Manchester, I was interested mainly in the Pre-Raphaelite paintings, of which the City Art Gallery in particular had a notable collection, including one version of Holman Hunt's *The Scapegoat* (the one *with* the rainbow), a reproduction of which hangs in my study at Sukhavati. Rather surprisingly, the original was much *smaller* than the reproduction, and mounted in a deep, wide frame that gave the whole picture a very different look, almost as though one was seeing the poor scapegoat, and the bottle-green Dead Sea, and the ridge of mauve-pink mountains behind him, through a telescope. Indeed, it was rather as though one was looking back into history — into the remote past. On our way to the City Art Gallery we passed a smaller gallery devoted to modern art. Kovida at once dived in, closely followed by Sthiramati and myself. As soon as we entered we were confronted by a bold, striking composition entirely in brown and white. It showed a table covered by a cloth (white) standing in the corner of a room (brown), and was by Patrick Caulfield, who apparently was one of Kovida's favourite modern artists. Having had our fill of bookshops and art galleries, as well as of walking round the still rather grandly Victorian city centre, we found a restaurant and had some lunch. The walls of the restaurant, I noticed, were covered with large, coarse-grained reproductions of really excellent old black-and-white photographs, mainly of local interest. Lunch over, we returned to where we had parked the car, Kovida and I said goodbye to Sthiramati, who walked off (a little sadly, I thought) with a wave of his hand, leaving us to find our way through the mazes of north-west Manchester (we got lost more than once) and out onto the M61 and then the M6.

It was a fine day, and after being on the road for an hour we were cruising through more or less open countryside. For some reason or other, this part of our journey north was much pleasanter than the first, and we actually seemed to be covering the slightly greater distance in less time. As we passed through the Lake District there was a sudden rainstorm, short and sharp, which set the windscreen streaming and the windscreen-wipers frantically swishing, after which all was bright and sunny again — until we reached the Border, where we were treated to another downpour. We were now driving up through green hills that seemed much bigger and rounder than those of North Wales, and were mostly bare except for a thin sprinkling of sheep.

Kovida was very glad to be back in his native Scotland, and crooned happily to himself as we drove along. I dozed off for half an hour. When I awoke, Kovida was still crooning, and we were beginning to enter the more outlying suburbs of Glasgow, which for the most part were not a pretty sight. Soon we were in the smoke-blackened city centre — in George Square — in Kelvinside — looking for the 'new' Centre, which neither of us had visited before, my own last visit to Glasgow having occurred more than two years earlier, when the Centre was still at Hamilton Park Avenue. Eventually we found the place, which was very picturesquely situated on the third floor of a handsome terrace house overlooking a tree-fringed river. As we parked at the side of the very steep road, there slid away down in front of us a small car through the back window of which I recognised a familiar head. It was none other than my old friend Anand Kaushalyayan, with three or four other Indians, one of them also a Buddhist monk. Those who are at all acquainted with Kovida will know that he is nothing if not quick on the uptake. Realising that I was not particularly keen to meet the visitors, who had obviously been enquiring for me at Heruka — it was a bit like the Black Riders looking for the hobbits at the Inn of Bree — he made no attempt to attract their attention, and I watched the car slide down the road and disappear round a bend with a feeling of some satisfaction. During the last few months Anandji had been trying quite hard to get in touch with me, and knowing him as I did I had wondered what was behind it all, especially as we had not seen each other for at least fifteen years. When I was in Poona, on the first of my recent visits, he had sent me several urgent messages to the effect that I should visit him in Nagpur, where he had established his headquarters in the small Vihara that had been built on the Diksha Bhumi, the site of the original mass conversion of ex-Untouchables to Buddhism under the leadership of Dr. Ambedkar. More recently, he had tried to get me to see him in London, where he had come for a few days from Wolverhampton. On that occasion we had just missed each other, and now it looked as though we had missed each other again. He and his friends would, I was sure, be back before long, but for the time being I was safe.

On our ringing the bell of Heruka, the door was at length opened by a young man who knew us even if we did not know him, and Kovida and I found ourselves in the spacious, colourfully decorated hallway of the large flat which accommodates both the present Glasgow Centre and its supporting community. At the far end of the hallway, on the right, was the kitchen-cum-dining-room. Here we found ten or twelve valiant Scots crowded round a small, uncomfortably low table having an early supper, as some of them were to take part in the class that was being held that evening. Among them were Ajita, Dhammarati, Susiddhi, Colin, and Kenny, plus Aryamitra and Joss (the only Sassenachs), besides two or three others whom I did not know, including the bearded lad who had opened the door. Everybody made us very welcome and we squeezed in round the table with them and partook of an excellent meal. One of the first questions was, of course, whether we had met the Indian visitors. Ajita explained that they had waited for me for an hour, as he had told them I was expected. Apparently he had not been very impressed by them. One of the laymen had tried to take him to task for not prostrating himself before Anandji and the other monk in the 'orthodox' manner, but Ajita had made it clear that, as a Western Buddhist, he did not consider himself bound to follow Eastern cultural traditions or social customs. He would shake hands with the monks, he said, which was the custom in *his* culture. Discussion revealed that the two laymen, who claimed to be followers of Dr. Ambedkar, were in some ways not very orthodox themselves. One of them was surprised that Ajita, as a Buddhist, did not believe in God, and tried to convince him that belief in God was an integral part of Buddhism. (Anandji himself, I knew, would not have agreed with this.) Moreover, it transpired that he and his friend had lived in Glasgow for eight or nine years and that they ran a liquor shop, which certainly was not very much in accordance with the principle of Right Livelihood. Ajita and I were still talking when the 'phone rang. It was one of the two Indian laymen. Realising that I was cornered at last, and that the fatal meeting could not now be delayed any longer, I told Ajita to say that I could see Anandji the following morning.

The following morning, therefore, along the old reprobate came — more than an hour late. I was waiting in the large reception room, which was decorated even more colourfully than the hallway, though the combination of bright red and bright green was a little too bold for my taste. On the wall was a selection of Dhammarati's posters, some of them quite attractive, but others, well ... Looking out of the window, one had a wonderful panoramic view of the city, which from that distance, and that height, seemed to contain an extraordinary variety of Victorian Gothic towers, steeples, and steeply pitched roofs. I had given Ajita instructions that only Anandji and the other monk were to be admitted to the reception room, and that the rest of the entourage was to be entertained elsewhere.

Anandji was genuinely glad to see me, and in the event I was, I think, glad to see him. Though I strongly disagreed with his narrowly rationalistic interpretation of Buddhism, which left no room for either meditation or faith, and though I had always been careful not to get involved in his various 'polictickings', we had been on amicable terms since the early fifties, and had enjoyed each others company whenever we happened to meet. Though more wrinkled and toothless than ever (he was now in his mid-seventies) he had not changed very much since I last saw him, and seemed to be wearing the same dingy yellow robe and the same knitted woollen cap. He was on his way to a conference in New York, he explained, in his usual slow, deliberate, circumstantial manner, and was spending a few weeks in England *en route*, waiting for the ticket for the next and final stage of his journey. The ticket was to be supplied by someone who knew me. This was Sujata Nataraja, formerely Sujata Hettiarachi, who had visited me in Kalimpong in 1950, when she had wanted to found an order of Buddhist nursing sisters. She would be getting in touch with me, Anandji said. Sure enough, a few minutes later the 'phone rang. It was Sujata, speaking from New York. At what must have been enormous expense, she told me at inordinate length about the wonderful conference she was organising. It sounded like the Buddhist nursing sisters, — and several other unsuccessful ventures of Sujata's, — all over again. What the purpose of the conference was, however, was by no means clear. Anandji himself did not seem to know, or even to care to know. After all, a conference was a conference, and as such well worth attending, especially if it involved flying from one country, — or one continent, — to another. Once again I was back, it seemed, in the world of perfectly useless, perfectly meaningless 'Buddhist activities' which did absolutely nothing except foster a sense of self-importance in the people concerned — a world with which I thought I had cut off all connection some years ago. At length Sujata rang off, and I returned to the reception room.

Having had enough of the conference, I changed the subject and tried to tell Anandji something about Buddhism in England — in which the plump, pleasant-faced young Indian monk accompanying him in fact seemed quite interested. Anandji, however, showed no interest in Buddhism in England at all, and insisted on rambling remorselessly on about the conference, giving me a highly circumstantial account of how he had come to receive his invitation, how he had nearly not been able to go, how he was now waiting for his ticket to New York, how the ticket might not come, how if it did not come he might have to go straight back to India, etc., etc. At one point I managed to get in a few words about Sukhavati, but this aroused not so much as a flicker of interest, and he clearly was no more desirous of seeing the place than he was of going to Timbuktu — if anything, rather less.

He did, however, show a gleam of interest when I spoke of Buddhist activities in India. Soon he was telling me about the troubles that had arisen at the Vihara in Nagpur, which in his usual fashion he had evidently made too hot to hold him. (I had heard something of these troubles when I was in India.) Fortunately he had heard that his good friend Sangharakshita had a plot of land in Nagpur, and that the land was not being used for any purpose, in which case ... I replied that it was true that I had a plot of land in Nagpur, but that I was planning to build a Vihara there in the not too far distant future. The reason why Anandji had been so eager to meet me was becoming a little clearer. It has something to do with my plot of land in Nagpur. Perhaps he wanted me to give him the land, so that he could build a Vihara of his own there, which would mean that he would still be able to have his headquarters in Nagpur, even if he was ousted from the Vihara on the Diksha Bhumi. Or he may have been trying to find out what plans I had for extending the activities of the TBMS to Nagpur, which with the possible exception of Bombay was the main centre of the Ambedkarite Buddhist movement and the scene of some of my own activities in the past. He was, as I well knew, an extremely crafty person, and much given to intrigue. (When, the previous evening, I had asked Ajita what his impression of Anandji was, he had instantly replied, 'He's a very shrewd man', which I thought quite perceptive of him.) Having sounded me out about my plot of land in Nagpur, Anandji returned to the subject of his ticket to New York, and was becoming more tedious than ever when Kovida put his head round the door and announced, with Scottish directness, 'Y'ur car's reeady!' The previous evening he had gone to spend the night in Dumbarton, leaving me to have a quiet read. Before his departure I had taken the precaution of arranging for this little interruption on his return, as I knew from experience how longwinded Anandji could be. However, though it was obvious I now had to go out, Anandji went rambling on, and it required another interruption from Kovida to bring the interview to an end.

A few minutes before his departure, as though by an afterthought, Anandji asked me to 'help' the young Indian monk, who was in charge of the Wolverhampton Vihara, and to whom I had already given a pile of FWBO literature. The remaining members of the entourage, in the form of two overweight young Punjabis in dark business suits, were then allowed in for purposes of *darshan*. They came half crawling in with glasses of water in their hands for Anandji (he had refused to have any tea), apparently not trusting Ajita to offer it to him in the proper manner. I asked them the usual questions about themselves, they were suitably apologetic about running a liquor shop, and at length, after more delays, and several false departures, — Anandji was still talking about his ticket to New York, — Ajita, Kovida and I managed to get them all through the Centre door and out onto the landing, where we said our last goodbyes. They had spent two hours at the Centre! Long before their departure, I was beginning to regret that I had agreed to see Anandji. Though I was quite fond of the old rogue, and initially had been glad to see him again, it was more evident than ever that we occupied two different worlds, and that we had even less in common than we did when I was in India. He had spent more than fifty years as a 'Buddhist monk' but for all his knowledge of Pali he still had no idea of what the Buddha, the Dharma, and the Sangha really were. What a pity! I was more glad than ever that the WBO and the FWBO had been brought into existence, and only felt sorry that Anandji was not able to find his way into them or even to see that they were there.

Having decided not to take the car, and setting out rather later than we had planned, Kovida and I spent the rest of the morning, and the early part of the afternoon, visiting the second-hand bookshops of Glasgow. We started off with the Voltaire and Rousseau, where we found copies of several works by Middleton Murry that I did not have, as well as other useful items. On the way I noticed that the Voltaire and Rousseau was situated in a street known as Otago Street. I had encountered the name in the course of my travels in South Island, New Zealand, and since it was not English had assumed that it was Maori. It now transpired that it was Scottish, probably Gaelic, though what it meant I was unable to find out.* Since I don't know Glasgow very well, and since Kovida and I passed and repassed through quite a lot of the inner city that day, I cannot give a very connected account of our wanderings.

Leaving the Voltaire and Rousseau, and taking in three or four other second-hand bookshops on our way, — Kovida's knapsack was now quite heavy, — we turned into Sauchiehall Street, which Glasgwegians proudly describe as the Oxford Street of Glasgow. In one respect at least Sauchiehall Street was not like Oxford Street. The healthy, vigorous people we saw there were, for the most part, not foreign visitors, but natives of the place. The further we progressed along the busy street, — the deeper we plunged

---

* Further enquiry has revealed that Otago is, in fact, a corruption of the Maori name Otaku. But how did 'Otago' get from South Island, New Zealand, to Glasgow? The Otago province, with its city Dunedin, was of course settled by immigrants from Scotland in the middle of the last century.

into the heart of the city, — the happier Kovida became. He was happy to be back in the city he knew so well, happy to feel the sheer vitality of the place, and to hear the uninhibited Scots voices ringing through the air.

When we were (I think) half way along the street, he pointed out to me the location of the new Glasgow Centre, — which Joss had pointed out to *him* the previous evening, before he went to Dumbarton, — which was on the opposite side of the road. It was situated on the first and third floors of a massive block of shops, offices and flats. Almost immediately underneath were *three* Indian restaurants. Opposite, on the side on which we were standing, was the Glasgow Arts Centre. Oxford Street of Glasgow or not, it certainly seemed that Sauchiehall Street was very centrally situated, and that the new Centre would be in the midst of the full stream of Glasgow life, work, and play. Slipping into the Arts Centre, we had a quick look round at an exhibition that was on, and then had a cup of coffee in the rather crowded café. From here it was half an hour's walk to our last second-hand bookshop, which was the famous John Smith's. Here I found another of Middleton Murry's works, while Kovida found the Complete Poems of Arthur Hugh Clough, for which he had been looking. Our outing was now almost at an end. We walked back through streets of massive, smoke-blackened red granite buildings with white Georgian porticos, found ourselves in Sauchiehall Street again, had a meal in a wholefood restaurant, — where I saw a very young man in a cherry-red kilt, the only time I saw a kilt during the whole of my visit, — and so returned to the tree-lined terraces of Kelvinside, and to the Centre, tired and footsore perhaps, but with our booty of second-hand volumes weighing down Kovida's bulging knapsack. The remainder of the day passed uneventfully. Kovida went off to Dumbarton to see his sister again, and to find out if his parents had yet returned from their holiday on the Continent. I gave interviews to various people who wanted to see me, and then read.

Next morning Ajita and I went to see the Glasgow Art Gallery and Museum. This was partly because I wanted to have another look at some of the exhibits, with which I was already familiar from my previous visits to Glasgow, partly because Ajita and I wanted to be able to talk freely and without interruption — and partly because it would give us the opportunity of walking through Kelvingrove Park, from which one had a splendid view not only of the Art Gallery and Museum itself (facing the wrong way round, so it was said, owing to the inadvertence of the architect), but also of the Camelot-like battlements of the University. What I had most wanted to see among the exhibits was the fine collection of precious and semi-precious stones. But try as we might we were unable to locate the collection, which I remembered as occupying a mysterious corner on the top floor of the building. Eventually, I was compelled to conclude that my memory had played me false, and that the precious and semi-precious stones of my recollection, — a truly magnificent hoard, containing numerous specimens of unusual size and beauty, — must be located in some other museum — perhaps the one in Edinburgh. I recalled another occasion on which my memory had played me false. When writing the memoirs of my early life which were *not* included in *The Thousand-Petalled Lotus* (the publishers thought they were not of sufficient general interest), I had described the Norman church at Besthorpe, the Norfolk village where my father's mother had been born, and which I had visited a number of times as a boy, as being situated on a hill. In my mind's eye I could see the church clearly standing on the hill, which though neither large nor steep was definitely a hill. On visiting Besthorpe a year or two after my return to England I was astonished to find that the countryside around Besthorpe was completely flat, without the least vestige of a hill, and that although there was a church there, and although the church stood a little way out of the village, the land on which it stood was as flat as the rest, if not flatter. Yet in my mind's eye I had an actual *picture* of the church standing there on its hill. One's memory could play one strange tricks, it seemed! However, though my search for treasure trove was unsuccessful, the rest of the morning went according to plan. Before leaving the Art Gallery Ajita and I had a good talk in the quiet and seclusion of the upstairs coffee bar, discussing various matters that needed to be discussed, after which we retraced our steps to Kelvingrove Park and from there returned to Kelvinside by a circuitous route that gave us a different — and more distant — view of the University. Back at the Centre I had a late lunch, then gave a few more interviews.

Kovida's cheerful face re-appeared just in time for supper. He had seen his parents in Dumbarton that morning, as well as what seemed an extraordinarily large number of old friends in the course of the rest of the time that he had been away. After supper came the Question and Answer meeting. This was to be my only 'public appearance' at the Centre, and people had come not only from Glasgow, but from Edinburgh and other places as well. By the time we started the reception room, big as it was, was full, and even overflowing. People sat on the floor, on chairs, on the arms of settees — wherever they could. Most of them were young, or fairly young, but there was also a sprinkling of people — nearly all of them men — who were definitely on the elderly side. From what I had heard earlier on, I knew that two or three of our Glasgow Friends had been quite outraged by some of the remarks I had made about Christianity in *Buddhism and Blasphemy*, and intended to challenge me on this score. In the event, nothing happened: no questions about Christianity, or about blasphemy, were asked, although more than once I deliberately gave an opening to anyone who wished to do so. On the whole the questions were not unlike those which I had been asked at similar meetings in India, in Malaysia, in Australia, and in New Zealand, earlier in the year, and my recollection of them is general rather than particular. Kovida, on being asked for *his* recollections a short while ago, could only say that I 'answered all the questions very well and gave some people more than they bargained for.' Whether some people got more than they bargained for or not, everybody seemed very pleased with the way the meeting had gone, and the resultant energy and emotional positivity flowed into the puja that followed. By 10 o'clock the next morning Kovida and I were ready to leave.

Before we left, Ajita gave me, as a present from him and the rest of the community, a beautiful multi-faceted Silver Crystal ball, nearly two inches in diameter, backed by all the colours of the rainbow. If I had been unable to locate the collection of precious and semi-precious stones at the Art Gallery and Museum, I now had something that would give me a lot of pleasure — and inspiration — long after I had left Glasgow.

Kovida and I had not been long on the road south when we decided that, as it was a reasonably fine day, and as we did not really need to be in Manchester until 4 or 5 o'clock, we had time for a quick visit to the Lake District. The Lake District is, of course, the area in which the poets Wordsworth, Coleridge and Southey all lived (Coleridge only in the earlier part of his life), and which figures prominently in their poetry, especially in that of Wordsworth. Half an hour after crossing the Border, therefore, we turned right at Penrith and headed south-west. Once off the Motorway, with its endless streams of north-bound and south-bound holiday traffic, we quickly found ourselves in a totally different world. The abruptness of the transition was astonishing. All around us were hills even more diminutive than those of North Wales, green fields enclosed by drystone walls, and thatched stone cottages of unbelievably uniform antiquity and picturesqueness. Kovida had not been in the Lake District before, and as we swung round bends, and drove up and down gently undulating hills, he looked around with special interest. After all, our visit was on the nature of a pilgrimage, and we were now on holy ground! That very tree, or that very stone, might have been the one apostrophized by Wordsworth in a famous poem.

I had been to the Lake District once before. In the Autumn of 1976, after giving my lectures on *The Sutra of Golden Light* in London, I had spent a week there, with Andy Friends, and had a reasonably good idea of the area. Even more than on that occasion, I was struck by how small the Lake District in fact was — at least, when one was driving round it by car, and not walking from place to place, as Wordsworth and Coleridge usually did. Soon we were driving down the gleaming length of Ullswater, glimpses of which we had every now and then through gaps in the trees on our left. Owing to some lack of clarity in the map, which did not show all the by-roads, we found ourselves coming in to Ambleside through a back way over some high hills partially shrouded in mist. From Ambleside we followed the Keswick road as far as Grasmere.

In Grasmere was Dove Cottage. It was situated a few hundred yards up a lane to the right of the main road, away from the village, which lay down a road to the left. Here Wordsworth lived for several years with his sister Dorothy and wife Mary, and here Coleridge came from Keswick to visit him, frequently walking the twelve miles there and the twelve miles back in one and the same day. Coleridge, and

De Quincey, also occupied it, independently, at different times. It was a tiny building of grey stone, slate-roofed, and stood back from the lane in a little garden. Adjacent to it were several other buildings of the same type, only bigger. Dove Cottage was, of course, now a national monument, and open to the public. Just as we arrived, it closed for lunch. Kovida did not really mind, as he was not very keen on going round the place in company with a party of tourists (the place was so small that people had to be admitted in batches), and I had been inside on a previous visit, and knew that the interior was pretty much as it had been in Wordsworth's time. We therefore contented ourselves with gazing at the building from outside, and visiting the bookshop opposite, where I bought a copy of Coleridge's *On the Constitution of the Church and State* ('We've sold one of them at last!' said one lady assistant to another), after which we went back to the village, where we had left the car, and started looking for something to eat.

Grasmere was full of restaurants and eating-houses of various kinds, but not one of them seemed to cater for the vegetarian. The large boards that stood outside their doors announcing the fare that was available within did not so much as mention an omelette, even. It was all steaks, steaks, and scampi. Eventually, we found a cup of tea and a sandwich in a pleasant riverside café from which we could look *down* at the water below and *up* at the people passing over the little stone bridge to our left.

From here we drove back to Ambleside, on the way stopping at Rydal. At Rydal, up another lane, on a ridge overlooking Rydal Water, stood Rydal Mount. This was the house in which Wordsworth lived for the last thirty-odd years of his life. It was much larger than Dove Cottage, and as there did not seem to be many tourists about we bought our tickets and went in, evading the guides. Though a drawing-room had been added, the rooms were furnished and decorated in much the same way as they had been when Wordsworth lived there, and contained many mementoes of the poet, his family and friends, including pictures, manuscripts, and printed books. There was even Wordsworth's own pen and ink-pot! After looking round the house, we explored the extensive grounds, which with their well-kept lawns and carefully trimmed shrubberies were certainly much less wild than they must have been in Wordsworth's own day. From the lowest point we could see, through a gap in the thickly growing trees, the mirror-like expanse of Rydal Water gleaming through the mist and sunshine below.

From Rydal to Ambleside, from Ambleside to Windermere, from Windermere to Kendal, and from Kendal back onto the Motorway, was only an hour's drive. It led, though, over hills that were almost mountains, through mist that was like fine rain, — or rain that was like thick mist, — and past a section of Lake Windermere. From the point at which we rejoined the Motorway, just outside Kendal, it was not much more than an hour's drive to Manchester, where we arrived at Gridhrakuta at about 4 o'clock — rather earlier than we had expected. Our trip to the north was beginning to draw to an end. After Kularatna had taken us to see the new Centre at Withington, and we had had a meal (prepared by Ratnaguna) with the Gridhrakuta community, I went for a walk in the Park with Sthiramati and Suvajra. At 10 o'clock the next morning we left for London, arriving six hours later after feeling ourselves being sucked with increasing rapidity down into the blackness of the megalopolitan drain. A bright spark at Sukhavati was Yuvaraj, with whom we spent part of the evening talking about evil spirits. (Kovida told some ghost stories.)

*Next* day, after breakfast, I left by train from Liverpool Street for Rayleigh, where I spent a few hours with my mother. Kovida collected me by car late in the afternoon, and after he had had a cup of tea we drove up through Essex and Suffolk to Norfolk. The trees were in their full Summer beauty. The fields were a waving expanse of ripened grain. I was glad to be back, even though I would not be able to spend many weeks at Padmaloka before returning to London to give my Autumn lectures. As we drove in through the paddock gate, I saw some of the retreat people strolling up and down the lawn, or standing round the lily pond, fingering their rosaries and waiting for the evening meditation to begin. *Boom, boom,* it was time, said the big Vietnamese gong in the courtyard, a few minutes later, as Kovida and I sat in the community kitchen having a meal. Before long the sound of chanting floated in from the shrine room ...

Later, upstairs in my study, I started settling in. On my big white bookcase was an elm tree section, about three inches thick, that had been smoothed and polished by Kulananda. On the section, which made a fine pedestal, sat a bronze figure of Avalokiteshvara, the Bodhisattva of Compassion, about twelve inches in height. He sat in an unusual attitude, with his right knee raised, and his left knee touching the ground, while his left hand, which rested on the ground behind his left knee, supported the weight of his body. His head, with its tiara and topknot, was inclined, and he *looked down*. His right elbow rested on the middle of his right thigh, and the fingers of his right hand, which was on a level with his navel, hung down in a relaxed fashion, the gently curved forefinger seeming to indicate a spot, not far from his right foot, on which his eyes, too, were fixed. *On this spot I put my Silver Crystal ball.* Sitting in my armchair, and looking across the room, I could see all the colours of the rainbow glittering in it, from red to violet through orange, yellow, green, blue, and indigo. If I shifted my position slightly, the colours of the ball would change. 'Look,' Avalokiteshvara seemed to be saying, 'the Jewel in the Lotus,' the potentiality that is at the heart of all sentient beings — and at one's own heart. Whatever one does, wherever one goes, one must never take one's eyes off that Jewel. I had brought back a good lesson with me from my wanderings.

## CHAPTER SIX

# THIRD LETTER FROM ENGLAND

I

SPACE and time are strange things. Whenever I write one of these Letters I write it sitting in a certain place, from a certain central point in a whole network of relationships with nature and with other human beings. Depending on where I am, England is 'near' and New Zealand is 'far', or England is 'far' and New Zealand is 'near'. I also write at a certain point in time, in relation to which August 13th, 1979, is yesterday, or last week, or last month, or six months ago — or, of course, tomorrow, or next week, or next year, and so on. At the moment I am once again sitting at my desk at Padmaloka, and it is 3 o'clock in the afternoon on Friday 29th February, 1980 — a leap day. England is 'near', and Finland, India and New Zealand are 'far'. August 13th, 1979, which is the point up to which I carried my last Letter, is now six and a half months ago. Time, as usual, has passed very quickly. Summer has ended, Autumn has come and gone, and Winter, it seems, is nearly over.

Much has happened during the six and a half months which have passed since my return to Padmaloka in the middle of the men's Summer Retreat, as related at the end of that *Second Letter from England*, and this time it will not be possible for me to give as full a description of my movements, activities, and reflections as I tried, at least, to give in the previous Letters. In any case, looking back over those Letters, three of them written from New Zealand and two from England, the thought strikes me that not only were they written in a certain place, at a certain time, not only were they a selection from a sequence of events strung out along a certain narrative line, but that the sequence itself represented a selection from the totality of my experience in — and out of — space and time. Like the Silver Crystal ball at which I sat and looked at the conclusion of my last Letter, my life has many different facets, many different aspects, of which the events so far described constitute a very small number indeed. For instance, — to take two extreme examples, — extreme in the sense that they represent facets on opposite sides of the multi-coloured sphere of my total life-experience, — in my Letters I said nothing about world events, or my 'reaction' to them, nothing about my own dreams, meditations, and insights. In other words, I said nothing about either the most 'objective', or the most 'subjective' factors in my experience, even though these were as much a part of my experience as going through the Passport Control and Customs at Santa Cruz, giving a lecture in the Pioneer Women's Hall in downtown Auckland, or walking on Hampstead Heath in London. *Some of the things that I have not written about may be more important than some of the things I have written about,* though generally speaking the fact that I write about a certain thing at all means that it is important to me in some way — that it has a *meaning* for me.

What I am trying to point out is that ordinary life, as we live it from day to day, is much richer and more complex than we generally realise, and that the account we give of it in words and images for the benefit of others represents an impoverished, not to say a misleading, abstraction from the multi-faceted and multi-dimensional totality of our experience. Even the fullest and frankest autobiography is no more than a thin cross-section, a narrow segment, of the whole which is the man himself as, for a certain length of time, he moves about in space, and wakes and sleeps and dreams. If such is the case with autobiography, what are we to say of biography, where one man is recounting the life of another after an interval of, perhaps, several hundred years — retracing events and reconstructing motives from incomplete and contradictory sources based, more often than not, on nothing better than speculation, rumour and gossip.

Even to find out the truth about events of national and international significance occurring in our own day is not always easy, even with the help of all the resources of investigative journalism. What really *did* happen at Dallas, at Watergate, and at Chappaquiddick — and why? What really *was* the understanding that Mr. Bill Sirs and Sir Charles Villers (or was it Mr. Bob Scholey?) came to in that hotel in Brussels (or was it Bonn?) last month? If it were not for the dead bodies that, in some cases, are undeniably but unaccountably there, one might be tempted to think that it is not so much that something happens but that a number of people *think* something happens and that the accounts they give have certain common features — features that are regarded as *being* the event which everybody thinks happens. But one does not need to go so far afield as American politics, or British industrial disputes, in order to find examples of the sort of thing of which I am speaking. What actually *was* decided at the FWBO Council meeting in 1978 when the reorganisation of Centre classes was discussed (yes, we have a set of minutes, but they are so brief as to be ambiguous and those who were present cannot agree on how they should be interpreted)? What *did* Upasaka A. really say to Upasaka B. when they had their exchange about communication at that Order meeting the other month (here we have no minutes to help us)?

When one passes from the life and experience of one individual to that of many individuals, from autobiography and biography to history, from modern history to ancient history, — to world history, — the degree of uncertainty becomes greater, and even total. Did Jesus really rise from the dead on the third day? Who — or what — was Jesus anyway? Was he a man or a myth or a combination of the two? Did Wellington or did Blucher actually defeat Napoleon on the field of Waterloo, or did they both defeat him, and if so did one play a more important part than the other, and to what extent? *Are* there definite 'trends' or 'tendencies' in history, in the light of which particular groups of social, political, economic and cultural 'facts' can be interpreted and explained? Is there such a thing as history, anyway? Is history a science? Or Politics? Or Economics?

But it is time we got back to me sitting at my desk at Padmaloka. The purpose of the excursion into autobiography and biography, into world events and history, was simply to emphasise the multi-dimensional richness and diversity of human experience, both individual and collective, and to underline the selective, segmental character of the narrative given in the previous Letters. In this Letter I hope to present a few more of the many different facets of the crystal, — the jewel, — of my life as, sparkling and iridescent, it goes rolling on. As my recent travels have been only between London and Norfolk, this account of the events of the last six months will not be following a single narrative line — not even a chronologically 'scrambled' one. But let me start at the beginning, from where I am now, sitting at my desk at Padmaloka looking out of the window.

The front lawn is almost as green as it was six months ago, when I last described it, but there are no roses blooming in the flower-beds, the soil of which is entirely covered by a layer of brown leaves. Through the window behind me to the left the low, mid-afternoon sun shines in diagonally through the room onto my desk, casting the shadow of my hand across the paper as I write, at the same time that, outside, the radiance of the same mild sun throws vague shadows across the grass. Ethereally blue sky looks down from in between fleecy white cloud on the naked, sunlit branches of the trees on the far side of the lawn — branches on which the buds have already started to appear. It has been a mild Winter, the mildest for more than twenty years, we are told, and Spring seems to be already on the way. It is three weeks and more since the first snowdrops appeared, and now they can be seen in little clusters all over the grounds, the white blossoms looking like drops of milk rather than of snow in the sunshine. Soon after the snowdrops came the aconites, like little yellow buttons, and then the purple crocuses, the biggest concentration of which, mixed with some of the yellow aconites, is underneath the spreading branches of the giant copper beech just inside the front gate. Looking out of the kitchen window today I saw a kind of miniature iris. The frail, spiky, intensely blue blossoms were perched, only a few inches above the ground, in the midst of tiny bunches of what seemed like the slender stalks of young onion plants. Clumps of daffodils have been coming up all over the grounds. So far there are plenty of slim green leaves, and, during the last few days, plenty of well-swollen buds, but so far no blooms. March is their month, and this year the brilliant yellow trumpets should be here early, no doubt 'fluttering and dancing in the breeze' in approved Wordsworthian fashion.

Since the Winter has been so mild, the birds have not needed much in the way of crumbs, nor have there been so many of them about, or very many different species. Apart from the usual blackbirds, thrushes, starlings, and sparrows, all of which are very numerous, there have been a few blue tits and robins, — the latter fiercely territorial, — as well as a plump, handsome bullfinch or two busily feeding on the flower-buds of the fruit-trees. Seagulls, moving in from the coast, have circled overhead at times, and at night there has been the long, wavering hoot of the owls, which are also very numerous, though usually unseen. (Soon after moving into Padmaloka we found one in the library one morning, sitting on the mantelpiece. He had fallen down the chimney in the night, and had been unable to get out. When we opened the french windows he flew out with a sweep of wings that was strangely noiseless for so large a bird.) Wood-pigeons and the much smaller stock-doves have come waddling across the lawn in quest of food and, in more leisurely and more stately fashion, the magnificent cock pheasant, sometimes attended by his drab little mate. During the open season these unfortunate birds are slaughtered wholesale by so-called sportsmen, and I like to think that some of them, at least, could find a refuge at Padmaloka. Whenever I saw them peacefully feeding, or heard the sound of a gun in the distance, I would involuntarily repeat to myself Pope's pathetic lines:

*See, from the brake the whirring pheasant springs,*
*And mounts exulting on triumphant wings:*
*Short is his joy; he feels the fiery wound,*
*Flutters in blood, and panting beats the ground.*
*Ah! What avails his glossy, varying dyes,*
*His purple crest, and scarlet-circled eyes,*
*The vivid green his shining plumes unfold,*
*His painted wings, and breast that flames with gold?*

Spring being on its way, as it would seem, it is not surprising that some of the birds should already have started pairing in the bushes. All through the Winter, in fact, there has been a certain amount of half-serious nest-building going on. Not only birds but animals too have been affected by the change. Padmaloka's prize black tomcat Tiger, so sleek and well-groomed all Winter, now returns from his nocturnal expeditions badly scratched and with lumps of fur hanging loose. Looking at poor Tiger, I recall the great description of Spring, and its influence 'on Vegetables, on brute Animals, and last on Man' by another 18th-century poet, James Thomson — particularly his description of the effect of Spring on the bull:

*Through all his lusty veins*
*The bull, deep-scorch'd, the raging passion feels.*
*Of pasture sick, and negligent of food,*
*Scarce seen, he wades among the yellow broom,*
*While o'er his ample sides the rambling sprays*
*Luxuriant shoot; or through the mazy wood*
*Dejected wanders, nor th'enticing bud*
*Crops, though it presses on his careless sense.*
*And oft, in jealous madd'ning fancy wrapt,*
*He seeks the fight; and, idly-butting, feigns*
*His rival gor'd in every knotty trunk.*

There is also a description of the effect of Spring on the horse, almost as fine, but perhaps it is time I started taking notice of the human beings at Padmaloka, who despite the fact that Winter is seemingly on the way out and Spring on the way in are still devoting themselves, for the most part, to the production of candles in order to raise funds for the proposed new centre and Vihara in Poona.

At present the community consists of ten members, not all of whom are always here. There are seven Order Members and three Mitras. Kovida is Secretary and Treasurer of the Padmaloka Co-operative (comprising Padmaloka Candles and Padmaloka Joinery), as well as being Treasurer of the FWBO Surlingham. In addition to all his desk work (assisted on the accountancy side by an electronic calculator of the very latest type), he helps out in the candle workshop. In his spare time he writes Shakespearean sonnets. Of all the members of the community Kovida has the largest number of local friends and acquaintances, all the pubs, cafés, bars, restaurants, discos and bookshops within a fifteen mile radius of Padmaloka being well known to him.

Kulananda works with the Padmaloka Co-operative, being busy creating new lines, obtaining large orders, and building up a nation-wide network of agents, besides which he does secretarial work for me, maintains the Order archives and files etc. Occasionally he finds time to read, his current favourite being Thackeray.

Sona is Chairman and Secretary of the FWBO Surlingham, which is technically responsible for looking after the Order finances (the Order as such has no legal existence), as well as being Order Convenor. As Order Convenor he is responsible for organising the Order Convention, and from time to time he functions as my medium of communication with the Order 'collectively', as when he makes announcements on my behalf at the monthly Order Days. At the moment Sona is away in Stockholm, Sweden, where, with the assistance of Kulamitra, he is spending a month leading a series of retreats and courses. Even when he is here the community does not see very much of him, as he usually has to go out to work three or four days a week in order to support himself and his family. Nonetheless, he manages to exercise a strong, unifying influence on the community. Not surprisingly, he hasn't much time for other interests, though he likes reading, and listening to music (mainly Classical and Baroque), usually having to listen to it while doing other things, such as sorting out the Order accounts and writing letters to people who have not paid their annual subscription. He is also an experienced Yoga teacher, though at present he is not, I think, doing any regular teaching.

Dhammapala spends most of his time in the candle factory. His real love, however, is gardening, to which he hopes to be able to get back before long, particularly as the Padmaloka flower garden is quite badly in need of attention. Apart from myself, he is the seniormost Order Member living at Padmaloka, and now leads the (optional) study group for community members.

Abhaya has the distinction of being the oldest of the seven Upasakas living here. When not producing doors and window boxes in the joinery workshop he is usually in his room turning out articles and book reviews for Nagabodhi. Formerly a teacher of English by profession, he helps members of the community with their grammar, spelling, and punctuation. As Convenor of (men) Mitras for the Norwich

Chapter of the Order, he visits Mitras in their homes, and leads a weekly study group at Vajradhatu. Once a week he also crosses the river to Brundall, a much bigger and more fashionable village than Surlingham, where he takes a Yoga class and spends some time with his wife and children, whom he continues to support. I have known Abhaya (and his wife) longer than I have known any other member of the Padmaloka community. They attended the second FWBO retreat at Quartermain in the late Summer of 1967, and though it was some years before he was ordained we have never been out of touch for long.

Virabhadra joined the community only two or three weeks ago and will be staying at Padmaloka for altogether six months. He works in a local hospital, where he is completing his final year before becoming a fully qualified doctor. Though sometimes we do not see him for two or three days together (he is often on night duty), he is very much a member of the community, and sometimes relates his hospital experiences to us at meal times. At breakfast a few mornings ago he told us how a young man had been brought in in an alcoholic coma. He was only sixteen years old. It seemed terrible that someone as young as that should be on his way, apparently, to become an alcoholic. Why is it that a growing number of young people in Great Britain feel that they have nothing better to do than to get drunk? The FWBO, I felt, should be making a much stronger effort to establish contact with such people, instead of waiting for them to come to the centres, which they probably would not do anyway, even if they did happen to hear about us.

Coming from Order Members to Mitras, Andy Friends is the housekeeper and general handyman, in addition to which he works regularly in the candle factory and looks after the vegetable garden, which he has organised very systematically. He also allocates community members their household duties and supervises the retreat work periods. One of the more athletic members of the community, he goes for a daily run and often walks into Norwich and back, scorning both public and private transport. Clive Pomfret works in the candle workshop, reads, and does karate. Colin Millar, who joined the community only a couple of weeks ago, at present works in the candle factory, but as soon as he can be spared will probably transfer to the joinery workshop. In his spare time he writes Shakespearean sonnets, though not nearly so many as Kovida.

In addition to regular members of the community we often have people staying with us for a few days, or a few weeks, at a time. Some come simply for a change and rest, others to see me. Already this year we have had Olle Mallander from Helsinki (the ten days immediately following the Winter Retreat, which he attended), Chintamani from London (one week), Brian, Derek and Kenny from Glasgow (the two days before the men's Order/Mitra Event, during which time they helped prepare the food), Tony Bowall from Croydon (the two days following the Event), Guhyananda from London (the three days following the Event), Kularatna from Manchester, who arrived a few days ago and who will be leaving us next week.

In the past some of the people who have stayed for a few days or a few weeks at Padmaloka have had quite a difficult time. One Mitra afterwards told me that his stay here had been the most difficult and painful period in his whole life. The reason for the difficulty is that all the community members are fully occupied with their own work, — with their own life and interests, — both individually and 'collectively', and have no time, and perhaps not the inclination, to spend several hours each day satisfying the neurotic demands for personal attention which have sometimes been made on them — in one or two cases to an extreme degree. Perhaps it would not be an exaggeration to say that there are, or have been, people who cannot bear the emotional positivity of Padmaloka, and who find its tendency to leave community members and visitors alike very much to their own devices threatening rather than liberating. Padmaloka is, in fact, a loosely knit, rather than a tightly knit, community — occasionally, perhaps, going to the extreme in that respect. (It is, of course, a men's community, allowing women visitors to come during the day but not to stay overnight.) Despite being so loosely knit, — perhaps even because of it, — Padmaloka is, in fact, a very friendly community, where people both work and play together, and where the atmosphere is one of ever-increasing emotional positivity. At the risk of giving them all swollen heads, I might even go so far as to say that if there was a little more mindfulness in such matters as closing doors (i.e. not allowing them to slam), and a little more regularity in puja and meditation, Padmaloka might be well on its way to becoming if not a perfect, at least practically a model, community.

In addition to those who actually stay with us, whether for a longer or a shorter period, there are the part-time workers who come out from the Norwich FWBO each day to help in the candle factory, and who take their meals with us, and what the members of the community refer to as 'Bhante's visitors'. Most of these latter are Mitras, and the Mitras mostly women, and I usually see them after lunch. Sometimes such interviews are satisfactory, sometimes not. Generally speaking, the better I already know the person, the better the interview goes, i.e. the more free and open communication is, though there are exceptions. A few people are able to communicate well the very first time we meet. Only too often, however, they are tongue-tied, confused, and anxious, and the meeting peters out in small talk or collapses in an embarrassed silence. Some people do not even know why they asked to see me. As a result of experiences of this kind I have become dissatisfied with the formal interview as an instrument of communication — even though it does, admittedly, have the advantage of bringing people sharply up against emotional blockages they had not realised were there. For me personally a formal interview can be as boring as it is, apparently, terrifying for some of my visitors. (A friend who subsequently became an Order Member refused to believe that I could be bored; but I can be. I can be bored by other people. Left to my own devices, I am never bored.) Most people seem to find it easier to communicate in the context of a more 'extended' situation, where they can get to know me, and where they can allow me to get to know them, without their being the exclusive object of my attention. For this reason I was glad to be able to get to know some of the newer women Mitras and Friends within the more relaxed framework of a seven-day Study Retreat at Padmaloka. — But more about this later on.

Part-time workers and 'Bhante's visitors' are supplemented by community guests, these being Norwich-based Order Members, Mitras and Friends whom one or another of us has invited out for a meal, usually in the evening. There are also visits from the FWBO Chairmen, including occasions when, as happened the week before last, they all get together with me, and with one another, for two days of informal consultation and discussion. With these gatherings we begin to approach the more 'organised', or at least the more public, aspect of my life and experience, that is to say, the aspect that involves a number of other people, — which I share with a number of other people, — and that tends to get reported in the FWBO *Newsletter*.

At this point, therefore, I think I had better give a brief chronological survey of my movements, and my main activities, during the whole period about which I am now writing, i.e. from the middle of August 1979 to the end of February 1980. This will not only bring this period into sharper focus for you, so far as *one* facet of the jewel is concerned, but also serve to refresh my own memory with regard to the actual sequence of events. Having done this, I shall deal with certain *other* facets of the jewel, facets of which no report ever appears in the *Newsletter*, and to which no direct reference was made in previous Letters. Before giving my chronological survey, however, I want to say a few more words about Padmaloka.

I have described, in brief, what each of the ten members of the community does, but I have not said what *I* do, or what my relation with the community is. Most of the day I spend at my desk writing, every now and then looking out of the window at the soothing green of the lawn, at the great trees beyond, and at the sky. Mornings are devoted to more 'creative' writing, whether article, book review, or one of these Letters, afternoons to correspondence (and interviews), as well as to 'organisational' matters connected with the Movement, while evenings are devoted to editing, — which usually means completely re-writing, — the transcripts of the lecture and seminar tapes. At 11 o'clock in the morning comes a cup of coffee; at 4 o'clock in the afternoon a cup of tea. In between, at 1 o'clock, comes lunch. (Members of the community take it in turns to cook, each person averaging three days kitchen duty every month. They are all good cooks, and generally take pride in producing palatable meals.)

Sometimes, if the weather is particularly fine, or if I am stiff from sitting at my desk for such a long time, I go for a walk round the garden, looking to see how the vegetables are getting on, or what flowers are in bloom. At one time I might linger near the small oval pond, admiring the delicate red of the water lilies, and trying to see how many more buds were making their way up from the murky depths to the surface; at another, I might take a stroll as far as the paddock, and stroke the noses of the horses as they came trying to nuzzle me over the fence. I might even venture into the candle factory, and watch Clive or Kovida rotating the great iron wheel and plunging batch after batch of red or yellow or blue taper candles into their bath of liquid coloured wax. Not that my day invariably follows the pattern I have described, though generally speaking I prefer to follow a regular routine, as this enables me to get more work done. Occasionally I spend the whole day reading, especially if I happen to light on a book of exceptional interest (such as Isaac Deutscher's *The Prophet Armed: Trotsky 1879-1921*, which Varjabodhi sent me recently), or if I have a book for review. When inspiration flags, I listen to a little music, usually an early Mozart symphony — or else sit in my armchair doing absolutely nothing for a while. (Doing nothing is itself a creative activity. Most people are incapable of doing nothing. They just sit and worry, their brains furiously ticking over while their bodies remain inactive.) Even more occasionally, I go out for a drive in the surrounding countryside with one of the lads, sometimes going as far as the coast, where one can walk along the pebbly or the sandy beach looking at the cold grey old North Sea that Heine loved to sing, and where one can sometimes see the bewhiskered face of a seal curiously regarding one from the surf.

From the way in which I spend my day it will be evident that I do not have much contact with the members of the Padmaloka community as such. They do their work, and I do mine. Indeed, though I live at Padmaloka, I do not consider myself, nor am I considered, a member of the community in the strict sense. Pujas and meditations, house meetings, study groups, meetings of the FWBO Surlingham Council, and meetings of the Padmaloka Co-operative, all carry on without me, though I am kept informed of everything that happens, and am consulted about anything of special importance — just as I am by other communities and centres.

The main reason why I do not consider myself a member of the Padmaloka community is that I am concerned with the well-being of the *whole* Movement, and therefore cannot identify myself with any individual community — not even the one with which I happen to be living. Letters arrive on my desk from all over the world. Batches of minutes come regularly from all the centres in Great Britain, New Zealand, and India, as well as from all the co-operatives. All these communications, — and I really do take them as such, — are carefully read, some of them more than once. Most of the letters call for some sort of reply. Some of the items in the minutes need to be commented on, or queried, either by means of a letter or a telephone call. Sometimes it may so happen that I am deeply concerned, perhaps for days on end, with happenings in a centre, or a community, in a distant part of the country, even a distant part of the world — happenings of which everyone in the Padmaloka community is completely unaware. Sometimes I may be envisaging the expansion of the Movement into realms that nobody has, as yet, imagined. Or I may be trying to foresee the difficulties that would be likely to arise in the future, if a certain line of action was followed, and considering how they could best be avoided. Or, on yet another occasion, I may be pondering the relations between the FWBO and certain Buddhist organisations with which we are in contact. Another reason for my not being a member of the Padmaloka community, in the strict sense, is that this might result in my overshadowing the other members of the community, or cramping their style, or, what would be worse, in their coming to rely on me to make all their decisions for them. At the same time, despite the fact that I keep separate from the community as such, with most members of the community individually I have a fair amount of contact, and of course I am always available to anyone who wants to talk to me about anything — just as I am available to anyone from outside the community. On the whole, the relation between me and the Padmaloka community is a quite satisfactory one. They help create the conditions which make it possible for me to get on with my own work. I, for my part, leave them to run their own affairs, intervening only to the extent that I intervene in the affairs of other communities — or if what they are doing impinges too much on what I am doing, as when they make too much noise, or leave me to answer the telephone.

Having concluded my impressions of Padmaloka with an account of what I do here, and what my relation with the Padmaloka community is, I must now give the promised chronological survey of my movements, and main activities, during the last six and a half months. Already earlier activities are beginning to loom indistinctly through the mist of minor incidents — and all are fast receding. The Summer Retreat, in the middle of which I returned again to Padmaloka, and on which Christer Starck was reborn as Ratnapriya, extended over practically the whole of August, and was succeeded, in September, by a ten-day and a seven-day men's Study Retreat. Both retreats were, of course, led by me. The first was a *double* study retreat, that is to say, the two dozen people who attended it were divided into two different groups, one of which I took in the morning, the other in the afternoon, the texts studied being Chogyam Trungpa's Commentary on the new, Freemantle-Trungpa translation of *The Tibetan Book of the Dead* and sections from the Evans-Wentz translation of 'The Precepts of the Gurus' in *Tibetan Yoga and Secret Doctrines*. While one group studied, the other had a work period and an extra session of meditation. (Each group had morning/afternoon study on alternate days.) First thing in the morning, and last thing at night, there was a joint puja-and-meditation session for both groups, and of course all meals were taken together. This was the first time that I had led a double study retreat, and the arrangement worked very well, even though I could not always remember in which group I had dealt with which topic. As usually happens, both this retreat and the one that followed a few days later, on which we studied more sections from 'The Precepts of the Gurus', have now merged with all the other study retreats I have led in the course of the last six years and I no longer have a distinct recollection of what particular points I made in the course of discussion. Some of the more important, or relevant, points arising in connection with our study of Trungpa's Commentary on *The Tibetan Book of the Dead* have been extracted by Subhuti and incorporated, in his own words, in his article *The Endless Round: The Six Realms* in *Mitrata 25*. Despite the absence of distinct recollections, from both retreats I retain a vivid impression of the many-faceted richness of human experience and spiritual life.

On September 27th I travelled from Padmaloka down to London via Rayleigh, where I spent the afternoon with my mother. This was my second or third visit since my return from New Zealand in June. Formerly I used to see her only once a year, on or around her birthday, but in recent years, owing to her advanced age (she is eighty-two), I have tried to see her more often. On this occasion I found her better than she had been on my previous visit, when she was still recovering from a painful swelling in the legs. As usual, she was glad to see me, and very cheerful.

In London I had only a few days in which to prepare the first of my eight lectures on 'The Inconceivable Emancipation: Themes from the *Vimalakirti-nirdesa,* a Mahayana Buddhist Scripture.' I had long admired this great work, which brings together, as though into a magnificent tiara, some of the brightest jewels of the Mahayana form of Buddhism, and had been thinking of lecturing on it for some years. Only towards the end of my stay in New Zealand did I finally make up my mind to do so. For a while I was undecided whether my first London lecture series for three years should be on themes from the *Vimalakirti-nirdesa* or on incidents from the life of the Buddha, and in the intervals of preparing my three lectures on 'A New Buddhist Movement: The Meaning of FWBO' I drew up a synopsis for both series. Order Members in London whom I consulted, however, on the whole favoured the *Vimalakirti-nirdesa,* and as this accorded with what had come to be my own feelings on the subject it was on the *Vimalakirti-nirdesa* that I eventually decided to speak.

The Movement in London having been so long preoccupied with the building of Sukhavati, with the setting up of co-operatives, and with the starting of classes at the London Buddhist Centre, it needed, I felt, to be lifted, at least for a few hours, to a totally different plane, a plane on which transcendental truth was conveyed by means of marvellous phantasmagoria, a plane of Buddhas, Bodhisattvas and Arahants, a plane on which Manjushri spoke with Vimalakirti, and on which the thunderlike silence reduced all discursive mental activity to nothing, and on which the 'Inconceivable' reigned supreme.

On this plane I had to remain for more than two months, while I prepared my lectures, descending from it only for interviews and in order to take part in the weekend

Order/Mitra Event at Padmaloka, which came between the third and fourth lectures, and in the Sangha Day celebrations, which came between the fourth and fifth lectures. Apart from the actual travelling up to Norfolk and back, the taking part in the Event involved not so much a descent from a higher plane as a translation from one dimension to another — from the world of Vimalakirti to the world of Padmasambhava. This was so far as my own study group, at least, was concerned, our text for study being Canto 103 of *The Life and Liberation of Padmasambhava* on 'The Advice Given to Three Fortunate Women Before the Departure', i.e. the departure of Padmasambhava for the Land of the Rakshasas, when he mounted the marvellous winged horse and, enveloped in rainbow-hued light, departed into the open heavens.

The Sangha Day celebrations unfortunately did amount to a descent, at least in the case of the poetry reading that was given in the evening at the East-West Centre, where my lectures were also being held. Some of the poems were well read, and some of the musical items were well performed, but the programme was badly produced and not very suited to the occasion. That part of the day's proceedings was really intended as an opportunity for Order Members and Mitras to bring along relatives and friends who had had little or no contact with the Movement. What was needed, therefore, was something more relaxed and 'social', which would encourage people to mingle and talk rather than sit back and be 'entertained'. Some of the poems read, moreover, were not in accordance with the ideals of the Movement. In organising such events, I reflected, we should always: (1) Have a clear idea of the sort of people we are trying to reach; (2) Adopt the best possible means of reaching them; (3) Make sure that the whole event reflects the spirit of the Movement, whether directly or indirectly; and (4) Organise the event, including ourselves, with the maximum care and efficiency.

Little as the poetry reading, at least, was suited to the Sangha Day celebrations, 'Themes from the *Vimalakirti-nirdesa*' proved to be very much in accordance with the current spiritual needs of the Movement in London and beyond. The lectures were well attended, — better attended, in fact, than any previous series had been, — and numbers kept up right to the very end. In view of the mind-baffling, even 'mind-blowing', nature of the *Vimalakirti-nirdesa*, this was rather surprising. At the first Order Day after the conclusion of the series, during the reporting in, I therefore asked those Order Members who were present to tell me why, in their opinion, the lectures had been so well received, and later on in the morning there was a discussion. (A report of this discussion appears in the January, 1980, issue of *Shabda*, pp. 16-19.) For my part, I found the lectures easy to prepare, and enjoyable to give. Indeed, I felt very much 'at home' in the world of the *Vimalakirti-nirdesa*, and came down from it with considerable reluctance. Apart from the Order/Mitra Event, and the Sangha Day celebrations, however, I came down from it only for interviews, which included meetings with Alan Ginsberg and Christmas Humphreys and a visit from my mother, sister, and niece. About each of *these* facets of the 'jewel' I shall have something to say later on.

The lectures ended on November 29th [1979], when the audience expressed its appreciation for the series with a magnificent bouquet — presented by Ratnaketu, presumably in his capacity as youngest Order Member — and three rousing 'Sadhus!' It was not until December 7th, however, that I was able to leave London for Padmaloka. The interval was filled with interviews and meetings of various kinds, as well as with dinner engagements with the little communities that have sprung up in the neighbourhood of Sukhavati. Indeed, as the day of my departure drew near, and people woke up to the fact that I was actually about to leave, requests for interviews and invitations to meals came pouring in. Kuladeva and Harvey (as he then was) were constantly running between the office and my flat with telephone messages. My last engagement was at Beulah, the women's community, where an excellent meal, tastefully served, was followed by a lively discussion.

The next day I returned to Padmaloka via Rayleigh. Though it was now early Winter rather than late Autumn, the trees still wore most of their leaves, and many of them had only just started turning yellow. Perhaps we could expect a mild Winter! At Padmaloka I did not do much for a few days, even a few weeks. The truth was that, after all my travels, and the seminars, lectures and meetings by which they had been followed, — not to mention the constant interviews and correspondence, — I was really quite tired, even though I did not always consciously feel it. I therefore decided to 'relax' for a while, not follow any particular routine, and do whatever I felt like doing.

This was made all the easier by the fact that the four-week men's Winter Retreat, led by Padmaraja, was now in progress. The Padmaloka community was, of course, still in residence, having shifted down to the small kitchen-cum-dining-room for meals, so as to leave the big kitchen, dining-room and lounge free for the retreat. As on previous occasions, the effect of the retreat was soon felt by the community and, in fact, throughout the house. It was as though the building was pervaded by a different atmosphere, or rather, by the same atmosphere as usual, only greatly intensified. I have often noticed, during retreats at Padmaloka (i.e. during 'general' retreats, in which I was not taking part), that I knew what the state of the retreat was, and how the various participants were getting on, even without having any physical contact with anybody — not even to the extent of seeing them from a distance. On this occasion the atmosphere of the retreat, — the atmosphere that pervaded the building, — was particularly strong, calm, and deep, and there was (I think) rather more silence observed than usual, particularly towards the end of the retreat.

Unfortunately, — from one point of view, though not from another, — only a week after my return to Padmaloka I 'had to' go down to London in order to attend the farewell supper that was being given in honour of Subhuti on the eve of his departure for the isles of Greece.

*The isles of Greece, the isles of Greece!*
*Where burning Sappho loved and sung,*
*Where grew the arts of war and peace,*
*Where Delos rose, and Phoebus sprung!*
*Eternal summer gilds them yet,*
*But all, except their sun, is set.*

'Having' to go down to London was unfortunate in that it meant an interruption of my enjoyment of the peace and silence of Padmaloka, but fortunate in that it meant that I could express my personal appreciation of everything that Subhuti had done for Sukhavati by being present at the farewell supper. Invitations had been sent out on the basis of the recipient's having 'lived and worked' with Subhuti at Sukhavati in the course of the previous four years. This meant the supper was, in effect, a 'men only' affair, since although several women had worked with Subhuti none of them had *lived* and worked with him. All the same, two or three of the women concerned had been approached, and asked if they would like to come, even though it would mean their being very much in the minority, but they had sensibly declined the offer. Subhuti himself knew nothing about the farewell supper until the last minute, or rather until fifteen minutes afterwards, when Nagabodhi found him wandering about the kitchen at Sukhavati wondering where everybody had gone, and steered him in the direction of the Annexe, where the farewell was being held.

When the time came forty-odd people sat down to supper at the long trestle tables, that had been arranged so as to form the three sides of a square. It must have been quite a reflection for Subhuti, to think that he had 'lived and worked' with all those people!

Even so, there were many more who were unavoidably absent. Phil Miller and Robert Gerke were in America, Lokamitra, Padmavajra, Purna, and Vajradaka in India, and Priyananda and Achala in New Zealand. What a lot of people had helped to bring Sukhavati into existence — not only those who had lived and worked together as a community in the actual building but everybody who had in any way contributed to the success of the project! Several of those present were so smartly turned out as to be hardly recognisable. One Mitra was resplendent in a black velvet suit, with frilled white shirt, while Nagabodhi, who presided over the occasion from the centre of the top table, wore a suit and an *enormous* bow tie — not to speak of a grin that positively stretched from ear to ear. Food was plentiful in quantity and superlative in quality. Towards the end of the meal the punch circulated, Devamitra rejoiced in Subhuti's merits in his most inspired fashion, Kovida (who had taken off his jacket and pullover) proposed the toast, and Ratnaketu came forward and made the presentation of a dictionary — to help Subhuti in his literary labours — and an envelope containing a sum of money. Subhuti was suitably overcome with emotion but managed to say a few words of thanks in reply. By this time quite a lot of people were being overcome with emotion in one way or another and a distinctly convivial — and very relaxed — atmosphere prevailed. Senior Order Members leaned back in their seats puffing cigars like privileged Sixth Formers.

But there was more to come. Chairs having been pushed back, and a cine-projector placed in position, Siddhiratna showed a film that he had put together from bits and pieces of footage taken at different times. It was, of course, a film of Sukhavati. Some of the sequences were quite hilarious and everybody in the room exploded with good-natured mirth. There was Subhuti himself (looking *ten* years younger, ferreting for bargains round the Sunday morning street market in Brick Lane, Ananda and Ashvajit between them carrying a door, and shadowy figures unloading things from off the backs of lorries, besides much else that for richness of (unintentional) comic effect was reminiscent of the Marx Brothers. Many of the sequences were of Sukhavati in the *very* early days of its development, and despite the derelict interiors with which Nagabodhi has regaled us, in the *Newsletter*, until quite recently, to me, for one, the truly appalling state of the building before we took it on came as quite a shock. The fact that it *could* come as a shock, even though I had myself been over the building with Subhuti before we took it on, showed the extent of the transformation that had since taken place — a transformation that would have been impossible without Subhuti's determined efforts. It seemed all the more appropriate, therefore, that on the eve of his departure for the isles of Greece we should show Subhuti our heartfelt appreciation for all that he had done. The 'official' farewell, at least, broke up at about 10 o'clock. As I left, I had a glimpse of a group of younger Order Members carrying off a flushed and perspiring Subhuti for further celebrations elsewhere.

## II

Though Sona, Kovida and I had come down from Padmaloka together for the farewell supper, the following day Kovida and I made the return journey by ourselves, since Sona had to go to Cambridge, where he was still working as a consultant heating engineer. On the way into London the three of us had spent a couple of hours at Kenwood House, where we had had lunch in the rather crowded new restaurant, taken a look at the pictures, among which there was a Vermeer and a Rembrandt self-portrait, and seen Dr. Johnson's summer-house. It had been Sona's first visit to Kenwood, though I myself had been to the place a number of times, especially when I was living at Highgate and at Muswell Hill.

Now, on our way back to Norfolk, Kovida and I decided to make a similar detour and stop off at Colchester, the second largest town in Essex and one of the oldest towns in Britain, with a history that goes back to Roman times. According to my guide book, fine streets of 17th-century and 18th-century houses had been progressively sacked by 'developers' (the single inverted commas are my own) and if one wanted to see Colchester before the whole town became a multi-storey car park one should go soon. Kovida and I felt that we had arrived in the nick of time. From the upstairs window of the shabby restaurant where we had lunch we could see cars, vans and lorries crawling nose-to-tail through narrow, boutique-lined streets that were hardly designed for horse-drawn carriages, the fumes from their exhausts rising in clouds. Despite modest 'finds' in the second-hand bookshops we were not sorry when, three hours after our arrival, we drove out of the ravaged, congested little town — half the size of Norwich, and twice as crowded — and back onto the A12. On our arrival at Padmaloka we found the retreat plunged into the same deep silence in which we had left it and it was not difficult for me to get back into the more relaxed routine that I had been following before we left.

One of the first things on which I had started working the previous week was the re-organisation, or rather the re-arrangement, of the Order Library. Since its removal from Aryatara, where it had been kept ever since my departure from London in 1973, this had been accommodated in the room below my study. During the two months that I had been giving my *Vimalakiti-nirdesa* lectures in London however, the room above the shrine had been converted into a special library room. (Hall, small kitchen and lounge had been redecorated at the same time.) Only the day before my return to Padmaloka Abhaya and Kulananda had put the finishing touches to the red and gold bookcases that had been built against two of the walls, and a couple of days later, the paint being dry, I had started to transfer the books to their new home, re-arranging them in the process. To this congenial task I now returned. It was a task which not only kept me pleasantly occupied, but also gave me some welcome exercise, as I had to walk up the stairs several dozen times a day with my arms full of books. Excluding paperbacks, the Order Library now contains some 2,000 volumes, about 1,050 of which are on Buddhism. Unfortunately, several irreplaceable books which were certainly part of the collection in 1973 now seem to be missing, and as soon as I can I shall have to make a final check and, if necessary, circulate a list of the missing items.

Besides re-organising the Library, I sorted out the contents of some of my personal files, and wrote letters. A number of these letters were addressed to New Zealand. This was not only because I wanted to keep up my contact with Order Members, Mitras and Friends in 'The Land of the Long White Cloud', many of whom are excellent correspondents, but because there were confusions to be cleared up in connection with an attempt by a 'Korean Zen' monk of New Zealand origin to form 'Another Buddhist Centre for Auckland' — an attempt that, in the event, did not come to anything. I was concerned about the matter inasmuch as the monk was supposed to have taken this step 'solely in response to people who [spoke] to him from among the Friends.' At any rate, in the course of his opening remarks at the preliminary meeting this monk claimed that 'many people' had said they were 'dissatisfied with certain elements in the FWBO whereby a Buddhist School ... was fast becoming anti-Christian, anti-family.' The 'certain elements' were apparently Purna and Udaya. However, in view of some of the remarks I had made in my recent lectures in Auckland, under the title 'A New Buddhist Movement: The Meaning of FWBO' (not to mention what I had written in *Buddhism and Blasphemy*!), it was clear that the monk was really attacking me, but did not dare to do so openly: Purna and Udaya were only the scapegoats. Fortunately, Vajradaka arrived on the scene at about this time, and it was soon obvious that whatever dissatisfaction a *few* Mitras and Friends *might* have felt with certain aspects of the FWBO represented no more than a temporary personal difficulty that genuine communication was able to resolve. Reflecting on the situation afterwards, I was more than ever confirmed in my conviction that (1) The less the FWBO is involved with 'Buddhist groups' and with individuals affiliated to existing Buddhist traditions the better (the Korean Zen monk had been allowed to stay at Suvarnaketu for several months, which had given him the opportunity of coming into contact with some of our Mitras and Friends), and that (2) The more uncompromisingly we maintain the principles for which we stand the more successful the FWBO will be, both materially and spiritually.

Though I had to spend quite a lot of time writing letters to New Zealand, as well as thinking about the situation that had arisen there, I was not really in the mood to deal with anything of a more 'organisational' nature. Whether because of the more relaxed routine that I was still following, or on account of the peace and silence with which the retreat was increasingly pervading the house, I felt my more 'creative' energies beginning to rise to the surface, displacing — to some extent — the 'executive' energies. Indeed, as the retreat, and the year 1979, started coming to an end, and as the Christmas season stole upon us, I found myself in a more strongly, and more exclusively, 'poetic' mood than I had known for quite a number of years.

It is difficult to describe this mood, which lasted for several weeks. First of all came a period of 'silence', both internal and external, during which there were no objective demands made upon me and no 'needs' to meet. This meant that I could allow the responses that usually arise in connection with such demands and needs to die down, so that whatever mental processes then went on were, on the whole, self-originating. Next, out of the silence, which was also a kind of creative rest, there arose a certain rhythm, or a poem without words — a poem that went on and on, without interruption. This rhythm, or wordless poem, seemed to blend with whatever I saw, or rather, with whatever it was to which I directed my attention, or on which I allowed my mind to dwell. It could blend with it because, whether it was a natural object like a tree, a realm of existence, or a figure from ancient Egyptian mythology, its rhythm was the same as the rhythm that had arisen out of my own silence, my own creative rest. As they blended, the two rhythms gave birth to words, words which were descriptive of the particular object on which I had allowed my mind to dwell and which formed, in some cases, complete poems, in others, only fragments of poems — perhaps a line or a couplet. At one stage it was as though the rhythm that arose within me was the same as, or at least in accordance with, the rhythm that arose within the depths of external nature and found expression in trees, flowers, houses, and human beings — in the whole objective order of existence. Whatever I allowed my mind to rest on became a poem, just as whatever Midas touched turned to gold. The whole world was material for poetry. In fact, the whole world was a poem. It was a poem, to the extent that the 'observer' was a poet.

I recollected that, when I was in my 'teens, I used to remain in this kind of 'poetic' state for months on end: it was my normal state. In that state, it was far easier for me to write poetry than not write it, and I wrote hundreds of poems. (The *nature* of the process, of course, tells us nothing about the *value* of the end result, i.e. the poem, considered from a purely 'artistic' point of view.) On this occasion, even, I managed to produce a couple of dozen poems, more than I had written in the previous half dozen years, though not all of them were as easy to produce as the account I have given might suggest. At any rate, a handful of poems I *did* produce, among them six sonnets on the six realms of sentient existence — one sonnet for each realm. Reflecting on the whole episode afterwards, I came to the conclusion that the 'poetic' state of mind is, as I had sometimes felt before, a state in which the subject assimilates the object in such a way that the duality between them is to some extent mitigated and that this mitigated duality finds expression in the 'poem', or work of art generally, which is both subject and object, or in which the subject-object duality finds expression on a higher, more refined level. Poetry is thus the mediator between the 'real' and the 'Ideal', the mundane and the Transcendental: it is the angel; it is the deva; it is the archetype.

By the time the New Year came all my poems had been written except one, the exception being the sixth and last sonnet in the series on the realms of existence, the one on 'The Realm of Men', which was written three days later. On Christmas Day I wrote a sonnet in which I tried to bring together in a single poem my experience of the snow-peaks of the Eastern Himalayas and my experience of the flat landscape of Norfolk and a sonnet on, appropriately enough, Holman Hunt's famous painting 'The Scapegoat', a reproduction of one version of which hangs in my study at Sukhavati, as well as a few odds and ends of verses.

In between writing poems I participated, with Kovida, Abhaya, Dharmapala and Andy (the rest of the community having gone away for the holiday period), and with Vajrakumara and Adrian Macro, — both of whom came out from Norwich for the occasion, — in our limited Padmaloka Christmas festivities. People sometimes ask to what extent we should take part in non-Buddhist religious festivals. In India the question arises in connection with Divali, and in England, New Zealand and Finland in connection with Christmas. Strictly speaking, we should not celebrate Divali or Christmas at all. That is, we should not celebrate them *as* Divali and Christmas, i.e. as religious festivals. In the case of Divali, it is hardly possible for a Buddhist to celebrate the return of a hero who had been victorious in battle and who, in any case, had once decapitated a low-caste man for daring to perform religious austerities — even if that hero *was*, allegedly, an avatara of the god Vishnu. In the case of Christmas, it is hardly possible for a Buddhist to rejoice at the advent of a 'saviour' in whose historical existence he finds it difficult to believe and who cannot, in fact, save him from his sins — even if the followers of that saviour had *not* time and again committed the most terrible atrocities in his name.

Participation in the purely social side of such non-Buddhist religious festivals is another matter. Such participation helps one to remain on friendly terms with non-Buddhist neighbours, colleagues, relations, acquaintances, clients, customers etc., and ensures that less energy is spent simply going 'against the flow'. (Even such social participation should not, of course, entail any violation of Buddhist ethical principles.) So far as the social side of Christmas is concerned, indeed, there is no reason why the (Western) Buddhist should not observe, as it were for their own ethnic sake, customs of pre-Christian, pagan origin that have, in fact, nothing to do with Christianity, and which became associated with Christmas only at a later date, i.e. after the introduction of Christianity into Europe.

Thus it was that, at 3 o'clock on Christmas Day, we could sit down to a rather more elaborate meal than usual that included 'Christmas' (really pagan) pudding, complete with sprig of (pagan) holly, with a clear conscience. We certainly did not go to midnight mass like those British Buddhists who, in their anxiety to demonstrate their 'broad-mindedness', only succeed in showing that they have not Gone for Refuge and do not know what Going for Refuge really means. As for the thirty or more people who were by this time on retreat at Padmaloka, they did not, I think, participate in the Christmas festivities even to the extent that the community and its guests did. Probably they did not notice that it was Christmas Day. Outside our gates, in the little village of Surlingham, life appeared to go on — or rather, not go on — just as usual. The only difference was that, with fewer vehicles on the roads over the holiday period, and no trains rattling along the line on the other side of the river, everything was much quieter.

On Saturday January 5th [1980], two days after I had written my last poem, came the public ordinations and, therewith, the end of the retreat. All nine Mitras being ordained had, of course, been on retreat for at least a week. Since there were so many people Going for Refuge at one time I decided to distribute the private ordinations over a period of three days. On each of the three evenings immediately preceding the day of the public ordinations, therefore, three people received their private ordinations. This meant that on these evenings there was a long period of silence, a long session before of the Metta-Bhavana practice, and a slightly more elaborate Sevenfold Puja led by me. As my custom now is, I inaugurated the Metta-Bhavana session before withdrawing to conduct the private ordinations upstairs, whither the ordinands followed me one by one in order of natural seniority, i.e. in order of biological age. What with the extra silence observed during the day, and the intensity Padmaraja brought to bear on the retreat anyway, the preparations for the public ordinations were more than usually thorough, so that when the morning of January 5th finally came it was, to an even greater degree than usual, very much the culmination of the entire four-week retreat. It was, in fact, one of those rare occasions on which joy is deepened into solemnity, and solemnity heightened into joy. While not unmindful of the distinctive individual characteristics of those being ordained, I had decided that, in giving them their names, I would emphasise three principles which, I thought, needed to be emphasised within the Movement generally, and especially within the Order. The three principles were the principle of victory, in the sense of rising triumphant over all adverse conditions, the principle of fiery, incandescent energy that consumes all obstacles, and the principle of playfulness or spontaneity. Three of the nine new Order Members therefore received names beginning with *jaya*, three of them with names beginning with *teja*, and three of them names beginning with *lalita*.

A fortnight after the men's Winter Retreat came the women's Study Retreat. In between I carried on with my literary work, attended to correspondence, and managed to catch a bad cold, cough and sore throat that persisted, altogether for about three weeks. The women's Study Retreat was the first event for women to be held at Padmaloka since Vajrakumara, Ratnapani and I set the place up as a Vihara and Retreat Centre in July 1976. However, I had not taken the women for a study retreat for nearly four years (the last one was held at Aryatara in June 1976), it was more convenient for me to hold the retreat at Padmaloka, the women had no objection to coming there, the community had no objection to moving out for a week, and so at Padmaloka the retreat was held. Abhaya withdrew to Norwich, Kovida and Kulananda went down to London, Dharmapala found refuge at Sea Palling (up on the coast), Andy crossed over to Manchester, Clive tucked himself away at White Row (the cottage near Brighton), while Jacek (who had stayed on from the Summer Retreat, and who was the only member of the community *not* to return to Padmaloka after the women had left) went to earth down in Croydon. Sona, of course, was still working in Cambridge.

Altogether twenty-two women came on the retreat, seven of them being Order Members and fifteen of them Mitras, which meant that for study purposes they had to be divided into two groups, one of which I took in the morning, the other in the afternoon. Halfway through the retreat the groups changed round, so that those who had studied in the morning now studied in the afternoon, and vice versa. (On the men's double Study Retreat, the previous Summer, the groups had changed round each day.) On the whole this arrangement worked quite well. In fact, the whole retreat worked quite well. In order to ensure organisational continuity, so to speak, Kovida and Andy had put up notices explaining how to look after the cats, which days the baker delivered, when to order milk, how the cooker worked, what vegetables to take from the garden, and so on. Moreover, Dhammadinna and Srimala had arrived a few hours before the other women, and Kovida had explained to Srimala, who was the retreat organiser, exactly how the place was run and where everything was to be found. The result was that the retreat functioned with seemingly effortless efficiency, and an extremely positive atmosphere prevailed.

This was particularly true of the study sessions, which were the main event of each day. Both study groups studied part of Gampopa's *The Jewel Ornament of Liberation*. One group studied chapters 7 and 10, on 'Benevolence and Compassion' and 'The Training in an Enlightened Attitude' respectively, while the other studied Chapter 13, 'The Perfection of Ethics and Manners'. The fact that emerged most strikingly from our discussions was, perhaps, the extent to which the positive emotion of metta is the essential factor in all human psychological and spiritual development, as well as being the indispensable basis of the Bodhisattva Ideal.

At the end of the retreat there were two Upasika ordinations, with Hilary Blakiston becoming Padmasuri and Anni Norman Asokasri. For the public ordinations, held on the morning of Saturday, 26th January, so many women turned up that, for a few hours, the number of people at Padmaloka was practically doubled. All too soon, however, the special shrine that had been set up for the occasion in the dining-room was being dismantled, carpets were being given a final hoovering and goodbyes said.

By mid-afternoon I was left alone in a silent and deserted building which, only hours before, had been thronged with happy faces and resonant with the music of happy voices. Kovida was the first member of the community to return. Since he did not feel like cooking he went out and got something to eat from the Chinese 'take-away' in Norwich, after which we sat down to a pleasant meal and he told me how he had spent his week in London. Some of the other members of the community did not return until the following day, while one of them, as I have already mentioned, did not return at all.

With the women's Study Retreat successfully concluded there lay ahead of me two whole months — the two months before the Order Convention — in which I was free to carry on with my literary work more or less without interruption. I say 'more or less' because a week later came the two-day informal Chairmen's meeting and a month later the quarterly weekend men's Order/Mitra Event, both of which were of course held at Padmaloka. These two happenings bring me to the end of this chronological survey of my movements, and main activities, during the last six and a half months.

The men's Order/Mitra Event followed a slightly different pattern from usual, at least as regards the symposium which, as on previous Events, was held over the two evenings of the weekend. Formerly there had always been three talks on the first evening and three on the second. This time there were two on the first evening and only one on the second. The subject of the symposium was 'Dimensions of Awareness'. On the First evening Mangala spoke on awareness of self under the heading of 'Inspiration' and Nagabodhi on awareness of others/the world under the heading of 'Being Aware of the World'. On the second evening Devamitra spoke on communication, as the synthesis of awareness of self and awareness of others/the world, under the heading of 'The Dance of the Dakini'. All three talks were extremely good. In fact they were the best that I had ever heard at an Event, and the best I had ever heard any of the three speakers give. It is, of course now almost customary in the Friends to say that the lecture we have just heard, or the retreat we have just attended, was the best ever, but strange to say this is almost invariably no more than the truth. Lectures, retreats, study groups, really are getting better and better all the time — which means, of course, that the FWBO is getting better and better all the time, and the people involved in it becoming more and more truly individuals.

The literary work with which I carried on during the weeks before and the weeks after the Event consisted mainly in the writing of my *Second Letter from England* and a review of a new biography of D. H. Lawrence, Keith Sagar's *The Life of D. H. Lawrence*, and the editing of the transcript of my three 1975 New Zealand lectures for publication in book form. There was also a certain amount of correspondence.

Mention of literary work reminds me that, in surveying my movements and activities over the last six months, I have said nothing about the new, American edition of *A Survey of Buddhism,* which should have been published about the middle of January but which has still not appeared. The revisal of the work for this edition, for which I wrote a new Preface and brought the Select Bibliography up to date, had been completed shortly before I left for New Zealand, and had been, in fact, one of the reasons for my having to delay my departure until the middle of February. Proofs should have reached me soon after my return to England in June, but it so happened that they did not start arriving until September, when I was busy with study retreats and already preparing to leave for London and my lectures on the *Vimalakirti-nirdesa.* To make matters worse, there also occurred a whole series of mishaps in connection with the compilation of the new index. If Michael Scherk had not come to the rescue, and helped me with proof-reading and in other ways, I could well have been in serious difficulties, and the publication of the fifth edition of the *Survey* might have been delayed beyond what it already has been.

Having completed the promised chronological survey of my movements, and main activities, during the period covered by this Letter, i.e. from the middle of August 1979 to the end of February 1980, I must now deal with some of the *other* facets of the iridescent jewel of my life — facets of a kind not featured in the *Newsletter* or directly referred to in previous Letters. Some of the facets have to do with people, others with the arts.

As you may remember, one of the things for which I had to 'come down' from the world of the *Vimalakirti-nirdesa* was interviews, including meetings with Allen Ginsberg and Christmas Humphreys, and a visit from my mother, sister and niece. Ginsberg I had known since 1962 or 1963, when he came to see me at my Vihara in Kalimpong, and when I had taken him to see the Chinese Buddhist Yogi C. M. Chen. How he came to know of my existence, living as I did in a remote corner of the Eastern Himalayas, I no longer recollect. He may have heard of me through the West Coast poet Gary Snyder, who had corresponded with me in the fifties, when he had already begun his own exploration of Buddhism and in particular of Zen. He may have heard of me in Calcutta, where he had called at the Maha Bodhi

Society's head-quarters, and where he had left his friend Peter Orlovsky, who was too ill to accompany him. Again, he may have been given my address by my somewhat eccentric old friend the *very* English 'Tibetan' Buddhist nun Sister Vajira, whom he had met in Darjeeling.

Our second meeting took place in London, in the decorous surroundings of the Hampstead Buddhist Vihara, where I was then staying. Ginsberg had come to London to take part in the 1965 International Poetry Reading Festival at the Royal Albert Hall, which had ended in chaos only the night before. When I asked him what had happened he replied, simply, 'I was drunk'. At the beginning of 1970 I was in the United States, conducting a hall seminar at Yale. While I was there Ginsberg visited the campus, and tried to get in touch with me; but that weekend I was away in New Jersey, visiting Geshe Wangyal. We had therefore not actually met for nearly ten years, though he had written to me, and I had not — for one reason or another — replied.

On the occasion of our first meeting in Kalimpong he had lent me one dog-eared collection of his poetry and given me another — *Howl* and *Kadish* I think the volumes were, though which was the one he lent and which the one he gave me I can no longer be sure. This was my first introduction to Ginsberg's poetry, of which I had not heard before. Indeed, I had not heard of the poet himself before his stooping, hirsute figure appeared on the verandah of the Triyana Vardhana Vihara. I had, so it seemed, missed out on twenty years of Western cultural developments! Later on, especially after my final return to England in 1967, I read more of Ginsberg's poetry, but I cannot say that he ever became one of my favourite poets — not even one of my favourite modern poets. Though I appreciated his poetic afflatus and his gift for imagery, and enjoyed individual poems and bits of poems, I thought his work on the whole uneven in quality and lacking in artistry.

The man himself was another matter. Some poets and artists are greater than their work, some smaller. Ginsberg was definitely greater than his poetry. From all that I had heard and read about him, as well as from his own writings and from our two meetings, I had a vivid impression of a genuinely human being of tremendous sincerity, selflessness, and even saintliness. Outside the circle of the Friends indeed, I knew of no Western Buddhist of greater integrity than Allen Ginsberg. He was one of the few people I had ever met who concealed nothing of himself. Like his much admired William Blake, he was a man without a mask. When I heard in the middle of November that he was again in London, this time for a poetry reading at the Roundhouse, I therefore asked Devaraja to get in touch with him — he had, in fact, already tried to get in touch with me — and invite him to Sukhavati. Perhaps it was time for us to meet again!

Apparently it *was* time! A few days later Devaraja met Ginsberg at Paddington Station, on his return from a poetry-reading foray into the West Country, brought him to Sukhavati, showed him round the Centre, and finally escorted him upstairs into my study. Thinking that he would be hungry after his long journey we had a meal waiting for him, which Devaraja proceeded to serve. For whatsoever reason the community cooking was not at its best that day, but Ginsberg did not seem to mind, and while we picked up the threads of communication he steadily worked his way through a large meal. We had already picked up quite a few threads when Kularatna stopped by, as the Americans say, and was introduced to the visitor. 'Are you a poet?' demanded Ginsberg, fixing our young friend with a beady eye. Kularatna, momentarily confused, had to admit that he was not. Once again, Ginsberg did not seem to mind, and our conversation continued, weaving now from Buddhism to Blake, now from Blake back to Buddhism, and taking in on the way such topics as visionary experience, psychedelic drugs, meditation, gurus, 'academic' poetry versus modern poetry, dialect poetry, and Tennyson. Devaraja and Kularatna listened eagerly and joined in from time to time.

In all essentials I found Ginsberg unchanged. He was the same simple, unaffected, open-hearted human being I had met on the two previous occasions and whom I had encountered in his poetry and other writings. His manner, however, was quieter, and he was more conventionally dressed — besides having shorn his long locks and shaved off his bushy beard. Since our last meeting he had come under the influence of Chogyam Trungpa, who seems to believe that the pursuit of wisdom is not incompatible with the American way of life, and this may have contributed to his apparent bourgeoisification.

Though he never actually said so, I got the impression that Ginsberg was not so much under Trungpa's influence as he once had been, and that for the last two years he had not seen much of him. Indeed, though he spoke of him as his guru, I detected a slight ambivalence in his attitude towards him, almost as though a process of reassessment was going on. To me such a process was entirely healthy, and while not wishing to disturb Ginsberg's genuine faith in Trungpa, I made it clear that so far as I was concerned the word 'guru' had been thoroughly discredited in the West, and that if it was used at all it should refer not to some kind of pseudo-spiritual 'position' that could be publicly claimed, even publicly enforced, but solely on that comparatively higher degree of spiritual attainment that, in the context of person-to-person communication, spontaneously manifests in one of the parties to the communication and is spontaneously recognised by the other. There is no need to establish, before the communication begins, who is guru and who disciple. All that one has to do is communicate. If the communication is genuine it will soon become apparent who is predominantly the giver and who predominantly the receiver in the exchange.

Before Ginsberg left, after spending nearly three hours at Sukhavati, I gave him a copy of *The Enchanted Heart*, half-jestingly assuring him that it was 'academic' poetry (he seem to doubt this), and he gave me an autographed copy of his recently published *Poems All Over the Place, Mostly 'Seventies* inscribed with the words 'Met again in West'. Opening the book after his departure, I saw on the title page a Zen style couplet:

*'Meeting, two friends laugh aloud;*
*In the grove, fallen leaves are many.'*

It was a fitting comment on our third meeting.

Two people more unlike each other than Allan Ginsberg and Christmas Humphreys it would be hard to imagine. Yet it so happened that, by an odd coincidence, on the very day that I had spent the afternoon with the one I passed the evening with the other. It was difficult for me not to relish the piquancy of this circumstance, and difficult not to wonder what it was that enabled me to remain on friendly terms with two such very different people as the American

Beat poet and the English judge — whether it was a Bodhisattva-like ability to be all things to all men or merely a mundane capacity for survival. So ludicrous, indeed, was the very idea that Ginsberg and Humphreys should be in contact with each other, even to the extent of having a common friend who saw both of them on the same day, that almost out of perversity I had enquired of Ginsberg whether he had been to the Buddhist Society and seen Christmas Humphreys. Strange to relate, Ginsberg seemed not to have heard of Christmas Humphreys. What was stranger still, when I told Humphreys that I had spent the afternoon with Allen Ginsberg, and asked if he had met him, he seemed not to have heard of Allen Ginsberg. Each, in fact, showed such a marked lack of interest in the other that I was obliged to drop the subject and talk about something else.

I had, of course, known Humphreys for much longer than I had known Ginsberg, in fact since 1944, when we met under circumstances described in the first part of my memoirs — the part rejected by the publishers as lacking in interest for the English reader. Since then we had met in New Delhi, in Bombay, in Kalimpong, and of course in London again, both before and after my final return to England in 1967. As a result of the events that preceded my return, however, — events that led to the founding of the FWBO and the WBO, — our 'friendship' had suffered an eclipse, and there was a period of six or seven years during which we did not see each other at all. Since about 1975, however, we had met at fairly frequent intervals, usually at his suggestion. Indeed, despite the mistakes he had committed in connection with the events of the Winter of 1966-67, — mistakes I could forgive, even if not forget, — his attitude towards me now seemed to be one of genuine goodwill. He had even convinced himself that he was my oldest and best friend and that he had always given me his full support! Though for the time being I might appear to acquiesce in this amiable delusion, I mentally reserved the right to tell one day the true story of the events preceding my final return to England — probably in some future volume of memoirs. I also hoped that eventually there would be sufficient confidence between us for him to be able to admit what part he had *really* played in those events.

Meanwhile, we continued to meet, and though he was not an easy man to get on with, — not nearly so easy as

Ginsberg, — I was glad that a more genuine relationship had now developed between us. One of the signs of this was that he had at last brought himself to recognise that I really was a vegetarian, and when I came to dinner — we usually met at his house in St. John's Wood, a select residential suburb of North London — no longer pretended to have forgotten that I did *not* eat meat, or that fish was *not* a part of normal vegetarian diet. On the present occasion he had not only caused his Italian cook to prepare me an excellent cheese omelette but actually had one himself — something he had never done before. He seemed, in fact, genuinely pleased to see me (we had not met since the previous year) and was more relaxed and open than he had ever been. As usual, we exchanged news of friends we had in common, such as the deposed Chogyal of Sikkim, and discussed recent happenings in the Buddhist world.

Though he was mentally as sharp as ever, I noticed that he now tired quickly, and that an hour and a half of sustained conversation was about as much as he could comfortably manage. I therefore did not prolong my visit. In any case, I had arranged for Devaraja to bring the car round for me at a relatively early hour. Before I left him Humphreys gave me a copy of *The Mountain Side*, his latest collection of poems. Both in form and content, they were very different from the poems Ginsberg had given me a few hours earlier. This was hardly surprising: in background, character, and tastes the two men were almost exact opposites. Nonetheless, both were Buddhists and both were poets. Having spent part of the day with each of them, it was difficult for me to believe that, on the ordinary human level, they really had no more in common with each other than their connection with me. My mother, sister, and niece (actually the younger of my *two* nieces) visited Sukhavati about two weeks before my meetings with Ginsberg and Humphreys. My mother, in particular, had wanted to see the place for some time. With the help of the *Newsletter* she had followed the long-drawn-out saga of the building of Sukhavati with mounting interest, and now that it was completed, and she had recovered from her illness, she was determined to see the place at least once before she died. She also wanted to see Bethnal Green, with which her second husband had been associated, but which she had never had the opportunity of visiting. 'Sid always spoke very highly of the people of Bethnal Green,' she told me.

Accordingly, on the morning of Monday 5th November, Ashvajit took the Cortina and after collecting the three women from my mother's house in Rayleigh chauffeured them down to Sukhavati, which they reached exactly at midday. Luckily they had a fine day for their visit. Though the air was quite cold, the sun shone brilliantly, and there was a clear blue sky. Since they were not vegetarians, I had decided to give them lunch in town, at the restaurant in the new YMCA building on the corner of Great Russell Street and Tottenham Court Road, where my mother would not have to walk up and down any stairs. First, however, I asked Ashvajit to drive us through the Victoria Park, so that they could see something of Bethnal Green. The YMCA restaurant turned out to be a good choice from the non-vegetarian point of view, and at the end of the meal my mother, sister and niece all declared themselves well satisfied with their lunch. Asvajit and I were less fortunate. Omelettes were not on the menu that day, and we had to be content with some rather musty ravioli with a rather dubious filling. However, our three guests had had what they wanted, and that was the main thing. On the way back to Sukhavati we drove through the City (on our way into town we had made a detour via Waterloo and the South Bank) and my mother pointed out places she had known years — in fact decades — ago.

The highlight of their whole visit was, of course, the seeing of the London Buddhist Centre, and in particular the two shrine rooms. Both my mother and sister were greatly impressed by the peaceful atmosphere of the Centre, and by the sense of light and space. What impressed them most of all, though, were the two great golden Buddha images. My mother, in particular, was quite transported with admiration, and could hardly take her eyes off the seated image in the main shrine room (my sister preferred the standing image in the small shrine room). This was interesting. My mother was in no sense an 'educated' woman, and knew very little about Buddhism, yet it was clear that, on account of her emotional positivity, and her general open-mindedness, the visual symbols of the Dharma could make a direct spiritual appeal to her — an appeal that had nothing to do with words and concepts. My sister was more reserved in expressing her admiration, but hardly less impressed. For many years she had been strongly anti-religious, and had realised that Buddhism was not a 'religion' in the usual sense of the term only after reading *Peace is a Fire*. Both she and my mother had read, and enjoyed, *The Thousand-Petalled Lotus*. Indeed, my mother had told me that during her illness last Winter she had read a little of it every evening, and that this had given her strength. Besides seeing the shrine rooms, my mother, sister, and niece all looked at the Centre bookstall, where my sister bought Windhorse T-shirts for her younger son and other members of the family. They then paid a visit to Friends Foods, buying there various items not available in Rayleigh.

By this time we had been back at Sukhavati for nearly two hours, and everyone was ready for a cup of tea. I was afraid my mother might not be able to climb the steps up to my flat, but taking hold of the handrail she managed the ascent quite easily, without any assistance. Her day's outing seemed, in fact, to have had a rejuvenating effect on her, and as soon as we had had tea she went across the road with my sister and niece to investigate Friends Trading. Here, to her delight, she found a gas cooker of the very type for which she had been looking, and at once bought it from Uttara. When they left the shop Uttara presented her and my sister each with an iridescent Art-Nouveau bowl -- an expression of goodwill which pleased both of them immensely. All too soon for my mother, sister, and niece alike the long-anticipated visit to Sukhavati was over, the gas cooker had been fastened down in the boot of the car, and Ashvajit was ready to drive them home to Rayleigh.

When I saw my mother a month later, on my way back to Padmaloka, she was still full of her visit, and it was clear that the atmosphere of the Centre, and the sight of the two Buddha images, had affected both her and my sister quite deeply. She had also been greatly impressed by the patience and skill with which Ashvajit had negotiated the heavy London traffic, and gave me a small Christmas present for him.

Among the facets of the jewel having to do with the arts, during the period covered by this Letter, one of the brightest had to do with the operas and oratorios of Handel, and with a brief reference to these I shall conclude. Handel had long been one of my three or four most favourite composers. Indeed, there were times when, with Samuel

Butler, I thought Handel the greatest of all (Western) composers. During the months that I was in London, giving my lectures on the *Vimalakirti-nirdesa,* I had the opportunity of attending live performances of no less than three operas (*Scipione, Hercules,* and *Julius Caesar*) and two oratorios (*Judas Maccabeus* and *Saul*). This meant coming down from the world of the *Vimalakirti-nirdesa* not so much to the *kamaloka* or realm of sensuous desire as to the *rupaloka* or realm of archetypal (sound and) form — a realm irradiated, perhaps, with reflections of the Transcendental. After attending these performances I decided that I definitely preferred Handel's operas to his oratorios. This was partly on account of difference of form, partly on account of difference of content. The operas were in *form* three-dimensional, so to speak, consisting of sound (solo voices, chorus, orchestra), spectacle (costumes, sets), and action (individual and group movements of various kinds), whereas the oratorios were one-dimensional, consisting of only sound (solo voices, chorus, orchestra). As regards *content,* the (dramatic) subject-matter of the operas was drawn from ancient Roman history and Greek mythology, whereas the (narrative) subject-matter of the oratorios was drawn from the Old Testament and the Apocrypha. Handel's genius, so it seemed to me, was dramatic and heroic, rather than narrative and 'religious', and as such had far greater scope for its expression in *opera seria* than in oratorio.

After seeing the operas, I was also convinced that it was possible to take the conventions of *opera seria* quite seriously — that is, to take them quite seriously *as conventions.* It was possible, in fact, to take quite seriously the conventions of heroic drama, the non-musical counterpart of *opera seria,* as well as the conventions of the romantic epic out of which both *opera seria* and heroic drama had, in a sense, developed. Elizabethan and Jacobean tragedy was not necessarily the highest form of poetic drama. A happy ending was not necessarily an artistic disaster. — These reflections led to so many others, and revealed so many more facets of the jewel, that further consideration of a very interesting subject will have to be postponed to some future Letter or article. Meanwhile, the jewel rolls on.

## CHAPTER SEVEN

# LETTER FROM WALES

### I

WE left Padmaloka after breakfast on Thursday 24th March [1983]. Prasannasiddhi was at the wheel, while I occupied what I believe is known as the owner's seat. The car was rather heavy, since the boot was tightly packed with suitcases and holdalls, cardboard boxes full of books, a white plastic tub containing wholefoods, box files, office equipment, a typewriter, and a tape-recorder. Bedding was piled on the back seat, together with raincoats and other items that might be needed on the journey. We were off to Wales.

Since the day of our return from Tuscany, three and a half months earlier, neither of us had spent a night away from Padmaloka. Indeed, we had hardly put our noses outside Norfolk. Now we were off to Wales for what we hoped would be three months of uninterrupted study and literary work. Prasannasiddhi hoped to get through an assortment of books on Buddhism, as well as H. G. Wells' *The Outline of History* and the poems of Wordsworth and Milton. I hoped to reduce the mountain of unanswered letters to something more like a molehill, to edit the transcript of the seminar on Dr. Conze's *The Way to Wisdom,* to write an Introduction to the new enlarged edition of *The Religion of Art* for Nagabodhi, to edit more transcripts of lectures given in India for Lokamitra, to edit more transcripts of seminars held in Tuscany and elsewhere for Subhuti and Vessantara, and to compose a condensed version of the White Tara mantra-recitation and visualisation practice for two newly ordained Order Members.

But meanwhile, here we were driving down the A140. Prasannasiddhi had his foot on the accelerator, and green fields and ancient villages went sweeping past. Once or twice the windscreen was obscured by rain. Norfolk was succeeded by Suffolk, Suffolk by Essex. We were not going straight to Wales. We were going to Wales via Winchester, where I was to speak that weekend at the Wrekin Trust's 'Mystics and Scientists' conference, to Winchester via London, and to London via Rayleigh, besides which we were breaking the journey from Winchester to Wales by spending a night or two in Bristol. In this way we would be seeing quite a number of Order Members and other friends before finally disappearing into the green foot-hills of North Wales.

Rayleigh is a small town, or overgrown village, near Southend, and so far as I know it has no claim to fame whatever. My sole reason for going there, as on all the previous occasions on which I had visited the place, was to see my mother, who has lived there for the last thirty years. Before making our way to her bungalow we drove up the hill to the main shopping centre so that I could buy some flowers. Despite the sunshine, the air as I stepped out of the car was quite icily cold, and I was therefore glad to be back in my seat, some fifteen minutes later, with my bunch of tulips and irises. I always took my mother flowers — probably because my father had always taken *his* mother flowers when he went to see her. Flowers or no flowers, my mother was always glad to see me, and the present occasion was no exception.

For my part, I was glad to find her in good health and spirits, and after Prasannasiddhi had been introduced, and we had all had a cup of tea together, the three of us drove to the nearby town of Rochford for a meal in an Indian restaurant. Since my mother is now in her eighty-sixth year, and lives alone, I see her as often as I can, which for the last few years has meant every three or four months (before it was once a year). She has also twice visited me in Norfolk, the second time being on the occasion of last year's Padmaloka Open Day, when she came with a friend even older than herself, attended the benefit dinner, and did not leave until after midnight, having thoroughly enjoyed herself. The year before she had paid her second visit to the LBC. Though not a Buddhist, she takes a keen interest in the work of the FWBO, especially in what we are doing among the Indian ex-Untouchables. Had she been thirty years younger, she once declared, she would have gone out to India and helped.

After the meal we drove back to Rayleigh, and while Prasannasiddhi rested in the spare bedroom my mother told me the latest news of the family. This mainly concerned my sister, whom she had not seen since before Christmas, her elder grandson and his family, who visit her every other Saturday and with whom she spends Christmas and other holidays, and my Uncle Dick and his ex-wife Audrey, with whom I stayed in Calcutta at the beginning of 1947 on my return from Singapore. There was also news of friends and amiable neighbours, of whom she has a good number, as well as news of the formation of a new Buddhist group in Basildon. She also spoke of Padmasuri, who had written to her from Poona. Before my last visit to Poona my mother had given me some money 'for the children', and this I had handed over to Padmasuri for her Sunday Dhamma class after they had given me lunch and I had given them a talk. Padmasuri had not only written thanking my mother on behalf of the children, but had also sent her, through me, a generous selection of the children's paintings, some of which were quite remarkable. This had pleased my mother very much, and she now gave me more money 'for the children' — as well as something for myself. In this way the afternoon passed until Prasannasiddhi rejoined us for an early tea, after which he and I, having bidden goodbye to my mother, left for London and Sukhavati.

My flat was pleasantly warm when we entered it, and as usual there were flowers on my desk by way of welcome. Prasannasiddhi and I had arranged to have supper with the community, and an hour after our arrival, therefore, we found ourselves ranged round the familiar table of the pleasant Sukhavati dining-room with a dozen or so bright-faced community members. Since my last visit, seven months earlier, the community seemed to have shrunk, some people having left, while others were either out or away. Kulananda, for instance, was in India. After a friendly and relaxed meal, during which news was exchanged, the community members and I adjourned to the sitting-room, where for the next two hours we had a useful discussion on matters of community interest. As usual, I was glad to be able to get together with them in this way, and they seemed glad to get together with me. I do not remember that we sounded any great depths, whether psychological or metaphysical, but it was good to renew our mutual friendship, and to exchange ideas on matters of common concern.

While I was thus engaged with the community Prasannasiddhi was in the flat with Chintamani talking, on my behalf, about something to which I had recently given much thought. It had all started a month or so earlier when Harshaprabha sent me — out of the blue — a clipping from an architectural journal giving details of a property that was for sale in the South of France, near Carcassonne. This clipping acted as a catalyst, bringing together a number of hitherto unrelated factors, and sparking off a series of events that is still continuing. To begin with, since my return from Tuscany, and even before, I had been on the look-out for a place to which I could retire for a while in order to get on, without interruption, with the literary work which, I had decided, was the best contribution I could, for the moment, make to the progress of the Movement.

Padmaloka was very dear to me. I loved the rambling, grey-tiled house with the white-pillared Georgian portico. I loved the spacious grounds, with their wide lawns and well-stocked flower-beds. I loved the centuries-old oaks, the gnarled old walnut tree, and the great copper beech. I loved the oval pond where the red lilies bloomed, and the nearby rockery where the face of the meditating Buddha caught the first rays of the early morning sun. I loved the walled kitchen garden, with its miniature greenhouse, and its neat rows of vegetables. I loved Padmaloka in the Spring, when crocuses and aconites covered the ground, and the yellow daffodils danced beneath the oaks and along the boarders of the lawn. I loved Padmaloka in Summer, when roses and jasmine bloomed, and in the Autumn, when leaves fell and the pale sunshine lingered week after week. I even loved Padmaloka in the Winter, when the snow lay dazzlingly white on the ground, on the roof, and on the leafless branches, and when the oval pond was frozen over, and when we put crumbs out for the blackbirds, thrushes, blue tits, robins and starlings. I loved my walk down to the River Yare. I loved the Order Library. I loved my study, which Buddhadasa had so lovingly decorated, with its red tartan carpet, its beige walls, and its light blue frieze. I loved my desk by the window overlooking the front lawn, at which I had sat for so many hundreds of hours and written so many thousands of words: letters, articles, book reviews, lectures, memoirs. I loved my books, which now filled all the available shelf-space and had overflowed first into my bedroom and then into the Archive room. I loved my images and thangkas and my small collection of semi-precious stones. Most of all, perhaps, I loved the members of the community, with some of whom I had been associated for many years, and with whom I wished to deepen my contact rather than disrupt it.

Nonetheless, during the last year or so Padmaloka — now a full-time retreat centre — had become a very busy place, the community had doubled in size, the Order Office had developed into a centre of activity in its own right, visitors were for ever coming and going, and the freedom from disturbance that I needed for my literary work had become increasingly difficult to obtain. I had therefore come to the conclusion that, much as I loved Padmaloka, I would have to retire to another place for a while, keeping Padmaloka as my official residence, so to speak, and permanent head-quarters. Padmaloka was very dear to me, but my work was dearer still. As an interim measure I had arranged with Hridaya to rent Tyddyn Rhydderch for three months, and thus it was that Prasannasiddhi and I came to be going not only via London to Winchester but also via Winchester to Wales.

The clipping sent by Harshaprabha had, however, suggested the possibility of a more permanent solution to my difficulties. Indeed, it had suggested a solution to the difficulties of several other people as well. Chittapala and Silabhadra, both of whom had just been ordained in Tuscany, had decided that for the next year they would devote themselves to organising the systematic transcription of the tapes of my lectures and seminars, and were looking for a place to live. Prasannasiddhi, who also had just been ordained in Tuscany, wanted to stay with me and devote himself to full time study. Chintamani, who had spent the past six months house-hunting in London, wanted to establish a small men's community in which he could settle down and finish writing his book. Why should the five of us not throw in our lot with one another and go and live together in the South of France, near Carcassonne?

In this way did Harshaprabha's clipping bring together a number of hitherto unrelated factors, and spark off a whole series of events. Indeed, in addition to those already mentioned, the hitherto unrelated factors thus brought together included one which, so far as I at least was concerned, invested the whole project with a very special significance. This was the fact that the property to which the clipping referred was situated not only in the South of France, not only in the Lanquedoc, but *near Carcassonne*. Carcassonne, as I well knew, was located in the heart of what had once been Cathar country, and in the course of the last eight or ten years I had not only read everything about the Cathars on which I could lay my hands but had also cherished an increasingly strong desire to go on pilgrimage to the former strongholds of the Cathar faith, especially to Monségur and Carcassonne.

Only three months earlier my desire had been partly fulfilled. On the way back from Tuscany Subhuti, Prasannasiddhi, Dhirananda and I spent a few hours within the walls of Carcassonne, which we found in a far better state of preservation (actually, nineteenth century restoration) than we had expected and almost unbelievably picturesque. Moreover, to our surprise we saw in the windows of the souvenir shops that lined the crooked, cobbled lanes a whole array of books, pamphlets and picture postcards dealing with the Cathars and Catharism, as well as with the culture of the region, including the *langue d'oc*. Unfortunately, since it was the off season for tourism, most of the shops were closed, but even from the limited number of items we were able to acquire it was evident that the traditions of the Cathars lived on in the consciousness of the local people, and were — together with the *langue d'oc* — the focal point of a good deal of local sentiment and local patriotism, some of it with distinctly 'nationalist' overtones. Indeed, something of a Cathar revival seemed to be under way, though how deep this went, and to what extent it was merely 'archaeological', it was impossible to tell. Nevertheless, the fact that seven centuries after their brutal extermination by the forces of Roman Catholic orthodoxy the Cathars could be, at the very least, the subject of sympathetic study and investigation, was in itself highly significant and even encouraging. The victories and defeats of the 13th century were not irreversible! A dent had been made in the Church's defences, massive though they were. Indeed, a breach seemed to have been made, and through that breach who knows what might not be able to enter. Perhaps the Lanquedoc would again be the centre of a flourishing non-Christian culture and spiritual tradition.* Subhuti and I, in particular, could not help thinking that perhaps it would not be very difficult for the FWBO to start up Buddhist activities in the region of Carcassonne. Indeed, as imagination took wing, we could see centres and communities — and even co-operatives — springing up all over the area, and as we drove off in the direction of Toulouse it was with the exhilarating sense of a breakthrough having been achieved.

All this — and much more — was in my mind as I studied the details of the property in the South of France, near Carcassonne. Perhaps it would be a more permanent solution to my difficulties, as well as to the difficulties of several other people, than Hridaya's cottage in Wales. For me to consult Subhuti and Prasannasiddhi, and for Subhuti to consult Chittapala and Silabhadra, as well as Chintamani and his father, was the work of a few hours. The hitherto unrelated factors were being brought together, and it was not long before the series of events had been sparked off. Speed was essential. Within twenty-four hours of a decision being taken, bank accounts had been raided, appointments made with lawyers in Limoux, Channel ferry passages booked, and Subhuti, Chittapala, Silabhadra and Chintamani were on their way to the South of France in the same red Volvo that was now taking the two of us to Wales.

While they were away Prasannasiddhi and I discussed the implications of the proposed move. They were indeed far-reaching. Carcassonne was situated on the crossroads, so to speak, between Italy, France, and Spain, and the establishment of a community or centre there would give us a bridge-head into the whole area surrounding the western end of the Mediterranean, from Gibraltar to Sicily, and even

---

* The Cathars of course regarded themselves as (the true) Christians. If Roman Catholicism is regarded as representing Christianity, however, the Cathars were *not* Christians.

into Switzerland and Germany. Initially, perhaps, a 'study and writing' community could be set up, and then, when we ourselves left for India and New Zealand in two years time, this could become a public centre from which the Dharma could be spread over as wide an area as possible. Eventually, perhaps, Nagabodhi, who speaks passable French, could come out and take charge of the place. Or perhaps Padmaraja, with his well known love of French culture, might like to take it over and run it as a southerly extension of Aryatara. In this way did the pair of us speculate, from time to time, during the five days that Subhuti and the others were away.

Nonetheless, it was *not* about anything to do with the property in the South of France, near Carcassonne, that Prasannasiddhi was talking with Chintamani that evening while I was engaged with the Sukhavati community. He was talking with him, on my behalf, about the property in Bungay, Suffolk, and it was into this property that we were hoping to move after our return from Wales.

Subhuti and the others had come back from their expedition tired but triumphant. As we already knew from the 'phone calls Subhuti had made from time to time, they had seen not one property but two, the second one being even more attractive, and much more secluded, than the first. They had, in fact, explored the area around Carcassonne as thoroughly as the time at their disposal permitted, and were full of information, impressions, and enthusiasm — especially Subhuti. Indeed, doing what I myself so much wanted to do, they had climbed to the top of the peak on which stand the ruins of Monségur. Since the second of the two properties was clearly the one more suited to our collective requirements, it was to the acquisition of this that Subhuti directed his energies. Letters were sent, 'phone calls made, to friends who might be able to help us financially. Different types of loan and mortage arrangements were considered. The rights of foreign nationals, under French law, in relation to such matters as permanent residence and payment of income tax were ascertained. At the end of one of the busiest and most interrupted weeks either of us had ever experienced (*he* was also having to take classes and attend meetings, and think about the launching of his book, while *I* was working on the paper I was to read at the 'Mystics and Scientists' conference) Subhuti had succeeded in stitching together an agreement and laid it on my desk for a final decision.

It lay there for two days. I then told Subhuti I had decided against acceptance. There were mainly two reasons for my decision. In the first place, although the agreement was certainly viable it would probably impose too severe a strain on our resources, and might even lead to worries on this account. In the second, much as the Movement in England needed to learn to stand on its own feet, for me to move at this stage to so distant a place as the South of France would probably be premature.

Yet even though I was not retiring to the property in the South of France, near Carcassonne, the journey that Subhuti and the others had undertaken, and all the investigations that had followed, had not, I felt, been a complete waste of time and energy. Provence, Carcassonne, and the Cathars, were now firmly stamped on the consciousness of at least a small number of people in the FWBO, and even if I myself never went to live in the South of France there were Order Members who would, sooner or later, do so, and the dream — or vision — I had had of the extension of our activities to that part of the world would eventually come true. Moreover, the exigencies of the situation created by the Carcassonne project had set up certain pressures, and it had been interesting to see how different people responded to these. Subhuti, in particular, had displayed extraordinary resilience and resourcefulness. Most important of all, perhaps, in the short term at least, was the fact that despite the collapse of the Carcassonne project the series of events sparked off by Harshaprabha's clipping was far from having run its course. The factors which had been brought together were together still, and though the momentum generated in the past two weeks had not carried Prasannasiddhi, Chittapala, Silabhadra, Chintamani and myself to the South of France it now seemed likely that it would carry us somewhere nearer at hand.

Suffolk had been mentioned as a county in which properties were still cheap, and while Chittapala and Silabhadra were away from Padmaloka in connection with the transcription work, Chintamani therefore continued his house-hunting in that part of East Anglia. Suffolk proving not quite so cheap as expected, his search led him to the Norfolk-Suffolk border and eventually to two isolated properties in the neighbourhood of Bungay. One very wet afternoon, less than a week before we were due to leave for Wales, Prasannasiddhi and I went with him to have a look at these. We were able to see over only one of them. It was in an excellent state of repair and decoration (three women lived there, it seemed), and in addition to the attractively gabled, half-timbered house there was an extensive range of outbuildings. However, the rooms were small and poky and it was doubtful if the place was really big enough for five people. The other property, which the three of us had seen only the day before (also on a very wet afternoon), on the very eve of our departure for Wales, was much more suitable, and it was about this property that I had asked Prasannasiddhi to talk to Chintamani while I was engaged with the Sukhavati community. It was sufficiently isolated, there was room for a community of five or more, and it was conveniently near to Padmaloka, so that I would continue to have access to the Order Library, and to the Order Office and the Archives, and would be able to see people there from time to time. As for Prasannasiddhi and the rest, though Suffolk was not quite such an attractive proposition as the South of France, they were well content, and already looked forward to life in the new community. I therefore asked Prasannasiddhi to confirm with Chintamani that we were prepared to move to Bungay on our return from Wales, and that he should go ahead with the purchase of the property as planned.

My discussion with the Sukhavati community having ended with the usual round of Barleycup, tea, etc., I returned to the flat to find Prasannasiddhi curled up on the sofa with a book. Chintamani had left some time ago, any uncertainty he might have felt as to my intentions regarding the Bungay project having been dispelled. More than twelve hours had elapsed since our departure from Padmaloka. Prasannasiddhi and I had had a busy day, and were likely to have an even busier one tomorrow. We therefore went to bed early.

In the morning, after I had seen two or three people, we took the tube into town and spent an hour in Foyle's. (For the information of the Indian Order Members I should mention that Foyle's, in Charing Cross Road, is the biggest bookshop in the world, with three million volumes in stock. I have known it since I was sixteen, and it is a favourite haunt of the more studiously inclined among the Order Members in England.) Since Prasannasiddhi wanted to read Milton while we were in Wales, we took the opportunity of acquiring a few more books on the great English poet, in case those we had brought with us from Padmaloka should prove insufficient. Prominent among our acquisitions was Christopher Hill's *Milton and the English Revolution*, which I had long wanted to read. We also bought a few newish books on Buddhism, including Trevor Ling's *Buddhist Revival in India*, which contains sections on 'Anti-Brahmanism and Dr. Ambedkar' and 'Ambedkar Between Marxism and Buddhism', and Michael Pye's *The Buddha*. After a cup of coffee in the restaurant at the corner of the new YMCA building, we returned to Sukhavati and prepared to leave for Winchester. Not wanting either to unload the car just for one night or to take the risk of leaving it outside all night loaded (Bethnal Green is not a dishonest place, but cars left with valuables in them are liable to be broken into, especially at night), we had parked it in the Centre courtyard. The great red gates were now unbarred, Khemavira waved goodbye, and we drove out under the wrought iron Nalanda crest on the next stage of our journey.

On our emergence from the Blackwall Tunnel we should have joined the South Circular Road and headed west, but somehow we missed our turning and continued south-east instead, going several miles out of our way before realising our mistake. Once we had realised it, however, it did not take us long to correct it, and before many minutes had passed we had gained the South Circular Road and become caught up in a tedious crawl through parts of South London that were unfamiliar even to me. It was not until we reached Clapham Common that I found myself back on familiar ground. From there we crawled on, in increasingly heavy traffic, through Battersea, Putney, and Wimbledon. Only when we were clear of Wimbledon did the traffic thin out, and the megalopolitan sprawl of Greater London start giving way to the pleasant Surrey countryside. Two hours had passed since our departure from Bethnal Green, and it was with feelings of something like relief that we now saw before us nothing but the open road.

An hour later we were in Guildford. This is the county town of Surrey, and Prasannasiddhi and I had been there the previous summer, on our way to Haslemere. On that occasion we had visited Guildford Cathedral, a fine example of '20th century Gothic', as it has been termed, that stands sentinel on a small hill outside the town and is, like the modernistic buildings of the new University, clearly visible from the road. This time we had no intention of visiting the Cathedral; we were looking for a restaurant, it being long past our usual lunch time. Like many another old English town, Guildford was simply not built for modern traffic, and it took us some time to master the one-way system, extricate ourselves from a cul-de-sac, and find parking space. Eventually we succeeded, and more by accident than design found ourselves outside a restaurant. After a quite good, though rather expensive, meal (asparagus quiche), we abandoned ourselves to the tender mercies of the one-way system and soon found ourselves heading west along a tree-lined minor road in the direction of Winchester.

In less than an hour we were in the ancient and venerable city. Ahead of us, to the left, rose the massive bulk of the Cathedral. On our right, at the entrance to the High Street, stood a statue of King Arthur brandishing a sword. The Wrekin Trust had, very considerately, sent us a map showing the location of King Alfred's College, where the conference was to be held, but unfortunately the map did not show which were the one-way streets. Once again, therefore, we had to master the intricacies of a one-way system. This was soon done, however, and in a matter of minutes we had found the road leading to the College and could see the buildings of the College itself rising before us on the hillside and shining in the late afternoon sun.

## II

The invitation to address the Wrekin Trust's annual 'Mystics and Scientists' conference had come six months earlier. It had arrived, in fact, in the middle of the Tuscany Pre-Ordination Course, having been redirected from Padmaloka. Every year the Trust spoṇsored a major conference concerned with 'different aspects of the emerging relationship between the mystical and scientific experience of the nature of reality', the letter of invitation informed me, a team of distinguished speakers was drawn from various disciplines, and the conference attracted over three hundred delegates from different parts of the world. Would I be prepared to address the conference to put forward a Buddhist viewpoint? It was Christmas Humphreys who recommended that I be approached. The letter was signed by Sir George Trevelyan, the Founder and Director of the Trust.

I did not know much about the Wrekin Trust, which had been founded in 1971 and was described, at the bottom of the official letterhead on which the invitation was typed, as 'An educational charity concerned with the spiritual nature of Man and the Universe.' All I knew was that it formed one of the better organised and more solidly established parts of the rather vague and undefined 'New Age' movement, and that I had met Sir George some years previously at Brighton, when we had attended a kind of inter-faith convention and been introduced to each other by my old friend Clare Cameron. Since nowadays I never speak under the auspices of organisations other than the FWBO (except when in India) I was at first more inclined to reject than accept the invitation. However, something prompted me not to refuse it outright, with the result that after giving a good deal of thought to the matter, and discussing it with Prasannasiddhi, I eventually decided that, on this occasion at least, I would accept, and replied to Sir George accordingly.

There were several reasons for this apparent *volte-face*. For the last ten years I had functioned almost exclusively within the context of the FWBO. Apart from one lecture at the Buddhist Society, and one lecture at the Caxton Hall under the joint auspices of the Buddhist Society and the FWBO, all my lectures (all my lectures in England, that is) had been given to audiences consisting almost entirely of Order Members, Mitras and Friends. In the same way, the numerous study retreats I had conducted had all been attended exclusively by men and women from within the Movement. Indeed, blood relations apart, except for the occasional journalist or visiting Buddhist dignitary I had hardly any personal contact with people outside the FWBO and no personal contact at all with other spiritual groups as such, whether Buddhist or non-Buddhist. Perhaps the time had come for me to see for myself what some of these groups, and the people connected with them, were now like. Perhaps it was time for me to see what changes had taken place in the course of the last ten years, and whether there was now more in common between ourselves and bodies like the Wrekin Trust than there once had been.

There was also the fact that the conference to which I was being invited was concerned with the relation between science and mysticism. In the clipping attached to the letter of invitation I read, under the heading 'Mystics and Scientists 6', 'Scientific exploration is pushing man's understanding far beyond the limitations of a materialistic conception of the nature of matter. Physicists, psychologists, parapsychologists, biologists and medical researchers are beginning to hold a vision of reality similar to that held by the mystics down the ages. The merging of these twin streams of science and mysticism can be seen as the most important event taking place today.' This was an area to which I had given all too little attention. Though I was far from convinced that the mystics down the ages had all held the same vision of reality, and therefore doubtful whether modern scientists were, in fact, beginning to hold a similar vision, perhaps the time had come for me to investigate the matter more closely, at least so far as the relation between Buddhism and science was concerned.

Moreover, there was a practical side to the *rapprochement* that the Wrekin Trust believed was taking place. 'The implication is that man's relationship to himself and his planet will fundamentally change,' the clipping continued, 'and out of this change a new society will emerge.' The emergence of a new society was certainly something that interested me very much. Perhaps the conference would be able to shed some light on the way in which the *rapprochement* between science and mysticism would bring about a fundamental change in man's relationship to himself and his planet, and how *this* would contribute to the emergence of a new society. If it could do that, it would certainly be worth attending. In any case, judging by the names of the speakers at last year's conference, the Wrekin Trust had succeeded in bringing together not just fringe or maverick figures but people who, whether as Mystics or Scientists, belonged to the mainstream of their respective disciplines and traditions. In the concluding words of the clipping, 'This annual conference has now become the most important yearly occasion for people working in the sciences and those following spiritual disciplines to meet and confer with each other. It is attended by figures of international repute.' Though I regarded myself as belonging no more to the Mystics than to the Scientists (the Wrekin Trust evidently classified me with the former) and would in a sense be attending the conference under false pretences, perhaps it would be possible for me to have a worth-while exchange with some of the speakers and other delegates. Such were the reasons for the apparent *volte-face* that had brought Prasannasiddhi and myself to King Alfred's College, Winchester, late that Friday afternoon.

Delegates to the conference were being received in the vestibule of the Conference Hall. While Prasannasiddhi waited in the car, I went and investigated. Upwards of a hundred people were queuing at the various trestle tables that served as reception desks. I joined one of the queues, but on being identified as a speaker was at once transferred to a special table at the end of the row, where a rather flustered lady who seemed unsure how she ought to treat me issued me with two round paper badges, a red one for me and a white one for Prasannasiddhi (we were supposed to write our names on them and wear them on our lapels) and told me that we would be staying at Christchurch Lodge. This was the most outlying of the College hostels, and was situated farther up the road from which we had turned off into the road on which the College itself was situated. Once there it did not take us long to settle in. We had been allocated two large rooms on the second floor, one containing three beds and the other four. Not knowing whether each of us had the exclusive use of one room, or whether all the beds in both rooms would eventually be occupied, we took the precaution of both moving into the larger and brighter of the rooms, from the windows of which there was a splendid view of the College roofs and, in fact, of the whole city, including the Cathedral. While we were unloading our suitcases from the car I saw a tall, thin old man with ruddy cheeks and a mane of white hair hovering uncertainly outside the front porch like a great gaunt bird. This was probably Sir George Trevelyan (not having seen him for so many years I could not be sure), but after eyeing me doubtfully he fluttered off in the direction of the College with another person for whom he had, apparently, been waiting. Whether Sir George or not, he clearly had a lot of things on his mind.

Prasannasiddhi and I had been hoping that on our arrival at the College a cup of tea would be forthcoming, but it was not, or else we failed to locate it. Perhaps the conference was going to be a highly spiritual affair, with not much attention paid to creature comforts! We therefore consoled ourselves by looking out of the window at the yellowing tones of the western sky, resting on two of the beds, and — in my case, especially — examining the books we had bought that morning at Foyle's. London already seemed very distant — what to speak of Padmaloka. Eventually, hoping that we would be luckier with dinner than with tea, we pinned on our paper badges and strolled down to the College, which was set amid trees on the hillside with flights of steps between buildings, and soon found ourselves outside the Conference Hall.

The entrance to the vestibule was thronged with people, rather like the entrance to a beehive on a warm summer's day. Amidst the throng I detected the tall, thin figure with the mane of white hair and flapping arms, who was just then emerging with a large black briefcase and a harassed look. Deciding that it *was* Sir George Trevelyan I stepped forward and introduced myself. He was very glad to see me. I was very glad to see him. We were still shaking hands, and I was trying to explain that we had met in Brighton not Preston (Sir George seemed a little hard of hearing), when there emerged a younger, robuster figure with an even larger black briefcase and an even more harassed look. This was Malcolm Lazarus, the Co-director of the Wrekin Trust, who had been in correspondence with me ever since my acceptance of Sir George's invitation. *He* was very glad to see me. I was very glad to see *him*. After a brief but cordial exchange, in the course of which Prasannasiddhi was introduced, I enquired the way to the dining hall, Malcolm gave us directions, and up a flight of steps (or was it down?) Prasannasiddhi and I went. Outside the dining hall there was a perfectly enormous queue, to the ever-lengthening tail of which we promptly attached ourselves.

All this time we were on the look-out for Subhuti. In fact, we had been on the look-out for him ever since our arrival. He was to have gone straight from Padmaloka to

Salisbury that same day, picked up the first copies of his book from the publishers, and then joined us at the College in time for tea or at least in time for dinner. He too was attending the conference, and Malcolm wanted his book to be on sale there at the Wrekin Trust's own bookstall along with books by me and the other speakers. As the queue snaked its way through a sort of exhibition hall and into the service area we remained on the look-out for Subhuti, but neither there nor in the dining hall did we see him.

When we had been in the queue for about ten minutes, however, and were looking at some of the dubiously modernistic paintings that hung on the walls, we did see Sir George and Malcolm again. As they brushed past Malcolm hissed in my ear that speakers should go straight to the head of the queue, where they would be served first. They should also sit at the high table. Not wanting to leave Prasannasiddhi on his own in the queue, I did not avail myself of the first of these privileges, and it was therefore another ten minutes before we emerged from the service area into the dining hall with our trays of food. Prasannasiddhi went in search of a seat, while I made my way to the high table. This was situated near the entrance, on a low platform, and was, I supposed, normally occupied by the teaching staff of the College. On the present occasion it was occupied by the organisers of, and speakers at, the Wrekin Trust's 'Mystics and Scientists 6', together with their wives and spiritual consorts. Before sitting down opposite Sir George and Malcolm I turned and — still on the look-out for Subhuti — slowly surveyed the dining hall. Tables for four, covered with white cloths, occupied the entire floor space, right up to the wide expanse of window-wall beyond. Most tables were already occupied, and a subdued buzz of cheerful conversation arose. The bees were inside the hive, and were humming contentedly over their nectar.

In the course of the meal I made the acquaintance of some of the other speakers. Our *curricula vitae* had appeared in the Trust's publicity brochure for the conference, and I had read about them, as they, no doubt, had read about me. I hoped that the Trust had not perpetrated in their case the sort of howler it had perpetrated in mine, when it glossed The Three Jewels as 'Buddha, Karma and the Path'. On the opposite side of the table, on Malcolm's left, sat a bulky figure with rather Nordic features and a patriarchal grey beard. This was Professor Arnold Keyserling. Besides being the son of Count 'Travel Diary of a Philosopher' Keyserling he was also, as Malcolm took good care to remind the company at our end of the table, the great-grandson of Bismark. Indeed, there *was* something faintly 'Bismarkian' about him. On my left sat a couple whom Prasannasiddhi and I had overtaken on our way down the hill from Christchurch Lodge to the College. The man turned out to be Dr. Rupert Sheldrake, a rising young biologist. The woman was not actually introduced. On my right sat a dark, diminutive woman of about thirty who, as if to justify her presence amongst us, explained to me that she was 'linked' with Professor Keyserling, and indeed, if one looked hard, and was at all sensitive to such things, one could see a thick psychic chain connecting the two of them. While she was speaking one of the cooks came and set down in front of Professor Keyserling a plate on which was a large steak. 'He only eats meat!' exclaimed Malcolm, with a deprecatory laugh, as Professor Keyserling, steel-blue eyes sparkling with pleasure, attacked his steak with gusto.

Between the end of dinner and the first formal session of the conference Prasannasiddhi and I had time for a little exploration. In the vestibule of the Conference Hall four or five 'New Age' organisations, including the Wrekin Trust itself, had set up bookstalls, and there was a broad range of publications to be browsed, from the solidly academic to the flightily Aquarian. On the Wrekin Trust's own bookstall, which was naturally the biggest, books by all five speakers at the conference were prominently displayed, and I was gratified to see stacks of *Surveys*, *Three Jewels*, and *Thousand-Petalled Lotuses*. As we progressed round the room, from bookstall to bookstall (at one of them I was cajoled into buying a magazine), I kept 'bumping into' people who recognised me and greeted me warmly but who, in most cases, I could not remember meeting before. Among those I definitely *had* met before were Diana McEwen, a Mitra attached to the Croydon Centre, and John Heape, also attached to the Croydon Centre, who handed me a note from his wife Marlene regretting her inability to attend the conference.

Prasannasiddhi and I were still browsing, and I was still bumping into people, when Malcolm started ushering everyone — especially the speakers — through the red velvet curtains of the doors that led from the vestibule into the Conference Hall. Speakers were to sit in the middle of the second row from the front. As I walked down the gangway (the hall was built as a theatre, with tiered seats, and stage with proscenium arch), I saw that the auditorium was practically full, and there was a distinct atmosphere of excitement and expectancy.

We did not have long to wait. Precisely at 8 o'clock Malcolm opened the proceedings by welcoming everybody (he was a very fluent and agreeable speaker), after which he dealt with the sort of things that are the subject matter of the organiser's announcements at the beginning of an FWBO retreat. In this connection he asked the different people who were helping with the running of the conference to stand up and identify themselves. This they did, but in some cases so self-consciously that I felt quite sorry for them and wondered whether people ought to be asked to exhibit themselves in this way. However, I learned that the flustered lady who had issued me with our round paper badges, and who was in overall charge of reception, was in fact Malcolm's wife. Having performed this part of his duty, Malcolm concluded by introducing Sir George, who hopped up onto the stage and harangued the conference vigorously to the effect that the New Age, the Age of Aquarius, was already upon us, and that the whole world was about to change dramatically for the better. (I hope I have not misrepresented him. This was the *impression* his words produced on me, regardless of what he may actually have said.) The audience seemed impressed, even if not entirely convinced. After he had harangued us for nearly an hour (the official title of his address was 'The Illusion of Separation and The Return to Wholeness'), and had enforced his message with some extraordinary gestures, Sir George concluded by introducing Professor David Bohm, who spoke for an hour in a much more sober and conversational style on 'Consciousness and the Unfolding Universe: Wholeness and the Implicate Order.' Once again Mystics and Scientists had come together. The conference had begun.

By this time it was well past 10 o'clock. Our second day away from Padmaloka had been even busier than the first, and all Prasannasiddhi and I wanted to do on emerging from the Conference Hall was to go straight back to Christchurch Lodge and straight to bed. But this was not to be. For the speakers, at least, the end of Professor Bohm's address did *not* mark the end of the day. We were to have a special meeting. Indeed, we were to have special drinks and sandwiches together in one of the adjoining buildings and discuss the programme for the weekend. Unfortunately, the door of the building was locked, the porter had gone off duty, and the key could not be found. After trying the back door, and even the windows, through one of which the drinks and sandwiches laid on for us were clearly visible, Malcolm led us in a ragged little procession down one flight of steps, then another, to the bar of the Students Union — Prasannasiddhi and I reluctantly bringing up the rear. The bar was not only crowded with people but dense with cigarette smoke and loud with rock music. A chorus of protest now arose from the long-suffering speakers one of whom proposed that we should forget all about the drinks and sandwiches and just have a cup of coffee together in somebody's room. This proposal having been carried unanimously, up the hill we trailed to Christchurch Lodge, where it seemed the speakers, as well as Sir George and Malcolm, were all staying. Having arrived at the Lodge, up the stairs we trailed to the room occupied by Professor Keyserling and the dark, diminutive woman 'linked' with him, which was situated next to the room occupied by Prasannasiddhi and myself. I did not want coffee at that time of night (Prasannasiddhi had gone straight to bed), but everyone else did, so off to the kitchen went the dark, diminutive woman, closely followed by the dark but by no means diminutive woman who accompanied Rupert Sheldrake (was she 'linked' too?), and coffee was soon ready. The dark, diminutive woman then offered to take a movement group during the weekend, but Malcolm (who was no doubt accustomed to wives and spiritual consorts trying to insert themselves into the programme) told her very firmly that there would be no time for additional activities. As if to underline his point, he took us item by item through the entire programme, which in any case we were supposed to be discussing. It was soon obvious that there was, in fact, nothing to discuss, and that Malcolm, having been totally absorbed in preparations for the conference for the last six months, had now reached the point where he was unable to stop thinking about it. The meeting might well go on all night! Saying I was tired and wanted to go to bed, I therefore wished everybody goodnight and withdrew.

Next morning I was up early, and while Prasannasiddhi attended the 7 o'clock meditation (he afterwards reported that there had been about fifty people present and that they had been asked to place the successive clauses of the Lord's Prayer in the different chakras or psychic centres) I ran through the text of my address, which I was to give immediately after breakfast ... But I have no intention of continuing in the circumstantial style in which I began this part of my Letter and giving an hour-by-hour narration of the events of the weekend. *That* is probably not desirable, and even if it was desirable would hardly be possible. Though the conference lasted no more than twenty-four hours (including the time we spent sleeping), so many things happened, and I met and talked with so many people, that a complete chronological account is out of the question. Indeed, I was kept so busy that Prasannasiddhi and I had no time to see the old part of the city, or to visit the Cathedral, which we had wanted to do ever since reading about Keats' association with Winchester ('the pleasantest Town I ever was in', as he described it) the previous Autumn, when we studied his poems together in Tuscany. We therefore contented ourselves with the distant prospect of the Cathedral that presented itself whenever we walked down the hill from Christchurch Lodge to the College.

Since I have mentioned my address, I may as well begin my less detailed account of the remainder of the conference with a few remarks on this topic, as well as on my other contributions to the proceedings. After all, it was in order to address the conference that morning on 'The Bodhisattva Principle: Key to the Evolution of Consciousness, Individual and Collective — A Buddhist View', that I had come to Winchester, and for me personally the giving of my address was (with one exception, which I shall mention in a minute) the main event of the weekend. The rather cumbersome title was not entirely of my own devising. It was to a great extent the work of Malcolm, who had been particularly keen that I should not prepare and read a formal paper, as I had told him I intended doing, but speak extemporaneously or from notes. 'The living word as it emerges in the creative moment,' he wrote, 'particularly in the case of such as yourself, is far more pregnant with life and inspiration than would be the more considered and weighty words presented from a read paper.' However, I stuck to my guns (is there not a more Buddhistic equivalent idiom?) and prepared a formal paper. This was a departure from my usual practice: indeed, I could not remember ever doing such a thing before; but I wanted to make a solid contribution to the proceedings of the conference, as well as to produce something that could be published immediately afterwards. I was also slightly suspicious of what seemed to me a tendency, on the part of the Wrekin Trust (a tendency deriving, no doubt, from Sir George, though Malcolm was certainly sympathetic to it) to use events like the conference to generate a sort of collective 'experience' that would carry everybody out of themselves and, presumably, straight into the Age of Aquarius. Fortunately, despite the title, and despite the fact that I was reading from a prepared paper, my address was well received, and I sat down to prolonged applause.

Nonetheless, in insisting on the importance of 'the living word' Malcolm undoubtedly had a point, and it was therefore fortunate that, as things turned out, having read my paper on the Saturday morning I should be given the opportunity of addressing the conference more or less spontaneously on the Sunday morning. The reason for this was that the only woman among the five speakers (six including Sir George) was unable to be present owing to illness, and Malcolm asked me (presumably because I was the only other 'Mystic' on the platform!) to take her place. The missing speaker was Monica Furlong, the well known Christian journalist and broadcaster, and she was to have spoken on 'Accepting the Relationship between Spirit and Matter, Its Integration and Redemption. Jacob Wrestling with the Angel' (had Malcolm had a hand in the title, I wondered?). There was no question of my speaking on this subject, and something had to be produced quickly. I therefore decided to take the opportunity of telling the conference something about the life and work of Dr. Ambedkar, and about the ex-Untouchable Buddhists, prefacing my account with a rapid survey of the development and decline — and revival — of Buddhism in India. Though this represented a departure from the theme of the conference, which was 'Reality,

Consciousness and Order' (I had genuflected in the direction of this imposing triad in the course of my paper), I did at least manage on this occasion to get a bit carried away and (I think) to carry my audience out of themselves a bit as well — if not into the Aquarian Age, at least in the direction of Maharashtra. At any rate, everybody seemed well satisfied, and if I am not mistaken my more or less extemporary efforts were applauded even more vigorously than my more considered ones had been. Indeed, several people told me afterwards that they had enjoyed my second lecture more than my first.

In addition to giving an address on 'The Bodhisattva Principle' etc. on Saturday morning I had been billed to take a 'Meditational Workshop (Optional)' on Saturday afternoon. Malcolm had, in fact, taken it more or less for granted that I would be happy to do this, and though I disliked the vogue term 'workshop' I had acquiesced in the arrangement, thinking that since it was optional very few people would want to attend anyway. In the event, at least three quarters of the three hundred and forty delegates attended the session, though both the organisers and the other speakers (who might have been considered as needing meditation most) were noticeably absent. However, I was not sorry that for one session, at least, I had the conference all to myself, so to speak. The 'workshop' was held in the Conference Hall, with everybody sitting, as usual, in the red plush tip-up chairs, and myself seated on the platform behind a table (I had asked the young man in charge of the tape-recorder to remove the lectern and the black-board and to lower the microphone). I had exactly an hour (not a minute more, so I had been warned), and decided to treat the session exactly like an FWBO Beginners' Meditation Class and take people through the first two stages of the Mindfulness of Breathing practice, with a short introductory talk and a short period for questions and answers afterwards. This format worked extremely well and was, in fact, exactly what was needed. Far from serving simply to fill in the time between lunch and tea, as I had feared might be the case, my 'Meditational Workshop' proved to be a definite contribution to the proceedings of the conference. As several people remarked, it was the only time during the whole weekend that they had had something practical to do, and they were correspondingly grateful for the opportunity.

For my part, I was agreeably surprised to find that so many of the delegates were interested in meditation and had, as it appeared, already practised it in one form or other. From the start to the finish of the session not a single person coughed or fidgeted or shuffled their feet. Perhaps only someone with considerable experience of taking meditation classes will be able to appreciate the significance of this fact.

What with reading my paper in the morning and taking the 'Meditational Workshop' in the afternoon, as well as meeting and talking to people, Saturday was quite a busy day for me. Sunday was no less busy. Besides standing in for Monica Furlong in the morning I took part, as one of The Lecturing Panel, in the 'Open Forum' that was spread in a sort of double session over the remainder of the morning and a good part of the afternoon. Malcolm was in the chair, with Professor Bohm and Dr. Sheldrake on his right, and Professor Keyserling and myself on his left. Sir George hovered in the wings. Written questions that had come in from the Hall lay on the table in front of each speaker (I had quite a pile) and we passed on those with which we particularly wanted to deal to Malcolm, who in turn made his own selection before reading out the questions and calling on the appropriate speaker (or speakers) for an answer. In this way we got through about thirty questions, though at least double that number had been submitted.

Some of the questions were quite technical (these seemed to come from 'people working in the sciences' and were addressed to Professor Bohm and Dr. Sheldrake), while others were of a more general nature. At least half the questions in my own pile related to the ex-Untouchable Buddhists, the subject of whom had clearly aroused a good deal of interest, and even of sympathy, but though I passed several of these on to Malcolm he did not read any of them out. This was a pity, but no doubt he felt that the subject was too far out of the main track of the conference to warrant any attention.

Towards the end of the session there was a brief intervention from Sir George, who hopped up onto the platform and flapped his arms vigorously for a few minutes, as well as a longer one from a portly, rather pompous and self-complacent clergyman who suddenly rose up from somewhere in the vicinity of Sir George to remind everybody, in effect, that the real answer to all our questions was Christ. As this unexpected figure got to his feet Malcolm hastily introduced him, in what I thought were rather fulsome terms, as a good friend of the Wrekin Trust, and I formed the impression that here was someone whom Malcolm did not wish to offend — perhaps dared not offend. I was under no such restraint, however, and when the clerical intervener tried to represent Lao Tsu's well known 'He who knows does not speak; he who speaks does not know,' as a saying of the Buddha I loudly disagreed. I also disagreed when, having accepted the correction with an ill grace, he nonetheless tried to use the saying to quash any discussion of the relative merits of Buddhism and Christianity. 'In that case,' I said, 'let's all stop talking and go and have a cup of tea!' (Prasannasiddhi has reminded me that the clergyman's intervention was in connection with a question as to whether there was, in Buddhism, anything corresponding to the Christian concept of the Holy Ghost. According to Prasannasiddhi, I dealt with this question rather too gently, and this may well have encouraged the clergyman to intervene in the way he did.)

Though I probably took a more prominent part in the conference than any other speaker, it was nonetheless the giving of my first address that was my most important contribution to the proceedings. Indeed, as I have already indicated, for me personally the giving of this address was the main event of the weekend — or would have been, if another event had not taken place at the same time. This was the publication of Subhuti's book. To me this was the main event not only of the weekend, not only of the month, but perhaps even of the whole year. Subhuti had not arrived at the College until 11 o'clock the previous night. For some reason or other he had travelled to Salisbury, and thence to Winchester, not straight from Padmaloka as planned but via London and Sukhavati. However, the first copies of his book were with him and one of these, suitably inscribed by the author, Prasannasiddhi brought for me on his return to the Lodge after attending the morning meditation session. At last I had the joy of actually holding in my hands a copy of *Buddhism for Today: A Portrait of a new Buddhist Movement* by Dharmachari Subhuti (Alex Kennedy)! Of the quality of the contents I was assured, having read the book in manuscript, but I was relieved to see what a large, handsome volume Element Books had produced. With its bright yellow cover with the sepia half-length reproduction of Chintamani's standing Buddha, it was indeed a first publication of which any author could be proud.

There were three reasons for my joy at seeing the book in print at last. The first reason was that, sixteen years after the founding of the FWBO, a guide to the Movement as a whole was badly needed, not only for the benefit of the outside world but even for the benefit of those within the Movement who, with the steady growth of the Movement, had been finding it more and more difficult to see the wood for the trees — or even to identify all the trees. The second reason for my joy had less to do with the book itself than with the author. Having seen Subhuti go off to Greece, there to write the first two thirds of his book in three months, I had been the witness — and the sharer — of his growing frustration as, for the next two and a half years, he struggled to finish it, find a publisher, see it through the press, and launch its publication, while at the same time functioning as my secretary and doing at least two other full-time jobs. Now Subhuti's frustrations were over (though he had already shown signs of wanting to write another book — in fact two or three books) and for this I was heartily glad. The third and last reason for my joy at seeing Subhuti's book in print was of a more personal nature. So far, whatever books the Movement had produced had been written by me. Order Members had written, at the most, a *Mitrata* or two. *Buddhism for Today* was thus the first full-size book on Buddhism to be written by someone in the Movement other than myself. In addition to possessing its own intrinsic value, the book therefore represented the devolution of yet another of my functions and responsibilities onto the 'senior and responsible' Order Members. Something more had been *handed on*.

Holding Subhuti's book in my hands I felt rather like a man who, in his old age, holds his first grandson in his arms and knows that his line will continue. (Strictly speaking, the line will continue only when Order Members are able to perform ordination ceremonies. Perhaps I could liken Subhuti's book to the first grand*daughter*, not the first grand*son*. The first 'grandson' will be the first person to be ordained into the Western Buddhist Order/Trailokya Bauddha Mahasangha by someone other than myself.)

Later that morning I had the satisfaction of seeing the bright yellow volume prominently displayed on the Wrekin Trust's bookstall, which occupied the right hand side of the vestibule. The proud father himself, with Prasannasiddhi's help, had set up an FWBO bookstall in between the two doors into the Conference Hall, on the same trestle tables that had done duty as reception desks. It was good to see the colourful spread of FWBO publications, and interesting to watch people picking them up and looking at them and, in some cases, buying them. The most popular publication, in terms of number of copies sold, was *Human Enlightenment*. This was at least partly because I had mentioned it, indeed recommended it, in the course of my Meditational Workshop, mainly on account of the chapter on 'What Meditation Really Is'. (Prasannasiddhi tells me that next to *Human Enlightenment* our most popular publication was *Peace is a Fire*.) At Malcolm's suggestion, I also mentioned and recommended, this time in the course of my second address, my volume of memoirs *The Thousand-Petalled Lotus*, copies of which were not disappearing from the Wrekin Trust's bookstall as fast as he would have liked. As a result, during the remainder of the day I was asked to autograph at least half a dozen more copies. With so much from which to choose, people seemed to need definite guidance as to what to read and, even, what not to read.

For my part, I had no difficulty making my selection. The only limiting factor was money. However, by the time the conference was over I had bought David Bohm's *Wholeness and the Implicate Order* and Rupert Sheldrake's *A New Science of Life*, as well as Monica Furlong's *Merton: A Biography*, the subject of which was the American Trappist monk who had written much — perhaps too much — on Zen. (Arnold Keyserling had not written anything, it seemed.) I also bought Ken Wilber's *Up From Eden: A Transpersonal View of Human Evolution* and Julian Jaynes' *The Origins of Consciousness in the Breakdown of the Bicameral Mind*, both of which promised to be of exceptional interest.

Besides buying the other speakers' books I also attended their lectures (with one exception) and got to know them personally (again with one exception). Professor Bohm's second address, which carried straight on from where the first had left off, was on 'Cosmos, Matter, Life and Consciousness as Projections of Multi-Dimensional Reality', while Dr. Sheldrake's was on 'Morphogenetic Fields and the Influence of the Past Memory and the Brain. Towards a New Science of Life.' So far as I could make out both addresses were based on material drawn from recently published books (the ones I had bought), and they both represented — like the books themselves — a definite move in the direction of a non-materialist interpretation of the nature of existence. In this respect Professor Bohm went farther than Dr. Sheldrake.

According to Professor Bohm, it was possible to see quantum physics as treating the totality of existence, including matter and consciousness, as an unbroken whole. This possibility was represented by the notion of what he called 'implicate order' which meant that, in the words of the 'blurb' on the back of his book, 'any relatively independent element contains within itself the sum of all elements, the totality of existence, as the points of contact made in the folds of a sheet of paper may contain the essential relationships in the total pattern displayed when the sheet is unfolded.' This notion 'makes possible a consistent account not only of the new properties of matter implied by quantum theory, but also of the activity of consciousness, and of its relationship to matter.'

According to Dr. Sheldrake (his was the lecture that I did *not* attend) the regularities of nature were more like habits than laws, depending on what had happened before, and also on how often things had happened. For this new type of causation across time and space he had coined the term 'formative causation', arguing that it is responsible for the shapes and instincts of all living things. According to him, moreover, the metaphysical theories of modified materialism, the conscious self, the creative universe, and transcendent reality, were all equally compatible with the hypothesis of formative causation. In other words, in the light of this hypothesis biology is not necessarily committed to a mechanist theory of life. An 'idealist' or 'spiritual' theory fits the facts of biology just as well.

Professor Arnold Keyserling (he was the speaker I did *not* get to know) was billed to speak on 'The Problem of Integrating Language Structures based on Separative Thought with a Holistic Appreciation of the Nature of Reality'. In this case the title of the address, which was even more cumbersome than the title of mine, definitely *was* the work of Malcolm, for Professor Keyserling began by telling us so, making a great joke of the fact and declaring that he would *not* be keeping to the subject. He did not keep to anything, in fact. His address was a hodge-podge of which I remember something about Shamanism, something about Kundalini, and something particularly abstruse (or was it merely muddled?) about the Twelve Signs of the Zodiac. Interspersed were a variety of droll stories, and a whole lot more jokes, some of them of a mildly suggestive nature. However, he was a highly experienced speaker, with a jovial, expansive platform manner, and had no difficulty whatever in holding the conference's attention. How seriously people took him it was difficult to say. Malcolm watched his performance with shining eyes, but I could not help thinking that he was a bit of a showman and that he resembled, in more respects than one, my old friend Panditji (see *The Thousand-Petalled Lotus*, Chapters 9-14).

Thanks to the high table, for the speakers to get to know one another was no less natural than it was for them to attend one another's lectures, and by the end of the conference I had not only struck up an acquaintance with both Professor Bohm and Dr. Sheldrake but had also managed to have a lengthy conversation with each of them. I was thus able to form some idea of what the two scientists were like. Both as man and as thinker Professor Bohm was definitely the more impressive figure. From the *curriculum vitae* that had appeared in the Trust's publicity brochure for the conference (as well as from the 'blurb' of his book) it was clear that he had done important work in the field of quantum physics. Ratnaprabha, who knows about such things, had indeed told me that he was one of the world's leading physicists, and had seemed surprised that he would be attending the conference.

I had not heard of Professor Bohm before, and was glad to have the opportunity of making good what was clearly a big gap in my knowledge. David Bohm was a man of my own generation, being perhaps five or six years older than I was. He was grey and balding, and inclining to corpulence, and according to Malcolm (who seemed to know a lot about everybody) suffered from a heart condition for which he had had open heart surgery. What was particularly noticeable about him was, in the first place, his entire lack of pretentiousness and, in the second, the quite exceptional quality of his intelligence. Not without reason did the Trust's brochure say of him that 'his lack of ego completely disguises the scale of his intellect'. He was probably the most intelligent person I had met since my return to England in 1964 (though my contacts have of course been rather limited). It was particularly interesting to see the way in which he dealt with questions, as on the occasion of the Open Forum. He gave them his absolutely undivided attention, listening without so much as a flicker of reactivity. Then came the answer, like a series of mildly brilliant lightning-flashes from a clear sky. Though his manner was unassuming almost to the point of diffidence, he went straight to the heart of a question, siezing hold of it and disposing of it with an effectiveness that was all the more devastating for being so effortless. But what the Trust's brochure said of him was true. His lack of ego really did disguise the scale (I would have preferred to say the calibre) of his intellect, and I am sure that most of the people in the Conference Hall failed to appreciate the extraordinary nature of his performance.

During our conversation it transpired that he knew Krishnamurti. I was not surprised. In the course of his lectures he had used a number of expressions that had a familiar, semi-Buddhistic ring to them, and it was now clear where they came from. He seemed, in fact, to know Krishnamurti quite well. At least, he offered to arrange a discussion between us, but not being sure whether he meant a private discussion (which I would have welcomed) or a public one (which I would not have welcomed) I gave a non-commital reply. As we talked I noticed that there hung over David Bohm a shadow that I could identify only as one of sadness. Perhaps the sadness was due to the fact that he lived — as the open heart surgery suggested — close to death. Or perhaps it was an existential sadness, due to the fact that some deeper part of him was still unsatisfied and unfulfilled. Be that as it may, the shadow that hung over him imparted a touch of wistfulness that, in some curious way, enhanced rather than detracted from his overall impressiveness.

No shadow hung over Dr. Sheldrake, who was at least twenty years younger than Professor Bohm and at the beginning rather than at the end of his career. From the Trust's brochure I had learned that in 1974 he had joined the staff of the International Crops Research Institute at Hyderabad in India where he was now Consultant Plant Physiologist, and this provided our conversation with a starting point. Hyderabad is situated in the State of Karnataka which is, of course, south of Maharashtra, and I asked Dr. Sheldrake if he knew of the ex-Untouchable Buddhists or had had any contact with them. Rather to my surprise, he was obliged to admit that he had no knowledge of them whatever, though it seemed he had heard the name of Dr. Ambedkar. I therefore gave him a brief account of the movement of mass conversion, and its implications for the social and economic life of Dr. Ambedkar's followers (this was before my second address), but he appeared to be no more than moderately interested in the subject. Indeed, he appeared to be no more than moderately interested in Buddhism. Unlike Professor Bohm, whatever religious sympathies he had were with Christianity rather than with Buddhism or Hinduism. According to the Trust's brochure, he had spent one and a half years in Dom Bede Griffiths' 'Christian Ashram' in South India, and had there completed his book *A New Science of Life*, which was, in fact, dedicated to Dom Bede. Nonetheless, we managed to find a certain amount of common ground, and had a reasonably satisfactory exchange of ideas. He was, in fact, quite an agreeable person, though perhaps somewhat lacking in definiteness of character.

One of the pleasantest things about him was his attitude to Professor Bohm. He clearly held the older man in very high esteem, and regarded personal contact with him as a privilege. I also noticed, particularly during the Open Forum, that he was not only clear in his thinking but highly articulate. Listening to the succession of beautifully constructed, almost pedantically precise sentences that flowed from his lips whenever he was called upon to answer a question, I thought of the incoherent ramblings to which I sometimes had to listen in the course of FWBO study retreats. In certain respects the FWBO falls very much below the standards of the outside world.

Keen as I was to get to know the other speakers I had no wish to limit myself to them. This would have been impossible in any case. For the majority of people who attended a conference of this sort, meeting and talking to the speakers is an essential part of the proceedings, and on this occasion there were certainly plenty of people who wanted to meet and talk with me. Out of the 340 people attending the conference I had personal conversations with at least 50, probably 60. Like the delegates as a whole, they tended to be middle-aged (even old) rather than young, middle-class (even upper-class) rather than working-class (I am not sure to what extent these clumsy categories are still applicable), while men and women were represented almost equally. Only a few of the people who wanted to meet me were in any way eccentric — like the stout, voluble Russian lady who assured me that she was in communication with certain high spiritual beings belonging to other planes and was herself the incarnation (or reincarnation) of certain others. Most of the people I met were neither Mystics nor Scientists, but fairly ordinary people who were well aware of the threat posed by unrestricted scientific development and who, while appreciative of spiritual values, tended to be suspicious of organised religion in its more orthodox forms. Though there were four or five Buddhists present (apart from those connected with the FWBO), most delegates seemed to be vaguely Christian in their religious sympathies, with a strong dash of occultism, spiritualism or whatever.

A few of the people I met and talked with were old Friends. Among these were Carmen Blacker, who teaches Japanese at Cambridge and who attended several of our very early retreats, and Anne Bancroft, who as Anne Lobstein took over 'Sakura' from the late Emile Boin in 1969 or thereabouts, neither of whom I had seen for several years. Carmen, a stately academic of uncertain years, still remembered the occasion on which she found herself doing the communication exercises with a young ex-coalminer from Yorkshire. As for Anne, she confided that she was now sixty and had just published a book on six mediaeval (Christian) mystics and their teachings.

Apart from the other speakers, probably the most interesting person I met at the conference was E. Lester Smith. For many years he had headed the physical science research group of the Theosophical Research Centre, and was part author of a book which sought to correlate the results of C. W. Leadbeater's clairvoyant investigation of the physical atom with the findings of modern science. As I had recently been dipping into Gregory Tillett's *The Elder Brother: A Biography of Charles Webster Leadbeater*, and was in fact taking the book with me to Wales, the subject was fresh in my mind, and we had an interesting discussion. He was attending the conference, E. Lester Smith told me, in order to write a report on it for the *New Scientist*. He also told me that a young Cambridge graduate had recently produced evidence that tended to confirm the objective validity of C. W. Leadbeter's clairvoyant investigations into 'occult chemistry' as it was known in Theosophical circles. When I asked if there was any similar evidence for Mme. Blavatsky's revelations concerning such things as prehistoric giant races endowed with the Third Eye, which Theosophists believed were derived from her reading of the Akashic Records, he replied that there was not, and from the way in which he said it I concluded he thought it unlikely there ever would be.

Whether in the Conference Hall or at the high table I was never far from either Malcolm Lazarus or Sir George Trevelyan, who in any case were almost always seen together, and in the course of the weekend got to know Malcolm as well, perhaps, as it is possible for a busy speaker to get to know the even busier organiser at a gathering of this sort. Sir George was more difficult to get to know, partly on account of his deafness, and partly because though obviously full of goodwill to all men he lived very much in a world of his own. In the course of one of our conversations Malcolm confided that he was drawn more to Buddhism than to any other spiritual tradition, and that he tried to do a form of Mindfulness of Breathing practice every day. Despite his harassed look, he was a man of some spiritual depth, as well as of considerable emotional positivity. As the Trust's publicity brochure explained, in 1974 he had had a series of profound psycho-spiritual experiences which had led to his joining the Trust. What these experiences were I did not enquire. Though sure he would have no objection to telling me, matters of that kind, I felt, were best left to emerge spontaneously out of deepening communication. Indeed, I was not quite happy that something like 'a series of profound psycho-spiritual experiences' should feature in a publicity brochure in the way it did (Monica Furlong was similarly credited with 'a series of mystical experiences'). It smacked too much of advertising, not to say of the making — on one's own behalf or on behalf of another person — of claims which by their very nature could not be verified. Perhaps it is really a question of spiritual good taste as much as of scrupulous regard for truth. At any rate, I was more happy with what the Trust's brochure had to say about Malcolm having been responsible for initiating the Mystics and Scientists conferences, and about his being 'particularly concerned in finding ways in which the traditional knowledge of the spiritual nature of Man can be grounded and applied in individual life and society.' There was no doubt about Malcolm's practicality, or about his organising ability. Despite the *contretemps* over the special drinks and sandwiches on the evening of our arrival, by FWBO standards the conference was very well organised indeed. The events all took place on time, the rooms in the College hostels were clean and comfortable, and the standard of vegetarian cookery was uniformly high. Characteristic of the general efficiency was the fact that cassette tapes of the lectures were on sale in the vestibule only minutes after the session in which they had been given was ended.

Naturally there was a price to be paid for the organisational effort all this entailed. Unless the Bodhisattva spirit takes over, efficiency is seldom achieved except at a cost in human terms. Malcolm had worked unremittingly for 'Mystics and Scientists 6' for the last six months, and the fact that he looked even more harassed than Sir George was due, it transpired, not only to the strains imposed by the conference itself but to the fact that there had been something of a crisis in his personal life. We were made aware of this when, at the commencement of one of the sessions, Sir George called Malcolm up onto the platform (Malcolm bounced up beside him with a pleased expression) and announced that he wanted to make a statement. Rumours had been going around, he said, to the effect that he and Malcolm had quarrelled, and that after the conference Malcolm would be leaving the Wrekin Trust. There was no truth in those rumours, the old man declared emphatically. He and Malcolm had *not* quarrelled. They were the best of friends (this was quite obvious). Malcolm would *not* be leaving the Wrekin Trust. What had happened was that Malcolm had put so much time and energy into the organising of the conference (the sixth that he had organised) that it had seriously affected his marriage and he was therefore going to have a complete rest for six months and spend more time with his wife and family. Whether there would be a 'Mystics and Scientists' conference next year remained to be seen. This said, Sir George shook Malcolm warmly by the hand, after which the two men patted each other on the back (getting as near to a public embrace as two Englishmen decently could), a demonstration of brotherly love that was received by the audience with evident satisfaction. Prasannasiddhi and I had not heard the rumours to which Sir George referred, but it was interesting to see how gossip could spread. I also appreciated the straightforward and positive manner in which Sir George dealt with the situation. Even within a socially conservative organisation like the Wrekin Trust, it seemed, conflicts between one's spiritual commitments and one's domestic responsibilities could arise. For the moment Malcolm was compromising, but I wondered how long the compromise would last.

Though I did not actually have a conversation with Sir George, I naturally saw a good deal of him, especially at the conference sessions and at meals. The Trust's brochure revealed a chequered career. Coming from a well known political family, and growing up against a background of liberal politics and progressive thought, he had read history at Cambridge, taught at Gordonstoun, and even served for a while in the army. After many years as principal of Attingham Park, the Shropshire Adult College where he had done his pioneering work in the teaching of spiritual knowledge in adult education, he had retired in 1971 and founded the Wrekin Trust. With his mane of white hair, his intense idealism, his transparent goodness of heart, his extraordinary gestures, his impassioned oratory, and his general vagueness and wooliness of thought, he was a figure that inspired a good deal of affection and respect, but rather less confidence. It was hard, in fact, not to think of him as the Michael Foot of the Aquarian Movement. Just as it was Sir George who opened the conference with an address on 'The Illusion of Separation and The Return to Wholeness' so it was Sir George who closed it with a similar address on 'A Sane Philosophy for a Sustainable Future'. Once again, what he said mattered less than the way in which he said it. At times he flapped and waved his arms so vigorously it seemed he really did think that, if he only flapped hard enough, he would literally launch himself into the air — and his audience with him. He certainly did his best to carry everybody into the Aquarian Age, whether literally or metaphorically or both. The climax of his address came when he asked everybody to stand for the Invocation of the Archangel Michael and the Angelic Hosts. Here the oratory became more impassioned, and the gestures more extraordinary, than ever, and for a moment it seemed that Sir George really expected something to happen. Perhaps the Holy Ghost would descend. Perhaps the heavens would roll open with a crash. Perhaps we would all see visions. As it was, nothing happened, Sir George seemed disappointed rather than surprised, we all resumed our seats (most people seemingly had joined in the Invocation more out of respect for Sir George than from genuine conviction), and the session came to an end in a more normal fashion. The conference was over. It was time for the Mystics and Scientists to depart. — Within an hour Prasannasiddhi and I had packed our bags, had said goodbye to Malcolm and Sir George, as well as to Subhuti, and were driving through the peaceful Hampshire countryside in the direction of Bristol.

Other Books by Ven. Sangharakshita

All obtainable from FWBO Centres or from
Windhorse Publications
136 Renfield Street, Glasgow, G2 3AU

## A SURVEY OF BUDDHISM

*A Survey of Buddhism* 'has the great advantage and rare distinction to have been written by an author who is a scholar as well as a poet and philosopher ... the poet in the author has embellished the book with well-chosen examples of literary gems and enlivened it with many excellent similes, metaphors and vivid descriptions.'
Lama Anagarika Govinda

This book is a systematic and detailed study of the entire field of Buddhist philosophy and practice. All the major doctrines and traditions are discussed in depth, both in relation to the whole of Buddhism, and to the spiritual life of the individual Buddhist.

This book will satisfy and stimulate both the student of comparative religion and the general reader.

ISBN 0 394 737326 £7.50

## THE THREE JEWELS

*The Three Jewels* begins with a biography of Gautama, the historial Buddha, in which the place of fact and legend are discussed. It then pursues the meaning behind the many different approaches to Buddhism and finally traces the spread of the Buddha's followers throughout the ages.

Sangharakshita has written a reliable and authoritative introduction to Buddhism that will provide the reader with a firm basis for further study.

ISBN 0 904766 05 5 £4.50

## BUDDHISM, WORLD PEACE, AND NUCLEAR WAR

This essay is remarkable for its insight into this most difficult of issues. It shows us that the threat of nuclear war and the need for world peace faces us with the problem of death and forces us to confront the fundamental questions of life.

ISBN 0 904766 16 0 £1.25

## MIND REACTIVE AND CREATIVE

The starting point of Buddhism is the Mind. In this essay Sangharakshita uses the Tibetan image of the Wheel of Life to show that the Mind can function either Reactively, endlessly repeating the same old patterns, or Creatively, continually reaching out towards ever new possibilities.

ISBN 0 904766 01 2 75p

About the FWBO
(The Friends of the Western Buddhist Order)

## BUDDHISM FOR TODAY: A PORTRAIT OF A NEW BUDDHIST MOVEMENT

by Dharmachari Subhuti

*Buddhism for Today* will be of interest to anyone who is concerned with the development of the individual human being and the transformation of society in accordance with the highest ideals. It explores the theory and practice of an expanding modern Buddhist Movement whose fundamental purpose is to establish the conditions under which as many people as possible can grow as individuals.

Element Books Ltd
ISBN 0 906540 32 1 £4.95

If you would like more information about Ven. Sangharakshita and his work contact the FWBO Centre nearest to you:

**England:**

**Brighton Buddhist Centre:** 15 Park Crescent Place, Brighton BN2 3HF Tel: 0273 698420
**Bristol Buddhist Centre:** 120 Long Ashton Road, Long Ashton, Bristol BS18 9LS Tel: 0272 392463
**Croydon Buddhist Centre:** 96-98 High Street, Croydon, Surrey CR0 1ND Tel: 01 688 8624
**Glasgow Buddhist Centre:** 329 Sauchiehall Street, Glasgow, G2 3HW Tel: 041 333 0524
**London Buddhist Centre:** 51 Roman Road, Bethnal Green, London E2 0HU Tel: 01 981 1225
**Manchester Buddhist Centre:** 18 Burlington Road, Withington, Manchester M20 9QA Tel: 061 445 3805
**Norwich Buddhist Centre:** 41a All Saints Green, Norwich, Norfolk NR1 3LY Tel: 0603 627034
**Padmaloka Retreat Centre:** Lesingham House, Surlingham, Norfolk NR14 7AL Tel: 05088 8112
**West London Buddhist Centre:** 7 Colville Houses, London W11 1JB Tel: 01 727 9382
**Vajraloka Meditation Centre:** Tyn-y-ddol, Trerddol, Nr Corwen LL21 0EN Tel: 0490 81406

**Abroad**

**Auckland Buddhist Centre:** PO Box 68-453, Newton, Auckland, New Zealand
**Boston Buddhist Centre:** 470 Centre Street, Boston, MA 021309
**FWBO Germany:** Rechtstr, 9, 43 Essen 11, W. Germany
**FWBO Stockholm:** Hillbersvagen 5, S-126 54 Hagersten, Sweden
**Helsingen Buddhalainen Keskus:** PL 288, SF-00121, Helsinki 12, Finland
**Sydney Meditation Community:** 13 Rocklands Road, Wollstonecraft, NSW 2D65, Australia
**TBMSG Ahmedabad:** c/o Bakul Bhavan, Behind Gujerat Vaishya Sabha, Jamalpur Road, Ahmedabad 38001, India
**TBSMG Aurangabad:** c/o Bungalow No 2, Cantonment, Aurangabad, India
**TBMSG Bombay:** 25 Bhim Prerana, Tapodhan Nagar, Bandra (E), Bombay 400051, India
**TBSMG Pune:** 'Dhammavijay', 32 Dr. Ambedkar Society, Pune 411006, India
**Wellington Buddhist Centre:** PO Box 12311, Wellington North, New Zealand

Or contact the **Office of the Western Buddhist Order:** Lesingham House, Surlingham, Norwich, Norfolk NR14 7AL Tel: 05088 310